EASY cuisine

gourmet cooking

300 treasured favorites for your special occasions

Nicole Alper

BORDERS®

EASY cuisine

gourmet
cooking

300 treasured favorites for your special occasions

Published by Adams Media, an F+W Publications Company
57 Littlefield Street, Avon, MA 02322 U.S.A.
www.adamsmedia.com

ISBN 10: 1-59869-224-0
ISBN 13: 978-1-59869-224-2

Printed in China.

J I H G F E D C B A

Library of Congress Cataloging-in-Publication Data
available from the publisher.

This publication is designed to provide accurate and authoritative information with regard to
the subject matter covered. It is sold with the understanding that the publisher is not engaged
in rendering legal, accounting, or other professional advice. If legal advice or other expert
assistance is required, the services of a competent professional person should be sought.
—From a *Declaration of Principles* jointly adopted by a Committee of the
American Bar Association and a Committee of Publishers and Associations

Many of the designations used by manufacturers and sellers to distinguish their products are
claimed as trademarks. Where those designations appear in this book and Adams Media was
aware of a trademark claim, the designations have been printed with initial capital letters.

Previously published as *The Everything*® *Easy Gourmet Cookbook*.

Contents

Acknowledgments

Special thanks to the many chefs from around the world who have shared their recipes, and also to Steve, for assisting me with the metric conversions.

Introduction

WHAT DOES "GOURMET" MEAN? When you think of the word, you probably have a sense of what it refers to, but you may find it difficult to explain. Some people associate gourmet with fancy ingredients, or an exacting recipe. Sometimes it is synonymous for French, and impossible to pronounce. We often ascribe "gourmet" to that which is both delicious and unfamiliar. Or it could be the thing adorning the plate that simply looks too beautiful to eat. And, of course, it can refer to the meal that cost as much as a home mortgage.

Today, the mystique of gourmet cooking has been replaced by something far more useful: knowledge. Gourmet cuisine is no longer reserved for celebrity chefs or the French. It can come in the form of a solitary ingredient that is not readily available, such as quail eggs or galanga root. It can be taking the extra time to think of presentation when you put a dish together. For instance, rather than throwing salad in a bowl, you can drizzle the dressing on the side of the plate, build a tower of mixed greens, and finish it with a chive garnish. It takes five minutes, but looks far more dramatic on the plate.

For the sake of this book, I am operating under a broad definition of gourmet. Some recipes incorporate the philosophy of layering and complexity, while others may simply include a unique ingredient. Some require extra care and time, while others test your talents at assembly. And some recipes are culinary icons, a dish quite common to a particular culture but which may very well taste "gourmet" to those unaccustomed to the cuisine.

Gourmet does not have to mean difficult, and I have therefore taken special care to include straightforward, easy-to-follow recipes. Though "easy gourmet" may sound like the ultimate oxymoron, just because something is elegant, with complex flavor, does not (as Chef Roland Passot noted) mean it must be difficult to make. And to that end I hope everyone reading this book comes away with a sense that they too can create a wonderful gourmet meal, from whichever country or region, whatever the occasion.

Chapter 1: Going Gourmet

Food. It's perhaps life's most universal necessity, as well as joy. Whether it is a mother preparing dinner for her family, a husband throwing prime rib on the grill, or a chef showcasing his or her skill at a fabulous restaurant, eating is about family and community. You use it to celebrate positive events, such as a new job or a raise, or even as a way to propose marriage. Sitting around the table together in the evening to share details about your day is a way to use the custom of dinner to bring your family closer together. You rely on food for nourishment, though it goes far beyond simple sustenance.

Small Beginnings

Over the years Americans have gained access to a rainbow of cuisines. *The Round-the-World Cookbook,* a collection of recipes compiled by Pan American Airways, spoke to wives in the 1950s as if they were on the culinary cutting edge by introducing the food of other cultures. The average housewife, suddenly armed with recipes from lands she had probably only caught pictures of in magazines, had a newfound sense of running an "international" kitchen, a far cry from today's traveled career woman, mother, and wife.

Another way of learning about food came from the diversity of people who make up the United States. You need only look to our own cultural melting pot to see how it overflows into your kitchens: countless immigrants brought with them a taste of their own cultures. If you grew up in California, Mexican food was de rigueur, and no one can live in New Orleans without reveling in French cuisine. Of course, the United States has its own unique culinary traditions, from good ol' Texas barbecue, to the hearty flavors of Soul Food, to the birth of the almighty California Cuisine.

There are many characteristics that can distinguish gourmet food from what is not considered to be gourmet, such as:

- Always using the freshest ingredients available.
- Daring to incorporate unique or hard-to-find ingredients.
- Not being afraid of unusual combinations, but never sacrificing taste for the sake of complexity.
- Concentrating on presentation, remembering that you eat with your eyes.
- Realizing that a great meal is an investment, and being willing to sometimes spend a bit extra for special ingredients.
- Cooking with enthusiasm, which is always infectious.

Food from Afar

Perhaps most influential of all on the education of the American palate, at least in recent years, has been travel. With the radical expansion of airline routes and lower prices, it's a good bet the average household has journeyed abroad, tasting foods that made firsthand impressions on their palates. Americans are opening their minds (and mouths) across the globe. Part of the excitement of travel is having the chance to eat beyond our usual menus. Memorable travel is often synonymous with great food. How many times do you, when recalling a destination, think back to an awe-inspiring meal, the pungent scents wafting through a food market, or even an explosively fresh fruit drink served on the side of the road?

Yet even with today's travel opportunities, a shocking number of people still do not journey beyond the borders of the United States. Only a small percentage of American citizens carry current passports. They may know of various cultures, but they have not experienced them firsthand. Food provides that opportunity. One way may be to visit a local international restaurant. Mexican, Italian, French, Thai, Japanese, and Chinese are all common restaurant choices, but now America is experiencing an upswing in even more exotic foods—Ethiopian, Persian, and so on—including a growing number of upscale fusion restaurants, such as Sushi Samba in New York City, which seamlessly blends Japanese and Latin flavors. These establishments boast eclectic cuisine that defies one simple geographical reference.

Food as Art

Over the years, cooking has developed into an art. Through the introduction of culinary shows (starting with Julia Child, now an entire network—the Food Network—is dedicated to the cause), through magazines, Internet sites, and books, American tastes are becoming more educated. Instead of simply following recipes in rote fashion, many cooks want to feel as though the kitchen is a place where they can experiment, learn, and create. Today's average cook wants the key to feeling innovative in the kitchen.

These vast sources and opportunities for learning about food gave birth to a new generation of "foodies." Baby boomers, one of the world's best-fed generations, went from frequenting exotic restaurants and lands to taking these experiences directly into their own kitchens. And why not? Today's average kitchen is well suited to inquisitive palates. Even markets play an important role in this global culinary education. The average upscale market, such as Whole Foods or Trader Joe's, nurtures this newborn culinary enthusiasm by stocking shelves with an ever-growing list of international staples and hard-to-find gourmet items.

France, with its increasing focus on painstaking preparations and dramatic presentation, was certainly the historical leader in the quest for sating complex culinary desires, and encouraged other countries to push their own culinary envelopes. The evolution of French cooking into an art form occurred through a combination of many historical factors—the ingredients available, the harsh discipline of the restaurant apprentice system, the royal court, the Revolution, the creativity of many individuals, the sharing (and stealing) of recipes and information, and, most of all, the love of good food.

Other cultures took notice and began experimenting. Nowadays, countries that were previously not known for noteworthy cuisine, such as England, Germany, and Scandinavia, are turning to more gourmet philosophies in the kitchen (as you will notice by the large number of recipes from these countries in this book). Of course, there are still some places in the world, such as many parts of Africa, where food and money are in short supply, and eating at all is more pressing than eating fine food. But even there, changes are taking place. Hopefully, as the world continues to mix and merge, one day people from all around the world will be able to celebrate one of life's most invaluable gifts together.

Getting Organized

Professional chefs have a philosophy called *mise en place*, which means "everything in its place." Quite simply, it's organization. Before you go shopping, it always wise to write a list of the things you'll need to purchase, and it's helpful to consider the best places to buy the ingredients you'll be using. You have a lot of options to explore these days with so many specialty food stores opening. You'll also want to take into account the before and after of making a meal—setting up your workspace and serving the meal.

Shopping

Read a recipe in its entirety at least once before starting your shopping list. Write your list to take advantage of items at the salad bar for prepped produce, the deli counter for sliced meats and cheeses, the produce counter for cleaned greens, the freezer section for prepped vegetables, and the dairy counter for specialty cheeses. As you get more familiar with your grocery store, you can begin to write your shopping list in the same organization of the store, grouping dairy together, produce together, deli together, and other categories.

Know your stores. There are many specialty stores out there, including gourmet shops, cheese shops, ethnic markets, butchers, restaurant supply houses, and local supermarkets. Plan to stop at one new store on shopping expeditions when you have time, and you'll be amazed at the different foods and products that are designed to save you time.

Never shop on an empty stomach. While shopping can be fun, the goal is to buy what you need and not have leftovers, and shopping while hungry is a recipe for buying more than you need.

Setup

A clean work area is a pleasure to be in. Give yourself counter space. Make sure your sink and dishwasher are clean, have a couple of clean cutting boards on hand, and you're set. Your products should be arranged in the order listed in the recipe—this is also the order in which you'll use them. Premeasure where possible, prepare baking pans if specified, preheat your oven when needed, and bring refrigerated items to room temperature if required. Now take a step back and put away anything that you're not going to be using, including spice jars, dairy containers, canisters, pans, or bowls. Trimmings and scraps should go into the garbage and dirty dishes should go into the sink, preferably in hot, soapy water to make cleanup easy. Good planning may seem like work, but it's actually a way to establish good habits that save time in the long run. Now is also a good time to think ahead and chill salad plates and warm serving platters.

Cooking

Your area is clean and your ingredients are prepared and you're ready to start. Take a minute and read the recipe in its entirety one more time. The worst time to realize you forgot something is in the middle of cooking. Have a few extra tasting spoons available and make sure there are paper towels and dishcloths easily accessible—just in case.

It's always a good idea to wash a few pots and pans when you have a minute, but don't let yourself become distracted from your priority, which is cooking. Follow the steps in the recipe and the suggested times provided for each step, but always keep in mind that the visual indicators noted in the recipe supersede the suggested times: if your fish is golden brown and cooked through in 6 minutes even though the recipe says 9 minutes, take it off the heat. Each oven and stovetop cook differently, pans cook differently, and meats, poultry, fishes, and vegetables each cook differently depending on age. Let your senses—not the clock—guide you.

Serving and Presentation

Even if you're cooking for just yourself, use a plate and sit at the table to enjoy your meal. It's just no fun to stand at the stove and eat your food from the pan. You deserve to be served, even if you're the one serving. Take a minute to chill salad plates and soup cups, if appropriate, and warm your dinner plates and serving platters.

Make sure you have a designated spot in the kitchen or a clean dishwasher so you have somewhere to put dirty dishes if you're serving a multicourse meal. It's better to have a place to put them temporarily than to leave them on the table. You can always take care of them later.

Cleanup

Cleanup is a necessary evil. Try not to leave everything for the end; put dirty dishes in the dishwasher as you use them. If you're going to leave a dirty pot on the stove to save sink space, fill it partway with hot soapy water so it can soak while you're enjoying your meal.

Restaurant supply houses, many of which are now open to the public, and larger discount chains sell a variety of aluminum disposable pans at a reasonable cost. Use these pans for any dishes that will be messy due to sauces, broiling, or roasting. You can run them through the dishwasher, and if they don't come out clean, toss them in the garbage. Place your broiler rack on a small rimmed baking sheet with sides or a small baking pan filled halfway with water—the drippings will fall into the pan, reducing your broiler cleaning time by at least half. Clean your broiler and grill after each use; it's disheartening to start preparing dinner and realize the broiler or grill was never cleaned from the previous use.

Kitchen Essentials

Your kitchen is where quality outweighs quantity when it comes to equipment. Your kitchen equipment will determine the efficiency of your workspace, which saves time in prepping, cooking, and cleanup. Having the right appliances makes your cooking experience efficient and easy. The right utensils for the right job also play a big role in how smoothly everything goes. Everything from what you use to cook to how you get rid of the scraps shapes the outcome of your cooking.

Basic Equipment

Freezer containers, food storage bags, freezer bags, and refrigerator bags in a variety of sizes, parchment paper, plastic film, and aluminum foil are staples that you should not be without. Ideal for storing leftovers for short or long periods of time, these items make it easy to handle any food that doesn't get eaten and provide versatility for storing depending on the type of food you're working with. For strainers and colanders, buy two different sizes of the metal type and you won't need to worry about heat resistance. A metal steamer basket is perfect for preparing vegetables, and the quality is usually consistent from brand to brand. Cutting boards are also helpful tools. Ideally, you should have two or three on hand. It's good to have one board for fruits, one for onions, garlic, etc., and one for meat and poultry. You can also have one for fish. Proper maintenance is mandatory, so be sure to follow the manufacturer's directions. They're available in wood and plastic, but the difference is simply one of personal preference.

A good cookware store will work with you to explain the pros and cons of each type of cookware for pots, pans, and ovenware. There are many manufacturers and each brand has its advantages. You'll know the types of foods you'll be preparing most and your style of cooking—braising, broiling, stovetop grilling, and sautéing. Invest in the cookware that you'll be using most.

There are many cost-effective cookware sets on the market, but make sure you analyze your storage space before bringing home that twenty-two-piece set that was just too good to pass up. Check with people you know who cook—ask what they use and what their likes and dislikes are and what they would do differently if purchasing a cookware set again.

Food Processors

Mini–food processors are huge timesavers for mincing garlic, shallots, herbs, and a number of other items. Many are now under $25, and if you watch for sale specials, you can get an extra work-bowl at no charge. You can also use a full-size food processor. Prices have come down on these appliances, so research before you buy to get the most for your money. Simple is better than complex—pay only for the accessories that you'll actually use. These appliances come with helpful manuals that provide tips for using them to get certain desired results. It's worth taking the time to get acquainted with the different ways you can use these products so that you know different ways to prepare food. In the end, these tips will make cooking much easier and save you time!

Handy Gadgets

One tool that every kitchen and cook should have is a hand mixer. Invest in a quality mixer with good motor speed. Several models also include a number of accessories including "wands" that are invaluable for puréeing soups, sauces, and fruit smoothies.

Citrus graters, which are also called *rasps,* are incredibly efficient tools that are excellent for grating the rinds of fruits for zest, and the larger version can be used for cheeses. Vegetable peelers are helpful, too. Buy two—you'll be glad you did (especially when you forget to run the dishwasher!). Can openers, whether manual or electric, are another must-have for any kitchen. A quality manual one is just as easy to use an electric one, and does the job all the same—it just depends on your preference. Pick one that's easy to hold and has rubberized handles. Instant-read thermometers are a sure way to test temperatures and doneness. Many thermometers now have the proper temperatures for meat and poultry printed right on them or their cover. Timers are also a must-have—it's just too easy to get distracted and a timer can save you from making countless mistakes.

Useful Equipment

When it comes to what you use to measure your ingredients, what you'll cook them in, and where you'll store them, there are some basic items that you'll need. Liquid measuring cups are essential. Don't count on just one big glass measuring cup to do everything. Have a variety of sizes and use the size that fits the job. There are several sets that nest, which saves on storage space. There is a difference between dry and wet measuring equipment, too. Dry measuring cups are available in plastic or metal. One advantage to plastic is that it's microwavable, but it will eventually stain. Metal cups are more durable, but lack the convenience of being microwavable.

In addition to measuring cups, you'll need measuring spoons. One set works for both liquid and dry measures and the metal spoons are worth the investment.

Brome Lake Duck Suprême

Serves 4

The following four recipes all come from Executive Chef Mélanie Gagnon, at the Auberg Ste-Catherine de Hatley in Québec.

1½ cup Mistral du Cep d'Argent (or another sweet wine such as Pineau de Charente)
⅓ cup sugar
½ cup fresh cranberries
1 grapefruit, zested and juice squeezed
1 orange, zested and juice squeezed
4 duck breasts

1. Combine the sweet wine, sugar, cranberries, grapefruit, and orange zest and juice together in a medium saucepan.
2. Simmer over medium heat for 7 minutes. If you prefer a thicker sauce, dissolve 1 tablespoon cornstarch in 1 tablespoon of cold water and add to the sauce when hot.
3. Cook duck breast in a sauté pan for 6 minutes on the skin side, 3 minutes on the other side. Finish in the oven for 10 minutes at 350°. Slice the duck breast and serve with the sauce.

Salmon Fillets in Sweet Wine with Orange and Fennel

Serves 4

This sweet twist on salmon is another recipe by Chef Executif Mélanie Gagnon, Auberge Ste-Catherine-de-Hatley in Quebec.

4 salmon fillets (approximately 7 ounces each)
2 tablespoons butter
¼ cup of Mistral du Cep d'Argent, or another sweet wine
¼ cup fish broth
1 orange, peeled and cut in fine, round slices
⅓ cup fennel bulb, finely chopped
1 teaspoon garlic, chopped

1. Season salmon with salt and pepper. Melt butter in frying pan. When butter starts to foam, fry fillets until they are golden and pink, approximately 3 minutes on each side. Finish in the oven for 5 minutes at 200°.
2. Splash fillets with 2 tablespoons of wine and flambé. Quickly transfer salmon to a plate and put near oven to keep warm.
3. Pour the remainder of the wine, fish broth, orange slices, fennel, and garlic into the pan. Bring to a boil and reduce by half. Season to taste with salt and pepper. Dress salmon on the plates and surround with sauce.

Escargots in Chablis

Serves 8

1 ounce garlic, chopped
½ ounce salt
½ ounce pepper
1½ ounces parsley, chopped
¾ cup butter
64 snails (8 per person)
4 cups Chablis (white wine)

2 cups water
Pinch nutmeg
2 onions, chopped
1 carrot, chopped
3 garlic cloves, minced
2 ounces shallots, finely chopped
1 bouquet garni

Chef Executif Mélanie Gagnon of Auberge Ste-Catherine de Hatley in Québec says you should soak the snails for 2 hours in salt water (4 cups of water plus 2 table-spoons ocean salt) before cooking them. Wash them thor-oughly after they soak.

1. For the escargot butter, combine the garlic, salt, pepper, parsley, and butter.
2. Boil the presoaked and washed snails for 10 minutes, then remove them from their shells and wash several times under running water.
3. Place the snails in a saucepan with half of the Chablis and 2 cups of water. Add salt, pepper, nutmeg, onions, carrot, garlic, and bouquet garni. Cook at 250° for 1½ hours. Leave to cool in water, then drain.
4. Sauté the snails with the shallots, then add ½ cup of Chablis. Leave them to absorb the wine vapors for a few minutes.
5. Replace the snails in their shell and butter on top with the escargot butter. Line the snails one against another in a heatproof pan. Pour the rest of the Chablis in the bottom of the pan and leave to cook until the wine has totally evaporated. Serve very hot!

One Flavorful Bouquet

A bouquet garni can be used in many dishes and is an easy way to impart flavor. To make, combine enough dried parsley, thyme, and rosemary to fit into the center of a small square of cheesecloth. Crackle a dried bay leaf on top of the mixture, then gather the cheesecloth and tie it together with a string. This way you can remove it easily when the dish is done.

Rabbit with Wild Thyme

Serves 4

In this rabbit recipe, Mélanie Gagnon, of Auberge Ste-Catherine de Hatley, uses wild thyme for added flavor. Wild thyme is more commonly found in Europe, and ordinary thyme can work equally well.

3 pounds rabbit, cut into pieces
4 cups Cuvée Louis de Montfort (or another red wine)
2 tablespoons thyme
1 bay leaf
2 tablespoons flour
1 ounce fatty bacon, chopped
18 pearl onions
3 small shallots, chopped
3 garlic cloves, crushed
3 sprigs wild thyme, chopped
1 pinch tarragon, chopped
1 ounce butter
1 rabbit liver (reserve the one in the rabbit), finely chopped
1 tablespoon cognac
Salt and pepper, to taste

1. Marinate the rabbit overnight in the red wine, thyme, and bay leaf (reserving the liver). Take the rabbit out of the marinade and sprinkle with flour.
2. Heat the bacon in a casserole dish for 5 minutes, then brown the rabbit in it. Add the onions, shallots, and garlic cloves. Allow to brown, stirring continuously, for 6 to 7 minutes.
3. Pour in half the marinade. Add the wild thyme and the tarragon. Season with salt and pepper and leave to cook over a medium heat for 1½ hours.
4. In a small pan melt the butter, then add the chopped raw rabbit liver and cognac. Add to the casserole and leave to simmer for 5 minutes. Serve.

The First Step Toward a Great Sauce

One of the most important steps in making a sauce is deglazing. Once your meat (pork, beef, chicken, etc.) has been seared or cooked in a pan, remove it and pour out any excess fat or oil. Then use a liquid such as wine or stock and pour it into the pan, scraping the bottom to remove all the tasty bits of meat. You can then add other things to the sauce, such as cream to give it body, or butter to give a rich flavor and sheen.

Corn Clam Chowder with Mulard Duck-Pan Seared Foie Gras

6 shallots, minced
1 sprig thyme
1 ounce olive oil
2 pounds small clams
5 ounces white wine
1 ounce butter
2 ears of corn, sliced off the cob
16 ounces heavy cream

1 white leek
3 carrots
3 celery stalks
2 tablespoons flour
6 slices of foie gras
   (approximately 2 ounces
   per person)
6 chives, as garnish

Serves 6

This recipe is provided by Chef Jean-François Méthot of Les Trois Tilleuls, in Québec. For this recipe, first soak the clams in a bowl of cold salt water for 24 hours to rid the mussels of any impurities.

1. Sauté 5 minced shallots with the sprig of thyme in the olive oil. Add the clams and the white wine. Cook covered for 2 or 3 minutes, stirring from time to time with a wooden spoon, until the clams open. Remove the clams; drain and reserve the cooking liquid.
2. Sweat the remaining shallot in the butter. Add the corn and the cooking juice of the clams. Add 4 ounces of water and reduce it to ¼, then add the cream. Let it cook for several more minutes, then mix it and check seasoning. Remove the clams from their shells, but reserve a few shells for decoration of the plates.
3. Cut a julienne of white leeks, carrots, and celery. Drop them in boiling water for about 20 seconds (this is called blanching). Then plunge them in cold water to stop the cooking and retain the bright color.
4. Flour the foie gras and pan sear it by itself in a nonstick pan on high flame. In 6 prewarmed bowls, place some clams and the vegetable julienne in the middle and add the seared foie gras on top. Pour the clam chowder all around. Garnish with some chives and an open clam shell.

Shallots and Leeks

Many French recipes call for both shallots and leeks. Members of the Allium family (which includes onions, garlic, chives, and scallions), leeks are perfect for sautéing, as well as steaming. Shallots, which are like small, teardrop-shaped onions, are used in soups, sauces, and braised and stewed dishes when a mild onion flavor is desired. Because they are small, they require some patience to peel and chop.

Truffle Oil and Brie Soufflé

Serves 4

This recipe is provided by Chef Roland Ménard, of Hovey Manor, North Hatley, Québec. The addition of truffle oil to this soufflé is an easy way to impart a gourmet flavor.

1 teaspoon unsalted butter
½ cup milk
2 drops truffle oil
1 tablespoon white flour
1 pinch salt

2 egg yolks
2 ounces Brie cheese
2 egg whites
Pinch freshly ground white pepper

1. Melt butter in a saucepan, add milk, truffle oil, flour, and salt. Cook it at a low temperature until it gets thick (a few minutes).
2. Remove the saucepan from the burner. Add the egg yolks and cheese, mixing well.
3. Whisk egg whites with the white pepper and add it to the truffle oil mixture.
4. Pour in 4 buttered ramekins and bake at 350° for approximately 15 minutes, until it has risen. Serve immediately.

Le Diamant Noir

Known as *le diamant noir,* or "the black diamond," a truffle is a fungus that grows underground. Only a small amount is needed to impart flavor, as truffles are very strong. You can also infuse oils with truffles to use in many dishes—to liven up salad dressings, add some depth to sautéed vegetables, and turn a simple egg dish into something gourmet.

French Onion Soup with Port

4 ounces unsalted butter
3 tablespoons olive oil
3 pounds Spanish onions, sliced
2 garlic cloves, chopped
1 pinch thyme
2 bay leaves
1 tablespoon sugar

1 teaspoon salt, or to taste
2 tablespoons flour
2 pints veal stock
1½ cup of port
1 teaspoon pepper, to taste
16 slices toasted French bread
1 cup grated Gruyere cheese

Serves 8

In this recipe Chef Roland Ménard of Hovey Manor in North Hatley, Québec, shares his variation of French onion soup, using port.

1. Melt butter and olive oil in a large heavy pot over medium heat. Add onions, garlic, thyme, and bay leaves and continue stirring until lightly browned. Reduce the heat to low, cover, and cook, stirring occasionally until onions turn golden, about 15 minutes.
2. Uncover, sprinkle with the sugar and ½ teaspoon salt. Raise heat to medium and continue cooking uncovered approximately 30 minutes, stirring often.
3. Sprinkle flour over onions and cook until flour is browned, 2 to 3 minutes. Pour in stock, a bit at a time, while stirring. Raise heat to high and bring to boil. Stir in port, ½ teaspoon salt, and pepper. Reduce heat to low and cover. Cook until onions start to dissolve, about 45 minutes.
4. Preheat broiler. Ladle soup into ovenproof bowls. Top each bowl with two slices of toasted French bread. Sprinkle with grated cheese.
5. Broil until cheese melts. Serve immediately.

Foods of the South of France

All manner of French gourmet treats come from the south of France: truffles from the Périgord region, foie gras from the Dordogne region, and cassoulet from Toulouse. Once you enter the Languedoc, Provence, and Pay Basque regions, there is a Mediterranean touch to the cuisine, using olive oil, tomatoes, eggplant, many types of wild mushrooms, and garlic.

Bouillabaisse

Serves 6

There are countless variations of this famous dish. Here is a very straight-forward version, offered by Chef Executif Maro Patry, of Château Bromont in Québec.

1 large onion, diced
4 tomatoes, diced
3 garlic cloves, chopped
1 medium-sized carrot
1 piece celery
¼ cup olive oil
2 cod filets, cut into medium-sized pieces
2 pike filets, cut into medium-sized pieces

¼ pound mussels
18 black tiger shrimp, deveined
14 scallops
½ teaspoon saffron
½ bottle dry white wine
1 cup water
1 sprig fresh thyme
½ sprig rosemary
Salt and pepper, to taste

1. Preheat the oven to 350°.
2. Place all the vegetables with the olive oil in a large heavy-bottomed pot. Then put the cut pieces of fish and shellfish on top of the vegetables. Sprinkle in the saffron, add white wine, water, thyme and rosemary.
3. Place pot in the oven for 45 minutes. Season with salt and pepper to taste. Serve.

Central France: From Escargots to Boeuf Bourguignon

Many famed French dishes come from central France: Escargot à la Bourguig-non (escargot stuffed with garlic butter), Boeuf Bourguignon (beef cooked in red wine), and Coq au Vin (Bresse chicken in red wine), to name a few. Burgundy wine is another world-famous product from the center of France, which has inspired countless chefs. Lyon, which consideres itself the gastronomic capital of France, boasts an impressive number of three-star Michelin chefs.

Chocolate Mousse with Goat Cheese Cream

3 ounces sweet chocolate
4 egg yolks
¼ cup sugar
4 egg whites
1½ cup heavy cream, whipped

1 recipe of Goat Cheese Cream
   (page 20)
½ pint of fresh raspberries, for
   garnish
A few sprigs of mint leaves, for
   garnish

This recipe, by Executive Chef Jacques Poulin, Chef of Lion D'or in Québec, combines a chocolate French classic with the unexpected taste of goat cheese.

1. Place the chocolate on a double boiler. (If you do not have one, put the chocolate in a medium-sized stainless steel bowl and set it over a simmering pot of water, being careful that no water splashes inside the bowl.) Stir until chocolate is melted. Remove from heat and set aside to cool.
2. Beat egg yolks until light in color. Add sugar and continue beating until light and fluffy. Stir in cooled chocolate.
3. Beat egg whites until stiff, slowly fold into chocolate mixture using a spatula.
4. Fold the whipped cream into the chocolate mixture. Pour mousse into 4 to 6 individual ramekins or small serving bowls. Chill in refrigerator for 2 hours.
5. Using two large service spoons, fill one with a scoop of the Goat Cheese Cream and push them against one another (rotating the spoons as needed) so that the cheese takes the shape of a miniature football (this is called a "quenelle"). Place 1 or 2 quenelles atop the mousse, and garnish with fresh raspberries and mint.

Goat Cheese Cream

Serves 4–6

Serve this delicious combination with Chocolate Mousse (page 19).

2 cups heavy cream
½ cup Chèvre des Neiges, or another mild goat cheese

1 tablespoon Mistral wine
1 tablespoon maple syrup

Blend all ingredients together. Use immediately.

Moules Mariniere (Mussels in White Wine)

Serves 4

One of the best parts of this dish is the broth, so be sure to serve it with some fresh French bread. Soaking up the remaining liquid is not impolite—it's part of the fun.

1 tablespoon unsalted butter
1 tablespoon extra-virgin olive oil
¾ small yellow onion, chopped
1 clove garlic, minced
½ teaspoon freshly ground pepper

5 pounds mussels, scrubbed and debearded
1¾ cups dry white wine
3 tablespoons minced fresh flat-leaf parsley

1. In a deep pot melt the butter with the olive oil over medium-high heat. Add the onion, and sauté 2 to 3 minutes, until translucent.
2. Add garlic, pepper, and mussels. Pour in wine, then sprinkle with half the parsley. Cover, cook on low heat until mussels just start to open, 10 to 12 minutes.
3. Uncover and stir in remaining parsley.
4. Using slotted spoon, scoop mussels into individual bowl, throwing away any that did not open. Ladle in a good portion of broth. Serve.

Crepes with Curaçao Strawberries and Oranges

4 large eggs
1¾ to 2 cups milk, as needed
⅓ cup all-purpose flour
1 teaspoon sugar
1 teaspoon salt
2 pints of fresh strawberries,
    sliced, plus extras for garnish

2 oranges, cut into segments
2 tablespoons brown sugar
4 tablespoons Curaçao
¼ cup butter
1 cup whipped cream
8 fresh mint sprigs

Serves 8

This is a delicious recipe created by Jacques Poulin, Executive Chef of Auberge au Lion D'or in Orford, Québec. If you find lumps when making the batter, pass it through a sieve lined with several pieces of cheesecloth. If your batter is too thick, just add a bit of milk.

1. To make the batter: In a large bowl whisk together eggs and 1¾ cups milk. Whisk in flour, sugar, salt, a bit at a time, until there are no more lumps. Cover and refrigerate for 2 hours.
2. In a medium bowl mix together the strawberries, orange segments, brown sugar, and Curaçao. Refrigerate for 30 minutes.
3. Place a 12-inch frying pan over medium-high heat (when you spatter a bit of water and it sizzles, it is ready). Drop in 1 teaspoon butter, tipping the pan so it distributes evenly on bottom. Pour in only ¼ cup batter and distribute evenly on bottom by tipping and rotating pan. When the batter bubbles and the sides appear cooked, approximately 20 to 30 seconds, flip with a spatula. Cook very briefly on second side, transfer to another plate, stacking crepes, one at a time.
4. To serve, place a heaping spoonful of the strawberry-orange mixture, inside the crepes. Add a dollop of whipped cream, and then roll up the crepe. Garnish with a small spoon of whipped cream, a few slices of strawberries, and a sprig of mint.

Raclette (Melted Cheese with Potatoes)

Serves 4

Raclette is also the name of a Savoyard cheese and is so common in France that many families own electric raclette grills, which have eight squares that can be filled with cheese to melt.

12 boiling potatoes, such as Yukon gold, Yellow Finn, or White Rose
1 teaspoon salt
1½ pounds raclette cheese, cut into 4 equal portions

1 pound prosciutto
4 gherkins, sliced
Freshly ground pepper to taste
2 sweet red peppers
1 cup Archer Porto wine, or any other port

1. In a large saucepan combine the potatoes, 1 teaspoon salt, and water to just cover.
2. Bring to a boil over high heat, reduce to medium and cook uncovered until potatoes can be easily pierced with a sharp knife (approximately 20 minutes). Drain, and then mash them. (You can use a food processor, but be sure to let them cool off a bit first.) Cover, and set aside.
3. Put a slice of prosciutto in a raclette cheese tray, add a scoop of mashed potatoes in the middle, and fold the prosciutto over. Put a slice of gherkin and a slice of cheese on top of each piece of prosciutto, sprinkle the pepper on top, and then put the cheese tray on the raclette grill.
4. Cut the sweet peppers into 1-inch cubes and place them in a medium pot over a medium-low heat along with the port wine, until the port has evaporated (approximately 15 minutes). Serve with the raclette.

The Story of Raclette

Long ago in the Swiss Alps, cowherds would carry potatoes and gherkin pickles up the mountainsides to eat with their cheese and milk. They'd bake the potatoes in the campfire and melt the cheese on a rock near the fire. As it melted, they scraped the cheese onto the potatoes and pickles. The word *raclette* comes from the French word "to scrape."

Shrimp and Melon Salad

Serves 4

2 tablespoons fresh lemon juice
1 teaspoon minced fresh baby
  dill, plus a few sprigs for
  garnish
½ cup mayonnaise
½ cup white wine

3 cups mixed honeydew and
  cantaloupe, ¼-inch cubed
1 pound baby shrimps, lightly
  chopped
Few leaves of Boston hearth
  lettuce, for garnish

In a medium-sized bowl stir together lemon juice, minced baby dill, mayonnaise, and wine. Add melon and shrimps. Cover and refrigerate for at least 1 hour. To serve, scoop a generous portion of shrimp and melon salad onto Boston hearth lettuce in a large pasta plate.

Executive Chef Jacques Poulin of Auberge au Lion D'or in Québec suggests you garnish his recipe with Boston hearth lettuce and a sprig of fresh baby dill.

Pesto Beurre Blanc

¼ cup shallots, minced
¼ cup red wine vinegar
¼ pound butter, softened

⅛ cup heavy cream
1 tablespoon pesto (can be store-
  bought)

Serves 8
(accompaniment
to fish)

Put the shallots in a pan with vinegar and cook over medium heat until the liquid is evaporated. Whisk in butter until a smooth emulsion is formed. Continue mixing and add cream. Continue cooking on low-medium heat for 1 minute. Add pesto. Serve with a fresh white fish of your choosing.

Beurre Blanc is a very adaptable white butter sauce.

Foie Gras-Stuffed Cornish Hens

Serves 12

Cornish game hens are young birds bred for extra flavor and tenderness. They are the perfect ingredient in this tasty dish!

12 ounces foie gras
24 ounces bread (no crust)
1 celery root
¼ cup chopped shallots
2 tablespoons garlic
Salt and pepper, to taste

4 ounces chopped cilantro
4 ounces chopped chives
6 Cornish hens
18 ounces Cornish hen jus
1 quart chicken stock

1. In a large, hot sauté pan add the foie gras and disburse evenly in the pan. Let cook for about 20 seconds. Add the bread. After the bread has absorbed the fat from the foie gras (about 30 seconds), add the celery root, shallots, and garlic. Allow the stuffing to cook for five minutes. Take stuffing off heat. Season with salt and pepper. Place on tray and sprinkle chopped cilantro and chives on top while still hot. Let the stuffing cool and mix thoroughly.

2. Bone the hen from the spine forward leaving the skin intact, and only half the wing bone and the leg from the knee down. Open the hen with the skin side to the cutting board and the wings at the top. (You can also ask your butcher to prepare the birds.) Season the inside of the hen with salt and pepper.

3. Place ⅙ of the stuffing on each hen. Using three toothpicks, close the hen beginning with the bottom working up the spine. Rest the hen on its legs and replace any stuffing that has fallen out. Close up the top with the final toothpick. Truss the hen with butcher's twine. Fold the legs around the front and wrap twine around the entire hen, tucking the wings under the string.

4. Sear the hen on every side in a hot sauté pan until dark golden brown. Deglaze the pan with Cornish hen jus and thin with chicken stock. Place the pan in a 350° oven using the sauce to baste the hen. Cook until the hen is heated through. Test with a thermometer. The temperature in the thickest part of the thigh should be at least 165°. Remove the hen from the pan. It should have a glaze to the top. Remove all toothpicks and twine. Slice in half and serve. Strain the basting liquid. If not thick enough, reduce further on the stove. Pour the jus on top of the hen.

Left Bank's Chocolate Fondant

6 ounces chopped bittersweet
    chocolate
1 cup unsalted butter, cut into
    cubes, plus 2 tablespoons at
    room temperature

8 eggs
1 cup granulated sugar
½ cup all-purpose flour
½ cup unsweetened cocoa
    powder

A signature dessert of the Left Bank, from chef/owner Roland Passot. "When your fork cuts into the cake and the warm, molten, truffle-like chocolate oozes out, it is irresistible! And it is even more heavenly served with vanilla or coffee ice cream."

1. Melt chocolate and 1 cup butter in small saucepan over low heat, stirring till smooth. Pour into large bowl.
2. In another large bowl, whip eggs and sugar together. Fold in flour.
3. Fold egg mixture into chocolate mixture. Refrigerate 2 hours.
4. Brush bottoms and sides of eight 4-ounce ramekins with 2 tablespoons butter. Dust with cocoa powder. Spoon chilled batter into ramekins.
5. Place ramekins on sheet pan and bake at 400° till firm to touch and just beginning to pull away from sides of ramekins, about 12 to 14 minutes. Cool 3 to 5 minutes if serving immediately. If serving later, or if you want to unmold before serving, cool to room temperature. To reheat, place on sheet pan and heat in 400° oven for 3 to 5 minutes.

Bakers' Breeches

In 1569, France passed a law that few bakers would stand for today. They were forbidden to wear regular pants other than on Sunday. The result? They were easily identified in their bakers' garb, thus forcing them to continue slaving away in the kitchen. But the strictness did not stop there. Bakers, who were highly prized at this period in France, were not allowed to gather in groups or bear arms, such as a sword. Though, they were, of course, allowed to handle kitchen knives.

CHAPTER 3
Belgium: More Than Just Chocolate

Cucumber Salad with Mint

Serves 6

Make sure to drain the cucumber slices well, or the salad will be watery. Feel free to jazz up the appearance of this simple dish by shaping the radishes into "radish flowers."

1 long European cucumber
1 teaspoon kosher salt, or as needed
2 Belgian endives
3 radishes
½ cup plain yogurt
1 tablespoon Dijon mustard

1 tablespoon freshly squeezed lemon juice
1 teaspoon granulated sugar
2 tablespoons chopped fresh mint leaves
Salt and pepper, to taste
Mint sprigs, for garnish

1. Peel the cucumber, remove the seeds, and cut in 1-inch slices. Place the cucumber slices in a colander and sprinkle with the salt. Let the cucumber drain for 15 minutes. Pat dry with paper towels.
2. Remove the stem from each endive, cut in half, and cut into strips. Thinly slice the radishes.
3. In a small mixing bowl, whisk together the yogurt, mustard, lemon juice, and sugar. Stir in the mint leaves. Season with salt and pepper, as desired.
4. To serve, lay out the cucumber slices on the outer edges of a plate. Working inward, lay out the sliced endive and then the radishes. Spoon the dressing into the middle. Top the dressing with fresh mint sprigs and serve.

Location, Location, Location

Considering its neighbors—France, Luxembourg, Germany, and Holland—it is easy to see why Belgium has had a myriad of culinary influences over the years. Belgium often boasts that its food is cooked with French refinement, while served with German-style generous portions. Due to its location, by the Middle Ages Belgium was at the center of the northern European spice trade. Everything from ginger to cinnamon, nutmeg, saffron, and peppercorns were used to season dishes. Today's Belgian cuisine still has its roots in medieval cookery. Spices, mustard, vinegar, and beer continue to be widely used in both savory and sweet recipes.

Beer-Braised Chicken with Endives

6 endives

4 chicken thighs

12 ounces beer, preferably
  Belgian, divided

1 tablespoon lemon juice

⅛ teaspoon garlic salt

Up to 2 tablespoons butter,
  if needed

⅓ cup heavy cream

¼ teaspoon freshly grated
  nutmeg

Salt and pepper, to taste

8 fresh parsley or mint sprigs, as
  desired

1. Remove the core from the endives, cut in half lengthwise, and cut into thin slices. Rinse the chicken thighs and pat dry with paper towels. Place the thighs in a resealable plastic bag. Add 6 ounces of the beer (use 2 bags if necessary). Marinate the chicken in the refrigerator for 1 hour. Discard the beer marinade.

2. Heat a frying pan on medium heat. Add the chicken thighs and sauté until cooked through (about 15 minutes), turning over halfway through cooking. Remove and drain on paper towels. Do not clean the pan.

3. Add a few tablespoons of the beer to the pan and deglaze, using a slotted spoon to stir up any browned bits. Add the endives to the pan. Sprinkle with the lemon juice and the garlic salt. Sauté the endives over medium-low heat until tender (about 30 minutes), taking care they do not burn and adding butter if necessary.

4. Add the chicken back into the pan. Add the remaining beer (about 5 ounces). Reduce the heat to low and simmer, covered, for 10 more minutes. Add the cream. Stir in the nutmeg. Simmer for 5 more minutes. Taste and season with salt or pepper if desired. Garnish with parsley or mint sprigs before serving.

Belgian Endives in Mornay Sauce

**Serves 6–8
as a side dish**

Rich Mornay
sauce cuts the
bitterness of
the endives in
this recipe.
For best
results,
choose
endives with
the whitest,
most tightly
packed heads,
and no discol-
oration.

8 Belgian endives
2 teaspoons freshly squeezed
   lemon juice
1 tablespoon white wine vinegar
2½ tablespoons butter
2 tablespoons all-purpose flour
¼ cup whole milk

¼ cup light cream
¼ teaspoon (or to taste) ground
   nutmeg
Salt, to taste
Freshly ground black pepper,
   to taste
½ cup shredded Gruyère cheese

1. Core from the endives and cut in half lengthwise. Half-fill a medium saucepan with the lemon juice, white wine vinegar, and water as needed. Fit the steamer in the saucepan. Make sure the liquid is not touching the bottom of the steamer. Bring the liquid to a boil. Add the endives, cover and steam until tender (about 20 minutes).
2. Melt the butter in a small saucepan over low heat. Make a roux by adding the flour and cooking on low heat for 3 minutes, continually stirring. Whisk in the milk and cream and bring to a boil, whisking continually until thickened. Stir in the nutmeg, salt, and pepper, and ¼ cup of the shredded Gruyère cheese. Stir until the cheese has melted.
3. To serve, lay the endives out in a serving dish and pour the Mornay sauce over. Sprinkle with the remaining ¼ cup of Gruyère cheese.

Making a Roux

Using a roux, a combination of cooked flour and fat, is an easy way to thicken sauces. Simply combine equal parts butter and flour, and cook over low heat until the roux has the desired color, whisking constantly. (Using 2 tablespoons of butter and flour, after 2 minutes you'll have a white roux, and in approximately 4 minutes you'll have a golden or blond roux.) But be patient and take your time cooking it. Using higher heat to get the roux done faster may cause it to lose its thickening ability.

Cream of Brussels Sprout Soup

½ pound (about 2 cups) Brussels
    sprouts
2 tablespoons butter
2 large shallots, chopped
3 cups chicken broth

¾ cup whole milk
¼ cup heavy cream
¼ teaspoon nutmeg, or to taste
Salt and pepper, to taste
Pinch of cayenne pepper, optional

Serves 6

Finish off this simple but elegant soup by topping with a Brussels sprout garnish made by blanching 6 Brussels sprout halves and plunging in ice water to stop the cooking process.

1. Trim the tough outer layer from the Brussels sprouts. Bring a large pot of salted water to a boil. Add the Brussels sprouts and boil, uncovered, until they are tender (about 15 minutes). Remove the sprouts, drain thoroughly, and cut in half. Reserve 1 cup of the boiling liquid.
2. Cut the drained Brussels sprouts in half and purée in the food processor.
3. In a medium saucepan, melt the butter over low heat. Add the shallots and sauté until tender. Add the chicken broth, milk, reserved boiling water, and the puréed Brussels sprouts. Bring to a boil, stirring. Reduce the heat and simmer, uncovered, for about 10 minutes.
4. Remove the soup from the heat. Add the cream. Stir in the nutmeg, salt and pepper, and the cayenne pepper if using. Serve hot.

A Surprising Fact

Belgium has the highest per capita number of restaurants earning Michelin stars and it is one of the few places around the globe where McDonald's loses money. What could be better proof that fresh ingredients and fine cuisine are a cultural must in Belgium?

Cream of Belgian Endive Soup

Serves 4

Having a dinner party and planning to serve an appetizer along with the soup? Reserve a few endive leaves to serve as an eye-catching receptacle for the appetizers.

3 Belgian endives
2 large carrots
1 large potato, peeled and diced
½ white onion, diced
½ stalk celery
3½ cups chicken broth

2 tablespoons butter
½ cup heavy cream
1 tablespoon fresh chopped basil, or to taste
1 teaspoon bacon bits, optional
Salt and pepper, to taste

1. Wash all the vegetables. Remove the core from the endives, cut in half lengthwise, and cut into thin slices. Peel and dice the carrots, potato, and onion. String the celery and finely chop.
2. Bring a large pot of salted water to a boil. Add the vegetables and boil until they are very tender, or even a bit mushy. Remove the vegetables from the pot and drain thoroughly. Purée the vegetables in a food processor.
3. In a medium saucepan, bring the chicken broth and the puréed vegetables to a boil. Add the butter. Reduce the heat and simmer, uncovered, for about 10 minutes. Remove the soup from the heat. Add the cream. Stir in the fresh basil, bacon bits if using, and season with the salt and pepper. Serve hot or cold.

The Belgian Endive

Accidentally discovered by a Belgian farmer, Jan Lammers, in 1830, the Belgian endive is a staple of Belgian cuisine. Upon returning from war, Lammers discovered that a stored chicory plant, which he'd previously grown and used for coffee, had sprouted white leaves. This bitter taste appealed to his palette. Thirty years later witloof, or endive, finally became a successful crop. In 1872 it hit Paris, and became so popular it was called "white gold." It is almost always served hot in Belgium, whereas in the States we usually eat it raw, in salads. Another good fact to keep in mind: the fresher the endive is, the sweeter and less bitter the taste.

Flemish-Style Red Cabbage

1 red cabbage
2 tart apples, such as Baldwin or
    Jonathan
½ Spanish onion
2 slices bacon
1 tablespoon butter

6 tablespoons red wine vinegar
3 tablespoons packed brown
    sugar
Salt and pepper, to taste
3 to 4 fresh parsley sprigs,
    chopped

Serves 6–8

To keep from losing the cabbage's rich red color, instead of rinsing it, wipe it down with a wet cloth.

1. Remove the core from the red cabbage, cut into quarters, and shred. Peel the apples, remove the core, and thinly slice. Peel and finely chop the onion.
2. In a heavy frying pan, sauté the bacon until crisp. Remove, drain on paper towels, and chop. Do not drain the pan.
3. Add the chopped onion to the pan and cook over medium heat until the onion is soft and translucent. Push the onion to the sides of the pan. Add the butter, melt briefly, and add the apple slices. Cook the apple in the melted butter for 1 minute.
4. Add the shredded cabbage. Sauté for 1 minute. Stir in the red wine vinegar and the brown sugar. Cook, covered, over medium-low to medium heat until the cabbage is tender (about 20 minutes). Mix in the chopped bacon. Taste and season with salt and pepper, if desired. To serve, garnish with the fresh chopped parsley.

Braised Squab with Caramelized Onions

3 slices smoked bacon
16 pearl onions, peeled
4 tablespoons unsalted butter, divided
2 teaspoons granulated sugar
4 squabs, 1 pound each
1 teaspoon salt
1 teaspoon pepper
½ cup dry red wine
½ cup homemade chicken broth
1 tablespoon finely chopped fresh parsley
1 tablespoon finely chopped fresh thyme

1. In a deep-sided frying pan, sauté the bacon until crisp. Remove, drain on paper towels, and chop. Clean out the pan.
2. Fill the pan with 1 inch of water. Add the pearl onions and bring the water to a boil. Cover and cook the onions over medium-low heat until tender and translucent (10 to 15 minutes). Use a slotted spoon to remove the onions. Drain the onions in a colander.
3. Melt 2 tablespoons unsalted butter in the frying pan. Stir in the sugar. Return the onions to the pan and cook over medium heat until they are sugar-glazed (5 to 7 minutes).
4. Rub the outside skin and the cavities of the squabs with salt and pepper. Melt the remaining 2 tablespoons of butter in the frying pan. Add the squabs and sauté over medium heat until browned all over. Remove the squabs from the skillet and set aside.
5. Pour the red wine and homemade chicken broth into the skillet and deglaze the pan over high heat, using a spoon to scrape up all the brown bits from the bottom of the pan. Add the caramelized onions and chopped bacon back into the pan with the squab. Stir in the chopped fresh parsley and thyme leaves. Cover and simmer over low heat until the squabs are tender (about 30 minutes). (The squab is cooked when its internal temperature reaches 150°.)

Glazed Turnips with Cinnamon

1½ pounds turnips
2 tablespoons butter
1 teaspoon ground cinnamon

1 teaspoon granulated sugar
1 tablespoon Italian flat-leaf
 parsley, finely chopped

Serves 4–6

For extra flavor, add a pinch of paprika when sautéing the turnips.

1. Peel the turnips and cut into 1-inch pieces. In a large frying pan place the turnips with enough salted water to cover. Bring the water to a boil. Reduce the heat to low and simmer the turnips, covered, until they are tender and can be easily pierced with a fork (about 10 minutes). Drain the turnips. Clean out the frying pan.
2. Melt the butter in the frying pan over medium-high heat. Add the turnips and toss with the cinnamon and sugar. Sauté until they turn golden brown (about 5–7 minutes). Stir in the parsley, and serve.

Simple Fruit Compote

1 cup strawberries
1 cup blueberries
1 cup Bing cherries
2 tablespoons Ruby port or
 Madeira

2 tablespoons granulated sugar
1 tablespoon lemon juice
8 mint sprigs, for garnish

Serves 4

Featuring various summer fruits, this simple light dessert makes the perfect finalé to a rich evening meal.

1. Wash and hull the strawberries. Rinse the blueberries and dry on paper towels. Pit the cherries and cut in half.
2. In a small bowl, combine the port, sugar, and lemon juice. Toss the fruit with the mixture. Chill, covered, in the refrigerator for 1 hour.
3. Spoon the fruit into individual dessert bowls. Garnish each dish with 2 mint sprigs.

Buttermilk Soup with Apples

Serves 4

Don't have buttermilk on hand? Create your own "buttermilk" by combining regular whole milk with lemon juice. Use 1 tablespoon of lemon juice for every cup of milk.

⅓ cup uncooked oatmeal
6 cups buttermilk, divided
½ teaspoon salt
2 good cooking apples, such as
    Golden Delicious
¼ teaspoon ground cinnamon
1 tablespoon granulated sugar
¼ cup molasses
¼ cup brown sugar

1. In a medium saucepan, bring the oatmeal and 3 cups buttermilk to a boil on medium-high heat. Stir in the salt. Reduce the heat and simmer, uncovered, stirring occasionally, until the oatmeal is cooked (about 20 minutes).
2. While the oatmeal is cooking, peel and core the apples. Cut the apples into thin slices.
3. Add the apple slices and the remaining 3 cups buttermilk to the soup. Bring to a boil. Reduce heat to low and simmer, uncovered, until the apples are tender (about 15 minutes). Stir in the cinnamon and sugar. Serve immediately, with the molasses and brown sugar in individual serving bowls on the side.

Frites on the Run

If you're in Belgium and in a rush, odds are you will grab a tiny cone filled with fresh frites (or, as we know them, French fries). These tasty treats are served with several condiments that may seem odd to our palette: mayonnaise, béarnaise, and even curry dipping sauce. Many argue that while beer is Belgium's national drink, frites are their national food.

Mussels in Wine

1½ pounds mussels
1 Belgian endive
½ stalk celery
1 tomato
4 shallots, chopped
2 cloves garlic, crushed
1 tablespoon olive oil

1 cup dry white wine
¼ cup low-sodium chicken broth
2 tablespoons light cream,
    optional
1 tablespoon chopped fresh
    parsley

Serves 4

When choosing mussels, look for ones with tightly closed shells. Make sure to clean the mussels thoroughly to prevent grit from settling at the bottom of the pan.

1. Clean the mussels by scrubbing them with a stiff brush while holding them under cold running water. Debeard, but do not remove the shells.
2. Prepare the vegetables: Remove the stem from the Belgian endive, cut in half lengthwise, and thinly slice. String the celery and cut diagonally into 1-inch pieces. Cut the tomato into 6 wedges. Peel and chop the shallots. Smash, peel, and finely chop the garlic.
3. Heat the olive oil in a large frying pan over medium-high heat. Add the garlic and shallots and sauté for 2 to 3 minutes, until the shallots are golden.
4. Add the cleaned mussels and the wine. Cover and cook on high heat until the mussels have started to open (about 5 to 6 minutes).
5. Remove the mussels from the pan. Add the chicken broth, vegetables, and cream to the pan. Stir in the fresh parsley. Simmer, covered, for 10 to 15 minutes to give the flavors a chance to blend. To serve, place with the mussels in a large casserole dish.

Big on Mussels

Without direct ocean access, Belgium relies on its neighbor, Holland, for its mussels—a food Belgians eat often. Mussel preparation varies quite a lot; one night you may dine on mussels escargot made with parsley butter, and the next sit down to an enormous pot of mussels steamed in broth. Other dishes include mussels gratiné, with tomatoes and cheese, and cold-marinated mussels.

Stoemp with Caramelized Shallots

Dieters
beware! The
combination
of butter and
cream makes
this a deli-
ciously rich
dish.

*4 large, baking potatoes, peeled
and cubed*
4 leeks
1 tablespoon salt
2 slices bacon
1 medium shallot, finely chopped
4 tablespoons butter

*3 tablespoons light or heavy
cream, as desired*
Salt and black pepper, to taste
¼ teaspoon nutmeg, or to taste
*2 tablespoons finely minced fresh
parsley*

1. Peel the potatoes and cut lengthwise into thin slices. Remove the outer
    leaves from the leeks and cut off the white stems. Fill a large saucepan
    with lightly salted water and add the potatoes, leeks, and 1 tablespoon
    salt. Bring to boil over high heat. Reduce the heat and cook the veg-
    etables, uncovered, for 20 minutes, or until the potatoes are tender and
    easily pierced with a fork.
2. While the potatoes and the leeks are cooking, cook the bacon in a
    frying pan on medium heat until crispy. Remove and drain on paper
    towels. Do not clean out the pan. Add the finely chopped shallot and
    sauté on low heat, until the shallot softens and begin to brown. Remove
    from the pan.
3. Finely chop the boiled leeks into thin slices ⅛- to ¼-inch thick. Finely
    chop the bacon.
4. Mash the potatoes in a large mixing bowl. Mix in the butter and cream.
    Season with the salt, pepper, and nutmeg. Stir in the chopped leeks,
    bacon, and shallot. Add the fresh parsley. Serve immediately.

Prune Tart

½ cup heavy cream
1 tablespoon buttermilk
12 pitted prunes, halved
6 tablespoons cognac

¼ cup granulated sugar
2-inch cinnamon stick
Flemish Yeast Dough (page 40)

Flemish Yeast Dough (page 40)

Serves 6–8

For added decadence, spread whipped cream or ice cream on top of the tart before serving.

1. The day before the tarts will be made, prepare the homemade crème fraîche: mix together the heavy cream and buttermilk and refrigerate, covered, for 24 hours.
2. On the day that the tart is to be made, in a medium bowl, combine the prunes with the cognac. Let sit for 30 minutes to soften.
3. Combine the cognac-soaked prunes, crème fraîche, sugar, and the cinnamon stick in a medium saucepan. Bring to a boil. Reduce the heat and simmer, covered, for 1 hour, stirring occasionally. Remove from the heat, discard the cinnamon stick, and cool.
4. Preheat the oven to 350°. Grease a 12-inch tart pan.
5. Turn the tart dough out onto a floured surface and roll out into a 12-inch circle approximately 1-inch thick. Carefully transfer the dough to the greased tart pan. Fold the overhanging dough over or trim as desired. For a better appearance, crimp the edges.
6. Purée the cooled prune mixture in a food processor. Spread evenly over the tart dough. Bake for 25 to 30 minutes, until the tart is browned. Cool and serve.

Flemish Yeast Dough

**Yields dough for
one 12-inch tart**

Spices such
as nutmeg
and cinnamon
play a major
role in Belgian
cuisine. Feel
free to add
extra flavor to
the dough by
adding up to
2 teaspoons of
either of these
spices to the
dry ingredi-
ents.

1 large egg
½ cup whole milk
1 package active dry yeast

¼ teaspoon salt
¼ cup granulated sugar
1½ cups all-purpose flour

1. Lightly beat the egg. In a small saucepan, gently heat the milk on low heat until it is warm but not hot (less than 120°). In a small bowl, pour the warmed milk over the yeast and let sit for 5 minutes to soften.
2. In a large mixing bowl, combine the salt, sugar, and flour. Use a wooden spoon to gradually stir the lightly beaten egg and the milk and yeast mixture into the flour. Adjust the proportion of wet and dry ingredients as needed to make a smooth dough: add 2 to 3 tablespoons flour if the dough is too wet, or a bit of water if it is too dry.
3. Turn the dough out onto a lightly floured surface and knead until smooth and elastic (about 5 minutes). Place the dough in a bowl, cover, and let rise in a warm spot for 1 hour. Use as called for in the recipe.

Belgian Chocolate

Belgium has long been a major producer of some of the world's finest chocolates. Godiva is undoubtedly a household name, and Neuhaus is another top brand, while Wittamer is considered the crème de la crème. Interestingly, Belgian praline is a general term for filled chocolates, but also refers to a mixture of milk chocolate and finely ground nuts or toffee. Nougatine is the same as praline, except larger pieces of nuts or toffee are used for crunchiness. True Belgian chocolates are made with the freshest cream, and last only a few days.

Belgian Waffles

1 cup milk
½ cup soda water, room
   temperature
1 package dry active yeast
2 eggs, separated

2 cups all-purpose flour
4 tablespoons granulated sugar
1 tablespoon cinnamon
1 teaspoon salt
½ stick unsalted butter, melted

Not sure
what to do
with leftover
waffles?
They freeze
beautifully—
just cool
and place in
resealable
plastic bags.
Reheat the
waffles in
the oven or
microwave.

1. In a small saucepan, gently heat the milk and the soda until it is fairly warm (more than 115°). Pour the warmed liquid over the yeast and let sit for 5 minutes to soften.
2. While the yeast is softening, prepare the eggs: use an electric mixer to beat the egg whites until stiff. Beat the egg yolks with a whisk. Set aside.
3. In a large bowl, combine the flour, sugar, cinnamon, and salt. Make a "well" in the middle of the flour mixture. Pour the milk, melted butter, and the beaten egg yolks into the well. Stir into the dry ingredients. Gently fold in the egg white. Place the dough in a bowl, cover, and let rise in a warm spot for 1 hour.
4. To make the waffles, heat the waffle iron. Cook the waffles according to the instructions on your waffle iron. Make sure to cook the waffles until steam is no longer escaping and they are crispy. Serve with your favorite fruit jam, powdered sugar, or even melted chocolate.

German Syrup

To make delicious German syrup, combine 2 cups brown sugar, 1 cup water, and 1 cup light corn syrup in a pot and boil for 3 to 4 minutes. In a small bowl, beat together ½ cup crème fraîche and 1 egg. Slowly add the cream mixture to the hot syrup. It yields 3 cups.

Bread Pudding with Belgian Beer

Serves 4

For extra flavor, plump the raisins by soaking them in beer (preferably Belgian beer) before using.

2 ounces dried cherries
2½ cups beer
1 loaf French or Italian bread
2 cups light cream
4 eggs, separated
¾ cup brown sugar
1 cup raisins
1 teaspoon grated orange peel
2 tablespoons confectioners'
*   sugar, or as needed*

1. Preheat the oven to 350°. Grease a 6-cup baking dish or a deep-sided casserole dish.
2. In a medium saucepan, heat the dried cherries with ½ cup beer over high heat. Lower the heat and simmer, covered, until the cherries are softened (10 to 15 minutes). Drain the cherries, reserving the liquid.
3. Slice the loaf of French bread into 1-inch pieces and place in a large mixing bowl. Whisk in the cream, egg yolks, egg whites, and brown sugar. Add the remaining 2 cups beer, cherries, reserved liquid, raisins, and the grated orange peel.
4. Pour the mixture into the greased baking dish. Let the pudding stand for 15 minutes to allow the bread to soak up the custard.
5. Bake for 45 minutes. Test for doneness by inserting a knife in the middle (if the knife comes out clean, the pudding has set). If the pudding is not ready, bake for up to 15 minutes more, covering the top with aluminum foil to prevent overbrowning. Lightly dust with the confectioners' sugar before serving.

Belgian Beer

We all know Belgian beer is famous, but perhaps we do not know why. First of all, how many countries have beer as their national drink? It is true that more beer than wine is consumed in Belgium—a fact that must horrify the French. Many beers are made by small artisanal brewers whose family recipes and techniques go back generations. Beer also features widely in the country's cuisine, even showing up in the national dish, carbonnades flamandes, a Flemish beef stew. The custom of using spices to flavor dishes also applies to beer—which may be one reason the Belgians chose to feature the often fruity and spicy brews as an ingredient in local dishes.

German Baked Apple French Toast

Serves 8

Despite its name, French toast is featured in many cuisines, including German cuisine. Food historians believe that the basic recipe was created by an 18th century New York tavern owner named Joseph French.

4 tart apples, such as McIntosh
8 slices crusty French bread
½ cup butter, softened
¾ cup brown sugar
¼ cup liquid honey
½ teaspoon grated lemon peel

4 large eggs
1 cup whole milk
1 teaspoon vanilla extract
½ teaspoon ground cinnamon
¼ teaspoon ground nutmeg

1. Peel and core the apples. Cut each apple into 6 to 8 wedges. Cut the bread into 1-inch cubes.
2. In a small saucepan over medium heat, combine the softened butter, brown sugar, honey, and the grated lemon peel, stirring, until the sugar dissolves. In a small bowl, lightly beat the eggs, milk, and vanilla. Stir in the ground cinnamon and nutmeg.
3. Lay half the bread cubes on the bottom of a deep-sided casserole dish. Pour the brown sugar–syrup mixture over. Lay the sliced apples on top. Add the remaining half of the bread cubes. Pour the beaten egg mixture over. Cover and refrigerate overnight.
4. Preheat the oven to 325°. Bake uncovered for 50 to 60 minutes. Cool and serve.

Drinking Apple Wine

It may not be to everyone's taste, but there is no denying that apple wine (Appelwoi) is more than just a drink—it is a way of life. Made mostly in Frankfurt's Sachsenhausen district, apple wine is delivered in patterned blue-and-gray earthen pitchers, and poured into tall ribbed glasses. You will find the homemade brew at taverns and garden restaurants throughout the area, and finding such garden restaurants is half the fun—simply look for a jug surrounded by a fresh wreath, hanging on the restaurant's outdoor sign. That translates as "apple wine made and served here." Used in some dishes such as apple wine soup, the slightly bitter and refreshing drink is most often drunk on its own, with sparkling lemonade, or sparkling water.

Beer-Basted Sausage with Caramelized Onions and German Mustard

1 white onion

2 tablespoons unsalted butter

3 tablespoons German hot
   mustard, such as Dusseldorf

8 German sausages

½ cup dark beer, preferably
   German

Serves 4–6

This hearty dish combines several ingredients typically associated with German cuisine, including sausage, beer, and hot mustard. Bratwurst, wieners, or knackwurst are all good choices for the sausage.

1. Preheat grill on medium-high heat. Peel the onion, cut in half, and finely chop.
2. Fill a deep 12-inch frying pan with 1 inch of water. Add the chopped onion and cook on medium heat until caramelized (about 10 minutes). Remove the onions from the pan and drain.
3. Melt the butter in the frying pan. Stir in the mustard. Return the onions to the pan and cook over medium heat until they are glazed (5 to 7 minutes).
4. Grill the sausages on medium-high heat, basting frequently with the beer, until browned and cooked through (8 to 10 minutes on each side). Serve with the caramelized onions.

What Is Brotzeit?

Famous in Munich, but served all over the German countryside, brotzeit can be eaten anywhere, at any time—and is most often shared by friends outside. Served on a cutting board, brotzeit is a rustic and traditional medley of regional specialties. Think smoked ham, sausages, liverwurst, blood sausages, wurstsalat, and local cheeses. The beauty of the dish is that it dramatically changes from region to region. Everything on the board is made by hand, and has a very homey, or hausmacher, quality.

Cold Wine Soup

Serves 4

Chilled soup makes a refreshing treat on hot afternoons. Serve with fresh fruit in season.

4 cups water
1 lemon, cut into wedges
¼ cup semolina
2 eggs, separated

8 tablespoons granulated sugar,
* divided*
1 cup white wine
1 teaspoon lemon juice
1 teaspoon ground cinnamon

1. In a medium saucepan, bring 3 cups of the water and the lemon wedges to a boil. Simmer for 5 minutes, uncovered, and remove the lemon.
2. Bring the water back to a boil. Mix the semolina with the remaining 1 cup of water. Slowly pour the semolina and water mixture into the boiling water, stirring continuously. Let boil for 1 minute. Reduce the heat and simmer, uncovered, until the semolina is cooked (about 20 minutes). Stir regularly.
3. In a medium bowl, whisk together the egg yolks, 2 tablespoons sugar, and the white wine. Stir into the soup. Simmer for 5 more minutes, stirring occasionally. Cool the soup and pour into a glass punch serving bowl. Cover and chill in the refrigerator.
4. Just before serving, beat the egg whites until they form stiff peaks. (Make sure to use eggs that are at room temperature.) Beat in the lemon juice, and gradually beat in the remaining 6 tablespoons of sugar. Drop small amounts of the beaten egg white into the soup. Sprinkle the soup with the ground cinnamon and serve.

Dark Bread Soup

1 clove garlic, cut in half
1 loaf German dark rye bread
4 cups water
2 beef bouillon cubes
1 cup cream

½ teaspoon caraway seeds
1 tablespoon freshly chopped
  chives
Salt and pepper, to taste
½ pound Mettwurst sausage

1. Rub the garlic clove over 3 slices of bread. Toast the bread in the oven or a toaster oven. Cut each slice into 8 equal pieces.
2. In a large saucepan, bring the water and the bouillon cubes to a boil. Add the cream and let boil briefly. Add the bread slices. Reduce heat and simmer, uncovered, for 5 minutes. Stir in the caraway seeds and the fresh chives. Simmer for 2 more minutes. Taste and season with salt and pepper if desired.
3. Place the remainder of the rye bread on a serving dish with the sliced Mettwurst sausage. Serve with the soup.

On German Cuisine

Many people think of German food as heavy, sausage-laden, potato-oriented fare. While that may be true, there is also a new revolution in German cuisine that reflects today's obsession with gourmet (and also lighter) cuisine. Germany has a myriad of fresh produce, wine, and particularly high-quality meats that impart complex and developed flavors. Germans are also masters of garnishing, from simple mustards, to rich hollandaise, to sauerkraut. With its roots as a rural country, the evolution of German cuisine reflected the needs of its people—mainly to sustain themselves during hard physical labor. Thus, many of the dishes are quite hardy. But today a new army of chefs, armed with the latest in training, phenomenal regional products, and a vivd imagination, are redefining traditional favorites with fresh, epicurian interpretations.

Westphalian Cabbage

Serves 4

Serve with a good German smoked sausage, or as a side dish with Holstein Duck (page 53).

1 head red cabbage
2 large McIntosh apples
3 tablespoons butter
2 tablespoons minced shallots
2 teaspoons brown sugar
¾ cup beef broth

¼ cup red wine vinegar
2 tablespoons lemon juice
1 tablespoon caraway seeds
¼ teaspoon salt
2 tablespoons chopped fresh
*   parsley*

1. Wash the cabbage, remove the core, and shred. Peel the apples, remove the core, and cut into thin slices.
2. In a large saucepan or Dutch oven, melt the butter. Add the shallots and cook over medium heat until softened. Add the shredded cabbage and the sliced apples. Stir in the brown sugar. Sauté until the apple slices are browned (about 5 minutes).
3. Add the beef broth, red wine vinegar, and lemon juice. Bring to a boil. Stir in the caraway seeds and salt.
4. Reduce the heat to medium. Cook, uncovered, stirring occasionally, until the cabbage is tender and most of the liquid has been reduced. (about 30 minutes). Stir in the chopped parsley. Taste and season with salt and pepper if desired. Serve hot.

White Asparagus Season

From the end of April until June 24, much of Germany's sandy-soiled flat regions (e.g., south of Frankfurt, areas around Berlin, the lower Rhine region) feature the famed white asparagus. Unlike its green counterpart, white asparagus must be peeled all the way to the tip—but the extra step is worth it. Once boiled with a dash of salt, sugar, and 1 teaspoon of lemon juice for about 20 minutes, white asparagus is juicy, tender, and has a sweet earthiness that truly sets it apart. Germans are very proud of their white asparagus—their summer's white gold—and eat it as main dish. You will most often find it served with ham, potatoes, and homemade hollandaise.

Fruit-Stuffed Pork Chops

4 pork chops, bone-in, about 1½-
inches thick
¼ teaspoon salt
¼ teaspoon black pepper
½ cup plus 2 tablespoons orange
juice
½ cup prunes, pitted and
quartered
1 tablespoon brown sugar

½ cup chopped McIntosh apple
½ cup dried currants
½ bunch fresh parsley, finely
chopped
⅛ teaspoon ground cardamom,
or to taste
2 tablespoons butter
2 tablespoons water

Serves 4

Tart fruit like
apples make
a perfect foil
for sweet
pork. Feel
free to sub-
stitute the
currants with
other dried
fruit—such as
cranberries
or apricots—
as desired.

1. Purchase pork chops already cut with a pocket, or slice open each pork chop yourself, cutting from the side and taking care not to go too near the edge. Season the outside of the pork chops with the salt and pepper.

2. In a medium saucepan, bring ½ cup of orange juice to a simmer. Add the prunes and simmer until softened (5 to 7 minutes). Remove the prunes with a slotted spoon. Stir the brown sugar into the orange juice. Add the chopped apple and simmer until tender. Stir in the dried currants, prunes, fresh parsley, and ground cardamom. Heat through. Remove the stuffing with a slotted spoon. Clean out the frying pan.

3. Stuff approximately ¼ cup of filling into the pouch of each pork chop. (Do not overfill.) Press down gently on the pork chop with a spatula to close.

4. Melt the butter in the pan. Brown the pork chops. Add the remaining 2 tablespoons of orange juice with the water. Simmer the pork chops, uncovered, over medium heat until the pork chops are tender (about 50 minutes). Serve hot.

Herbed Potato Salad

Serves 6

This recipe offsets the starch of the potatoes with the sharpness of red wine vinegar, flavored beautifully with bacon, shallots, and herbs.

2½ pounds small new or red potatoes
6 slices bacon
1 tablespoon olive oil
3 large shallots, peeled, finely minced

3 tablespoons extra-virgin olive oil
2½ tablespoons red wine vinegar
½ teaspoon granulated sugar
2 tablespoons chopped fresh dill
1 teaspoon mustard seed
Salt and pepper, to taste

1. Place the potatoes in a large saucepan with just enough salted water to cover. Bring the water to a boil. Reduce the heat and simmer, uncovered, until the potatoes are tender (about 20 minutes). Cool and cut into quarters.
2. While the potatoes are cooking, heat a large frying pan on medium-high and cook the bacon until crispy. Remove the bacon, drain on paper towels, and finely chop.
3. Clean out the pan and add 1 tablespoon olive oil. Add the shallots and sauté on medium-high heat until they are softened (3 to 4 minutes). In a small bowl, whisk together the extra-virgin olive oil, red wine vinegar, sugar, chopped fresh dill, and mustard seed until well blended.
4. Transfer the potatoes to a large bowl. Toss with the cooked shallot, bacon, and the salad dressing. Season with salt and pepper to taste. Serve warm.

Buttered Fillet of Sole

2 sole fillets
1 tablespoon freshly squeezed
   lemon juice
4½ tablespoons butter, divided
1 teaspoon dried dill

½ teaspoon German mustard
4 fresh parsley sprigs
1 lemon, cut into wedges

Serve this simple dish with good French bread and boiled or mashed potatoes.

1. Rinse the sole fillets and pat dry. Sprinkle the lemon juice over the fish and set aside.
2. In a frying pan over medium heat, melt 2 tablespoons of the butter. Add the fillets and sauté for 5 minutes, or until they are lightly browned and flake easily when tested with a fork. Turn each fillet over halfway through cooking.
3. Transfer the fillets to a hot platter. Add the remaining 2½ tablespoons butter to the pan. Stir in the dried dill and the mustard. As soon as the butter melts, pour it over the sole fillets. Serve, garnished with the parsley sprigs and lemon wedges.

Reading a German Wine Label

Producing about as much wine as the United States, Germany is a major force in the world of wine. Germany has thirteen wine-growing regions, 75 percent of which concentrate on white wines, most importantly Rieslings. To read a German wine label effectively, there are a few things you should know. The common classification is known as qualitatswein bestimmter anbaugebiete, or Q.b.A. for short. This refers to wines of good quality, destined for everyday consumption. A step up is the Q.m.P. (quality wine with distinction), most of which come from a specific wine-growing district. This category is divided into six subcategories, steadily increasing in natural sugar content and quality: Kabinetts, Spätleses, Ausleses, Beerenausleses, Eisweins, and Trockenbeerenausleses.

Elderberry Soup with "Dumplings" and Apples

Serves 6

The "dumplings" in this soup are beaten egg whites that float on top of the soup.

8 cups elderberry juice
2½ teaspoons freshly squeezed lemon juice, divided
1 cup plus 1 teaspoon granulated sugar, divided
3 tart apples, chopped (unpeeled)

1 teaspoon ground cinnamon, divided
2 tablespoons Jamaican dark rum
2 egg whites

1. In a large saucepan, bring the elderberry juice, 2 teaspoons lemon juce, and 1 cup sugar to a boil. Add the chopped apples. Stir in ½ teaspoon ground cinnamon. Reduce the heat and simmer, uncovered, until the apples soften (4 to 5 minutes). Stir in the rum. Keep the soup warm on low heat while preparing the dumplings.
2. To make the dumplings: beat the egg whites until they form stiff peaks. Beat in ½ teaspoon lemon juice and 1 teaspoon sugar.
3. Remove the soup from the heat. Drop in large spoonfuls of the egg white mixture, turning lightly so that the dumplings absorb some of the liquid. If desired, sprinkle the remaining ½ teaspoon ground cinnamon on top of the dumplings. Serve immediately.

Holstein Duck

1 duck (3–4 pounds)
½ teaspoon marjoram
¼ teaspoon salt
¼ teaspoon pepper
5 tart apples, such as McIntosh
1 sweet apple, such as Granny
   Smith

2 slices smoked ham
¼ stick unsalted butter
¼ cup minced shallots
2 tablespoons breadcrumbs
2 eggs
1½ cups sour cream
Italian flat-leaf parsley sprigs

Serves 4–6

Before placing the duck in the oven, prick holes in several parts of the body, including underneath the wings. This allows the fat to drain during roasting.

1. Preheat the oven to 375°.
2. Remove the liver and fat from the body cavity of the duck. Rinse the duck under hot running water and drain well. In a small dish, combine the marjoram and salt and pepper. Rub the spice mixture over the outside of the duck and sprinkle inside its body cavity.
3. Remove any connecting tissue from the duck liver and slice. Peel and core the apples and chop finely (keep the chopped Granny Smith separate). Dice the smoked ham.
4. Melt the unsalted butter in a frying pan over medium heat. Add the minced shallots and cook until softened. Add the duck liver, cook briefly, and add the ham and the chopped McIntosh apples. In a large bowl, combine the breadcrumbs with one of the eggs. Use your hands to mix the breadcrumbs with the duck liver, ham, apple and shallot mixture, and the other egg. If necessary, add a bit of water so that the stuffing is neither too dry nor too "mushy."
5. Fill the duck cavity with the stuffing. Place the duck on a rack in a shallow roasting pan. Cook the duck for 1½ hours, basting frequently with water. Drain off the fat and baste the duck with water again. Add the chopped Granny Smith apple to the roasting pan and cook for another 15 to 20 minutes, as needed. (The duck is cooked when the internal temperature of the fattest part of the thigh is 180°.)
6. Remove the duck and slice. Mix the roasted chopped apple with the sour cream. Slice the duck and garnish with the parsley sprigs. Serve with the sour cream–apple mixture.

Black Forest Cherry Cake

Serves 8

There are numerous versions of this popular cake that originated in Germany's Black Forest region. Feel free to beat 1 or 2 tablespoons of kirsch brandy liqueur into the whipped cream filling if desired.

1 cup all-purpose flour, sifted
1 cup granulated sugar
¼ teaspoon salt
¼ cup cocoa powder
3 eggs
1½ teaspoons vanilla extract, divided

1¼ cups sour cherry juice, divided
2 tablespoons granulated sugar
1½ cups whipping cream
¼ cup confectioners' sugar
2 cups canned sour cherries
1 ounce semisweet chocolate

1. Preheat the oven to 350°. Grease two 8-inch cake pans.
2. To make the cake, sift together the flour, sugar, salt and cocoa powder. Beat the eggs and 1 teaspoon vanilla extract until light and fluffy. Carefully fold the flour into the beaten egg. Pour the cake batter into the greased pans. Bake for 30 minutes, or until a toothpick inserted in the middle comes out clean. Cool the cakes completely.
3. To make the syrup, in a small saucepan bring 1 cup of the sour cherry juice and the granulated sugar to a boil. Cook, stirring, until the sugar dissolves.
4. To make the filling, beat the whipping cream until stiff peaks form. Beat in ½ teaspoon vanilla extract, the confectioners' sugar, and the remaining ¼ cup of sour cherry juice.
5. To assemble the cake, turn the cakes out onto 2 cake plates. Spread ½ of the syrup mixture over each cake. Let sit for 5 minutes, then spread ⅓ of the whipped cream filling over 1 cake. Add ½ cup of the cherries. Place the other cake on top. Spread the remaining ⅔ of the filling over the top and sides of the cake. Place the cherries on the top of the cake and the sides.
6. Grate the chocolate and sprinkle on top of the cake. Chill until ready to serve.

Hazelnut Torte

8 large eggs, separated
1½ cups granulated sugar
1 teaspoon vanilla extract
1 cup finely ground hazelnuts

4 ounces semisweet chocolate, grated
¼ cup kirsch brandy liqueur
2 cups whipped cream

Guests are certain to be impressed by this delicious dessert. For an added touch, sprinkle a bit of confectioners' sugar or grated chocolate over the whipped cream topping.

1. Preheat the oven to 350°. Grease two 9-inch springform pans and line the bottom with wax or parchment paper.
2. Beat the egg yolks until smooth and set aside. In a separate bowl, beat the egg whites until they form stiff peaks and are very light (about 5 minutes). Gradually add the sugar during beating. Beat in the vanilla extract.
3. Fold the egg white mixture into the yolks. Use a rubber spatula to carefully fold the chopped hazelnuts into the mixture. Fold in the grated chocolate.
4. Pour the batter into the cake pans, dividing it evenly between them. Bake for 35 to 40 minutes, until the cake is browned and springs back from the sides of the pan. Remove the cakes from the oven and cool on a wire rack.
5. Finish the torte by lightly brushing 2 tablespoons of the kirsch over the top of each cake. Place one of the cakes on top of the other. Spread the whipped cream on top and chill until ready to serve.

How to Grind Hazelnuts

First, blanch the hazelnuts by boiling them for 5 minutes. When they are cool enough to handle, remove the skins. To grind, place about ¼ cup at a time in a blender, or chop as finely as you can with a sharp knife.

Swabian Stuffed Pockets (Maultaschen)

Serves 4

The German version of ravioli, Maultaschen are traditionally served with a simple salad.

2¾ cups all-purpose flour
6 eggs, divided
¼ teaspoon salt
Water, as needed
⅓ cup breadcrumbs, or as needed
2 slices prosciutto, thinly sliced

¼ pound fresh sausage meat
½ pound ground pork
½ cup cooked spinach
¼ cup chopped fresh parsley
½ teaspoon grated nutmeg
Salt and black pepper, to taste

1. To make the dough, place the flour in a large bowl. Make a "well" in the middle and add 4 eggs and ¼ teaspoon salt. Combine the egg with the flour to form a dough, adjusting the level of flour and water as necessary: if the dough is too wet, add a bit more flour. If too dry, add 1 tablespoon of water at a time as needed. Keep kneading for at least 5 minutes, until the dough is smooth and elastic. Cover the dough and let rest for 30 minutes.
2. To make the filling, in a small bowl combine the breadcrumbs with 1 tablespoon water to soften. In a large bowl, combine the softened breadcrumbs, prosciutto, sausage, ground pork, spinach, parsley, the nutmeg, and the remaining 2 eggs, using your hands to mix everything together. Add a bit of water or milk if the filling is too dry. Season with salt and pepper as desired.
3. To make the ravioli, knead the rested dough for a few minutes more. Turn onto a floured surface and divide in half. Roll both halves out very thinly (⅛-inch if possible). Lay out one of the halves and use a pastry cutter to cut into 4-inch squares. Stack the squares, cover with a damp towel to keep from drying, and repeat with the other half.
4. To fill the ravioli, place a heaping teaspoon of filling in the middle of a square. Moisten all the edges of the square with water. Lay another square on top and press down to seal. Continue with the remainder of the ravioli.
5. To cook, bring a large saucepan of salted water to a boil. Cook the ravioli in the boiling water until they float to the top (7 to 10 minutes). Take care not to overcrowd the saucepan. Serve hot with tomato sauce or melted butter.

German Cucumber Salad

2 medium cucumbers
1 red onion
3 tomatoes
½ cup sour cream
1 tablespoon German mustard
2 tablespoons granulated sugar

1 tablespoon red wine vinegar
2 tablespoons minced fresh dill
⅛ teaspoon salt, or to taste
⅛ teaspoon pepper, or to taste
4 sprigs fresh parsley, to garnish

For maximum flavor, chill the salad for at least 1 hour to give the flavors a chance to blend.

1. Peel the cucumbers and thinly slice. Peel and thinly slice the red onion. Cut each tomato into 4 to 6 wedges. Combine the vegetables in a salad bowl.
2. To make the dressing, combine the sour cream, German mustard, sugar, red wine vinegar, fresh dill, and salt and pepper in a small bowl. Pour the dressing over the prepared vegetables and chill. Garnish with the fresh parsley sprigs before serving.

A German Ravioli

Maultaschen is a Swabian stuffed noodle with an amusing history. Swabia is a region and language in southern Germany, and long ago once included what is now modern Switzerland and Alsace. Swabians liked to eat meat, and they did not want to give it up for Lent. So in order to get around this challenging situation, they resorted to camouflage. They ground the meat, mixed it with spinach and onions, wrapped it in a thin pasta dough, and added melted cheese as a final cloak. This, they thought, would hide their secret ingredient from God. It is still served today, though in some restaurants you may find a modern "open-faced" interpretation.

CHAPTER 5
Greece: Gourmet Island Hopping

Roasted Potatoes with Garlic, Lemon, and Oregano

Serves 4–6

This dish is a specialty on the Greek island of Naxos, where it is frequently served with roast chicken or leg of lamb.

12 small red potatoes
4 tablespoons freshly squeezed lemon juice (2 lemons)
½ teaspoon garlic salt
1 tablespoon dried oregano
1 teaspoon salt

Freshly ground black pepper, to taste
¼ cup olive oil
1½ tablespoons chopped fresh oregano
4–6 fresh parsley sprigs

1. Preheat the oven to 425°.
2. Cut the unpeeled potatoes into quarters. In a medium bowl, toss the potatoes with the lemon juice, garlic salt, oregano, salt, and freshly ground black pepper.
3. Pour the olive oil into a shallow 9 × 13-inch baking pan. Use a paper towel or cloth to wipe the olive oil across the pan so that the pan is evenly coated. Spread out the potatoes on the pan.
4. Bake the potatoes until they are browned and pierce easily with a fork (about 30 minutes). Turn the potatoes 2 or 3 times during cooking. Garnish with the fresh oregano and parsley sprigs and serve.

The Greek Diet of Longevity

Greeks used to relate stories about the men and women of Crete who lived past the age of 100, thanks to a diet of little meat and that was rich in olive oil, greens, and grains. Strangely enough, those stories have now been proven true—this diet does increase lifespan. Although a large percentage of Greeks are still heavy smokers and the country doesn't enjoy one of the highest standards of living in Europe, the inhabitants of Greece have one of the world's highest life expectancies.

Squid in Wine

Serves 4

1 whole small squid, 1½ pounds
¼ cup olive oil
2 cloves garlic, minced
1 cup dry red wine
2 tablespoons balsamic vinegar

¼ cup water
1 chopped green onion
2 tablespoons chopped fresh
  parsley
2 (3-inch) cinnamon sticks

Shellfish play a prominent role in Greek cuisine. In this dish, balsamic vinegar and red wine bring out squid's natural sweet flavor.

1. To clean the squid, pull out the entrails (body contents) and cut off the tentacles, making sure to remove the beak in the center of the tentacles. Discard the ink sac and the head. Lay the squid flat and carefully scrape off the dark outer skin. Rinse the squid body and the tentacles under cold running water. Pat dry with paper towels. Cut the tentacles in half lengthwise. Cut the main body into rings.
2. Heat the olive oil in a deep-sided frying pan. Add the minced garlic and squid pieces. Cook over medium heat, until the squid is lightly browned (about 5 minutes). Remove the squid from the pan and drain on paper towels.
3. Deglaze the pan by bringing ¼ cup of the red wine to a boil, using a spatula to scrape up the browned bits. Add the squid back into the pan. Add the remaining ¾ cup of red wine and balsamic vinegar. Add the ¼ cup water, or as much water as is needed to cover the squid. Stir in the chopped green onion and fresh parsley. Add the cinnamon sticks.
4. Bring to a boil, then reduce the heat and simmer, uncovered, until the squid is tender (about 60 minutes). Stir the squid occasionally, and add more water or wine if necessary to cover. Serve warm (remove the cinnamon sticks before serving).

Pan-Fried Fish with Rosemary

Serves 6

Besides red
snapper, the
sweet and tart
sauce in this
recipe works
well with
many types of
fish, including
mullet and
trout.

4 red snapper, fillets
¼ teaspoon salt, or as needed
5 tablespoons flour, divided
2 teaspoons dried rosemary
2 teaspoons dried thyme

5 tablespoons olive oil, divided
2 cloves garlic, minced
⅓ cup balsamic vinegar
1 lemon, cut into wedges
6 to 8 rosemary sprigs

1. Rinse the fish under cold running water, and pat dry with paper towels. Rub the salt over the fish. Set aside.
2. Combine ¼ cup flour, dried rosemary, and dried thyme on a piece of parchment or wax paper.
3. In a 12-inch frying pan, heat ¼ cup of the olive oil over medium-high heat. Cover the fillets with the seasoned flour mixture, pressing to coat. Lay the fish in the frying pan and cook until golden brown and crispy (2 to 3 minutes on each side). Remove the fish from the pan. Place on a serving dish and keep warm.
4. Add the remaining 1 tablespoon oil in the pan. Add the minced garlic and sauté on medium-heat until the garlic is lightly browned. Turn the heat up to medium-high and add the remaining 1 tablespoon of flour and the balsamic vinegar, stirring continuously to thicken. Pour the sauce over the fish and garnish with the lemon wedges and rosemary sprigs. Serve hot.

Macaroni—a Greek Pasta?

Making pasta was an ancient way of preserving grain. Though most of the words related to pasta are Italian, there is one—macaroni—that has its roots in Greece. It likely originated from the tradition known as the Feast of the Makarion (the Blessed) in Ancient Greece—festivals dedicated to the honoring of dead souls. It was (and still is in many places today in Greece) a tradition where, on that particular day, they cook grain and mainly pasta, since the seeds from the grain (Demeter and Persephone) symbolize death (sowing) and resurrection (sprouting).

Lemon and Egg Soup

¾ cup white or brown rice
6 cups chicken stock
6 tablespoons freshly squeezed lemon juice, divided
3 large eggs

2 teaspoons dried oregano
Salt and freshly ground black pepper, to taste
Lemon slices as desired, for garnish

Serves 6

The Greek version of chicken soup is made with egg for extra protein. Feel free to use your favorite type of rice, including long-grained or short-grained white rice.

1. Rinse the rice if desired. Bring the chicken stock to a boil in a large saucepan. Add the rice and 4 tablespoons lemon juice. Return the soup to boiling, reduce the heat, and simmer, uncovered until the rice is tender (10 to 15 minutes). Remove 1½ cups of the soup and set aside.
2. In a large bowl, use an electric mixer to beat the eggs until they are fluffy. Beat in the remaining 2 tablespoons of lemon juice. Whisk in the reserved 1½ cups of soup.
3. Pour the egg and soup mixture back into the saucepan, whisking continuously to thicken. Cook for 5 more minutes to give the flavors a chance to blend. Stir in the dried oregano. Taste and season with salt and pepper if desired. Serve hot with lemon wedges.

The Greek Leaf

Phyllo, which literally translates as "leaf" in Greek, is made of finely rolled and stretched sheets of dough. Practically see-through, these paper-thin sheets are stacked, rolled, wrapped, and then frozen. Phyllo dough is available at most supermarkets and at Greek and Middle Eastern specialty food stores (making your own is tricky). Because the dough is already rolled and precut, phyllo is relatively easy to work with.

Braised Octopus with Onions

Serves 6

Don't worry about adding olive oil when you first add the octopus to the pan— the octopus releases its own liquid while cooking. Sprinkle the dish with parsley before serving.

4 sun-dried tomatoes (not oil-packed)
½ cup dry red wine
2 pounds octopus, cleaned
2 tablespoons olive oil
6 shallots, finely chopped
2 cloves garlic, finely chopped
2 tablespoons red wine vinegar
2 tablespoons chopped fresh basil
1 bay leaf
Salt and freshly ground black pepper, to taste

1. Reconstitute the sun-dried tomatoes by placing in a bowl with the red wine and enough water to cover. Soak in the wine and water mixture until softened (25 to 30 minutes). Pat dry with paper towels and cut into 1-inch slices. Reserve the soaking liquid.
2. Place the cleaned octopus body and tentacles in a saucepan. Do not add water. Cook, covered, over low heat, until the octopus is tender and easily pierced with a fork (about 20 minutes). Remove from the saucepan. Cut the octopus into 1-inch pieces. Cut off the suckers if desired. Reserve the cooking liquid.
3. Clean out the saucepan, and add the olive oil. Add the shallots, chopped garlic, and the sun-dried tomatoes. Sauté over medium to medium-high heat until the shallots have softened and the garlic starts to brown.
4. Add the octopus back into the pan, with the reserved tomato soaking liquid, reserved liquid from cooking the octopus, and the red wine vinegar. Bring to a boil. Stir in the basil, bay leaf, and salt and pepper to taste. Cook, covered, over low heat until the sauce has thickened and the octopus is tender (40 to 50 minutes). Remove the bay leaf before serving.

Tzatziki
(Cucumber, Garlic, and Yogurt Dip)

Serves 4–6

1 English cucumber
½ teaspoon salt
2 cups Greek yogurt
4 cloves garlic, finely chopped
5 teaspoons virgin olive oil

2 teaspoons red wine vinegar
2 tablespoons chopped fresh
    sweet herbs (dill or mint)
Freshly ground black pepper, to
    taste

Thick and
creamy
Greek yogurt
has a higher
percentage of
milk-fat than
other types
of yogurt.

1. Peel and grate the cucumber. Drain the liquid from the cucumbers by placing them in a colander and sprinkling the salt over. Place a small plate on top of the cucumbers to help push out the liquid, and let drain for 1 hour.
2. Combine the yogurt, grated cucumber, chopped garlic, olive oil, red wine vinegar, and the chopped fresh herbs in a medium bowl. Season with the black pepper. Cover and chill until ready to serve.

Feta and Mint Dip

Serves 6–8

4 ounces feta cheese, crumbled
¾ cup plain yogurt
¾ cup sour cream
1 green onion, diced
1 tablespoon freshly chopped
    mint

Juice of 1 freshly squeezed lemon
⅛ teaspoon salt, or to taste
¼ teaspoon freshly ground black
    pepper, to taste
Mint leaves for garnish

Serve
this light,
refreshing
dip with
crudités or
toasted slices
of Greek pita
bread.

In a food processor, purée all the ingredients except for the mint leaves until you have a smooth, creamy dip. Cover and refrigerate for at least 1 hour to give the flavors a chance to blend. Garnish with the fresh mint leaves before serving.

Moussaka

Ground beef makes a convenient substitute for lamb in this variation on classic Greek moussaka. Be sure to use truncheon-shaped western eggplant, and not the thinner Japanese eggplant.

2 medium eggplants
5 tablespoons olive oil, divided
1 medium white onion, finely chopped
1 pound lean ground beef
2 large cloves garlic, minced
¾ cup canned tomatoes
¼ cup dry white wine

1 teaspoon dried oregano
1 tablespoon chopped fresh parsley
3 tablespoons butter
2½ tablespoons all-purpose flour
1 cup half-and-half
1 egg, lightly beaten
½ cup grated Parmesan or Gruyère cheese

1. Preheat the oven to 350°. Grease a 9 × 9-inch baking dish.
2. Peel the eggplants and cut into slices between ¼- and ½-inch thick. Degorge the eggplant slices by placing them in a colander and sprinkling with salt. Let the eggplant slices sit for at least 1 hour to release their liquid. Remove from the colander, lay on paper towels, and press down to remove the liquid.
3. Heat 3 tablespoons of olive oil in a frying pan. Add the eggplant slices and sauté over medium heat until they are browned. Remove and drain on paper towels. Clean out the frying pan.
4. Add 2 tablespoons olive oil to the frying pan. Add the onions and cook over medium heat until they are soft and translucent. Add the ground beef, using a spatula to break it up. Cook over medium heat until the beef is browned. Drain the fat from the frying pan. Add the garlic, tomatoes, and the white wine. Stir in the oregano. Reduce heat and simmer, uncovered, for 20 minutes, stirring occasionally. Stir in the fresh parsley.
5. While the meat is simmering, prepare the white sauce: melt the butter in a small saucepan over low heat. Add the flour, stirring continuously until the flour is mixed in with the butter (2 to 3 minutes). Slowly add the half-and-half. Continue stirring over medium heat until the sauce is thick and bubbly. Remove from the heat and stir in the lightly beaten egg.
6. To cook, add the eggplant and meat sauce to the dish: lay out half the eggplant in the bottom of the baking dish and half of the meat sauce mixture on top. Repeat with the remaining eggplant and meat sauce. Spread the béchamel sauce over top. Sprinkle with the grated cheese. Bake until the moussaka is heated through (about 45 minutes). Cut into squares to serve.

Galaktoboureko (Greek-Style Pie)

4 large eggs
1 tablespoon lemon juice
1¾ cups granulated sugar,
*   divided*

6 cups whole milk
1½ cups semolina flour
12 sheets phyllo dough, thawed
⅔ cup unsalted butter, melted

Serves 6

Finish off this delicious Greek dessert by topping with a simple sugar and water syrup, made by boiling 1¾ cups water and 1 cup granulated sugar, stirring to dissolve the sugar.

1. Preheat the oven to 350°. Grease a 9 × 13-inch pan.
2. In a large bowl, beat the eggs until fluffy, beating in the lemon juice and ¼ cup of sugar. In a large saucepan, heat the milk on medium-low heat until it is at a near boil, taking care not to burn or scorch. Remove the saucepan from the heat.
3. In a medium bowl, combine the semolina flour and the remaining sugar. Whisk the flour and sugar mixture into the warm milk. Gently stir in the beaten eggs.
4. Lay 6 of the phyllo sheets in the bottom of the pan. Brush with half of the melted butter. Carefully spread the egg custard mixture over the phyllo sheets, using a rubber spatula to make sure it is spread out evenly. Lay the other 6 phyllo sheets on top and brush with the remaining melted butter. Make horizontal cuts in the top layer of the phyllo, taking care not to cut through into the custard. Bake until the custard is firm and the topping is golden brown (45 to 50 minutes). Cool before serving.

Roasted Leg of Lamb with Lemon-Garlic Potatoes

Serves 6

Robust Yukon potatoes flavored with tart lemon and garlic make a perfect foil for lamb. For extra flavor, feel free to add a pinch of garlic salt when seasoning the potatoes.

¾ cup olive oil, divided

3 teaspoons minced garlic, divided

2½ tablespoons dried oregano, divided

4 teaspoons dried thyme, divided

2 sprigs chopped fresh rosemary

6–7 pound leg of lamb, bone in

3 pounds Yukon gold potatoes

Juice from 3 freshly squeezed lemons (6 tablespoons)

¾ teaspoon salt, or to taste

1. In a cup or small bowl, combine ¼ olive oil, 2 teaspoons minced garlic, 1½ tablespoons dried oregano, 1 teaspoon dried thyme, and rosemary, Rub the marinade over the lamb. Place the lamb in a large, deep container or shallow roasting pan. Cover and refrigerate overnight.

2. Preheat the oven to 325°. Remove the lamb from the pan and discard the marinade. Clean out the pan if this is the pan that will be used for roasting.

3. Wash the potatoes and cut into quarters. (Do not peel.) Place the potatoes in a large roasting pan and toss with ½ cup olive oil, lemon juice, 1 tablespoon oregano, 1 tablespoon thyme, 1 teaspoon minced garlic, and the salt. Place the lamb over the potatoes.

4. Roast the lamb, allowing 20 minutes per pound, until it reaches the desired level of doneness. Check for doneness by inserting a meat thermometer in the thickest part of the lamb: for medium-rare, the internal temperature should be 140°; it should be 170° for well-done. Baste the lamb with the juices and turn the potatoes occasionally during cooking.

5. To serve, remove the lamb from the oven and let stand for 10 minutes before carving. Check the potatoes: if they are not tender, continue cooking while the lamb is standing. Serve the lamb with the roasted potatoes.

Greek-Style Rabbit Stew

3½ pound rabbit, cut into 6
   serving pieces
½ cup all-purpose flour, or as
   needed
1 medium yellow onion, finely
   chopped
2 blood oranges or other sweet
   orange

¼ cup olive oil
1¼ cups dry red wine
1 bay leaf
10 juniper berries
1 (3-inch) cinnamon stick
Salt and black pepper, as needed

Serves 4

Sweet blood
oranges and
cinnamon
combine to
give this stew
a unique
fruity flavor.

1. Rinse the rabbit pieces under cold running water and pat dry with paper towels. Dredge each piece in the flour. Peel and chop the yellow onion. Peel the orange and cut into 6 to 8 segments.
2. In a heavy saucepan, heat the olive oil. Add the rabbit and sauté over high heat until browned all over. Remove the rabbit from the pan. Add the chopped onion to the pan and cook over medium heat until the onion is soft and translucent.
3. Drain any excess oil out of the pan. Add ½ of the orange segments and ¼ cup wine. Simmer for 2 to 3 minutes. Add ¾ cup of the wine and bring to a boil. Add the bay leaf, juniper berries, and the cinnamon stick. Add the rabbit back into the pan. Cover and simmer for 30 minutes, turning the rabbit occasionally. Add the remaining ¼ cup of wine and simmer for 15 more minutes, or until the rabbit is tender and cooked through. Remove the bay leaf and the cinnamon stick. Taste and season with salt and pepper if desired. Serve on a warm platter garnished with the remaining orange wedges.

Baklava

Serves 6–8

Although Baklava is associated with Greek cuisine, it is found in many Middle and Near Eastern countries. Feel free to use any combination of chopped nuts.

2 cups warm water
1 cup granulated sugar
2 tablespoons honey
1 tablespoon rose water
4 sticks unsalted butter
2 cups walnuts, coarsely chopped
1 cup almonds, coarsely chopped

1 cup pecans, coarsely chopped
½ cup packed brown sugar
1 teaspoon ground cinnamon
½ teaspoon ground cloves
1 pound (24 sheets) phyllo
*   dough, thawed*

1. Preheat the oven to 350°. Grease a 9 × 13-inch baking pan.
2. To prepare the sugar syrup, bring the water, sugar, and honey to a boil, stirring to dissolve the honey and sugar. Add the rose water. Simmer for 1 minute longer; cool and refrigerate until needed.
3. In a medium saucepan, melt the unsalted butter over low heat. Keep warm. In a medium bowl, toss the coarsely chopped nuts with the brown sugar, cinnamon, and cloves.
4. Lay 12 of the phyllo dough sheets at the bottom of the baking pan. Spread a portion of the sweetened nut mixture over. Lay 1 phyllo sheet over the nut mixture. Use a pastry brush to brush the phyllo sheet with the melted butter. Spread more of the nut mixture on top. Continue layering in this way, alternating between a nut mixture and 1 phyllo sheet brushed with butter, until the filling is used up. Lay any remaining phyllo sheets on top. Brush with any remaining melted butter.
5. Use a sharp knife to cut through the first few layers of the baklava, cutting into triangle or diamond shapes as desired. Bake until the baklava is golden brown and cooked through (about 1 hour). Pour the syrup on top. Let sit for a minute to let the syrup sink through and serve.

Milk-Fed Veal Cutlet
with Parmesan and Truffle Crust

Serves 1

Swiss-born Chef Marco Mazzei has made Danieli's, at St. Regis Beijing, one of the best Italian restaurants in town. If you can't find black truffles, use button mushrooms instead.

2 tablespoons olive oil
10½-ounce veal chop,
*   with bone*
Salt and pepper, to taste
½ red bell pepper, trimmed and
*   cut in triangles*
1 celery stalk, trimmed and cut in
*   1-inch pieces*
½ red onion, peeled and cut
*   lengthwise in wedges*

1 tablespoon sun-dried tomatoes
½ cup butter
½ cup breadcrumbs
½ cup grated Parmesan cheese
¼ cup sliced black truffles
2 tablespoons dry white wine
3 tablespoons chicken stock
Dash dried rosemary
Fresh rosemary sprig

1. Preheat the oven to 375°. Heat the olive oil in a cast-iron skillet. Season the veal chop with salt and pepper, and pan-fry the chop for approximately 3 to 5 minutes on each side.
2. Transfer the veal chop to a roasting pan along with the bell pepper, celery, red onion, and sun-dried tomatoes. Roast for 7 to 8 minutes.
3. Transfer the veal chop to a plate and tent with foil to keep warm. Add the butter to the vegetables in the pan and bake until the vegetables are tender and lightly caramelized. Season with a pinch of salt, then transfer the vegetables to a plate and keep warm. Increase oven temperature to 400°.
4. In a small bowl, combine the breadcrumbs and Parmesan. Place the sliced truffles on the meat and cover with the bread mixture. Drizzle with a little olive oil and bake for a few minutes in the oven until golden brown.
5. Pour the white wine and chicken stock into the roasting pan and heat on medium-high on the stovetop. Use a wooden spoon to scrape up the leftover meat bits from the bottom of the pan (this is called deglazing). Flavor with a touch of rosemary and season with salt and pepper to taste. Place the roasted vegetables on a serving plate, top with the veal chop, and surround with sauce. Decorate with fresh rosemary and serve.

Penne with Scallops, Bacon, and Chili Pepper

1 strip bacon
¼ cup extra-virgin olive oil
1 garlic clove, peeled and
    crushed
⅛ pound fresh scallops
Salt and freshly ground black
    pepper, to taste

4 ounces penne pasta
Cherry tomatoes, cut into
    quarters
Arugula leaves or fresh spinach
    cut into strips
Dry or fresh chili, to taste

Serves 1

Here, Chef Marco Mazzei combines classical Venetian food items. "The dish is so well received," he says, "because local citizens in Beijing have a passion for seafood and pasta."

1. Cut the bacon into strips and fry gently over medium-high heat for several minutes until all the fat is rendered. Set aside the bacon and drain and discard the fat from the pan.
2. Add the olive oil to the frying pan and heat on low. Add the garlic and sauté, stirring continuously, for about 1 minute (make sure not to burn the garlic, otherwise it will be bitter). Add the scallops and sauté gently until opaque in the center, about 2 to 3 minutes. Season with salt and pepper, and transfer to a plate to keep warm.
3. Bring a pot of salted water to a boil, and cook the pasta until al dente. Drain, and add the penne to the frying pan.
4. Add the bacon, scallops, cherry tomatoes, and arugula leaves, and toss gently. Season to taste with chili and serve very hot.

Italy's Role in Gourmet Cuisine

When considering the roots of gourmet French cuisine, there is a marriage that must be credited—that between Catherine de Medici and Henry d'Orleans, who became Henry II, king of France. Catherine de Medici, niece of Laurence de Medici, duke of Urbino, had a reputation of being a gourmet and fond of her homemade Florentine cuisine. When she moved to France, her cooks and ingredients came with her, including artichokes, beans, peas, spinach, and olive oil. These ingredients appeared on the French cooking scene and helped define it.

La Pasta d'Angelica

Serves 3–4

For extra flavor, add several large kalamata olives with the pine nuts and other seasonings.

12 ounces angel hair pasta or spaghetti
½ white onion
2 garlic cloves
2 large tomatoes
¼ cup pine nuts
3 tablespoons olive oil

¼ cup red wine vinegar
½ cup golden raisins
¼ cup chopped basil
⅛ teaspoon ground cumin, or to taste
Salt and freshly ground black pepper, to taste

1. Fill a large saucepan with just enough salted water to cover the pasta. Bring to a boil. Add the pasta and cook, uncovered, until al dente (10 to 15 minutes). Drain the pasta thoroughly.

2. Peel and chop the onion. Smash, peel, and chop the garlic. Chop the tomatoes, reserving 2 tablespoons of the juice.

3. Heat a large frying pan over medium heat. Add the pine nuts and sauté, shaking the pan occasionally, until they are browned (about 2 minutes). Remove and set aside. Wipe the pan dry.

4. Heat the olive oil in the frying pan. Add the onion and cook over medium heat until the onion is soft and translucent. Stir in the garlic, chopped tomatoes, reserved tomato juice, and the red wine vinegar. Reduce heat and simmer, uncovered, until the tomatoes have softened (about 5 minutes).

5. Stir in toasted pine nuts, raisins, chopped basil, and the ground cumin. Heat through. Taste and season with salt and freshly ground pepper as desired. Add the pasta, tossing well to combine with the sauce. Serve hot.

Marinated Olives

*1 pound large kalamata or oil-
   cured black olives*
3 large cloves garlic, thinly sliced
¼ teaspoon cayenne pepper
1 tablespoon dried oregano

1 teaspoon dried rosemary
2 tablespoons red wine vinegar
1 teaspoon lemon juice
*⅓ cup extra-virgin olive oil,
   or as needed*

**Serves 4–6
(as a snack)**

In a large bowl, combine the olives with the sliced garlic, cayenne pepper, dried oregano, dried rosemary, red wine vinegar, and lemon juice. Toss with ¼ cup of the olive oil. Add as much of the remaining oil as needed to lightly coat the olives. Cover and refrigerate for at least 1 hour before using, to give the flavors a chance to blend.

Ripe black olives, such as kalamata, have more flavor than green olives and are a better choice for marinating.

The Italian Olive

Olives are grown all over Italy, and each part of the country has its own way of dressing them. They are often served with aperitifs, along with salted almonds, and, in the home, olives are almost always offered with a glass of wine before a meal.

Pan-Roasted Swordfish
with Plum Tomatoes

Serves 4

This sword-fish dish can be on the table in less than 30 minutes. Feel free to use the same recipe to prepare fresh tuna.

4 large plum tomatoes
4 (5- to 6-ounce) skinless
   swordfish steaks
2 tablespoons capers
2 cloves garlic
4 tablespoons olive oil, divided
¼ cup balsamic vinegar
½ cup chopped fresh basil
1 tablespoon dried oregano

1 tablespoon granulated sugar
2 tablespoons fresh-squeezed
   lemon juice
Salt and freshly ground black
   pepper, to taste
Italian flat-leaf parsley,
   to garnish
1 lemon, cut into wedges,
   to garnish

1. In a medium saucepan, add enough water to cover the tomatoes. Heat to boiling and blanch the tomatoes briefly until the skins loosen (about 1 minute). Use a slotted spoon to remove the tomatoes from the boiling water. Drain thoroughly, peel the skin, and cut into thin slices. Cut each swordfish steak into 3 to 4 pieces on the diagonal. Rinse the capers. Peel and mince the garlic.

2. In a large frying pan, heat 2 tablespoons olive oil over medium heat. Add the garlic and cook until lightly browned. Add the tomatoes, capers, and the balsamic vinegar. Heat through; then stir in the basil, oregano, sugar, and lemon juice. Add the salt and pepper. Cook slowly over medium-low heat until the balsamic vinegar is reduced by half.

3. Brush 2 tablespoons olive oil over the swordfish pieces. Add to the pan. Cook over high heat until the fish is golden brown on the outside and cooked through (about 3 to 5 minutes). Transfer to a serving platter. Garnish with the parsley and lemon wedges. Serve immediately.

Braised Veal Shanks
with Porcini Mushrooms

1 ounce dried porcini mushrooms
¾ cup all-purpose flour
½ stick unsalted butter
4 veal shank cuts, 1½ pounds
    total
½ cup dry white wine

1 small white onion, finely
    chopped
2 carrots, chopped
2 tablespoons tomato sauce
2 cups beef broth
Gremolata Seasoning (see below)

Delicate porcini mushrooms add an earthy flavor to the braised veal. Serve with Classic Risotto (page 81) for a complete meal.

1. Reconstitute the porcini mushrooms by soaking in water for 20 minutes. (Make sure the mushrooms are completely covered.) Remove the mushrooms, drain thoroughly, and chop.
2. Spread out the flour on a piece of wax or parchment paper. Dredge the veal in the flour. Melt the unsalted butter in a large frying pan. Add the veal and sear over high heat, until browned on both sides. Remove the veal to a large shallow baking dish.
3. Deglaze the pan by heating ¼ cup of the dry white wine on medium-high heat, using a spatula to scrape up any browned bits. Reduce the heat to medium, and add the chopped onion, carrots, and the porcini mushrooms. Stir in the tomato sauce. Heat through, and add the remaining ¼ cup of wine and the beef broth.
4. Return the veal to the pan. Reduce the heat and simmer the veal and sauce, covered, for about 1½ hours, until the meat is tender and cooked through. (The meat should be so tender that it is almost falling off the bone.) Add more beef broth or water if necessary.
5. While the veal is cooking, prepare the Gremolada seasoning. To serve the veal, place the shanks on a platter, spoon the sauce over them, and sprinkle with the seasoning.

Gremolata Seasoning

To make the seasoning, combine 3 minced cloves garlic, finely grated zest of 2 lemons, 2 rosemary sprigs, and 2 tablespoons chopped fresh Italian parsley.

Pasta alla Puttanesca
(Pasta with Harlot's Sauce)

Serves 4

Legend has it that this flavorful sauce was invented by an Italian "lady of the evening." Roma tomatoes give the sauce its fiery color, and the heat comes from the red pepper flakes.

6 Roma tomatoes
10 Italian or Greek oil-cured olives
1 tablespoon capers
4 ounces canned anchovies
2 cloves garlic

1 pound spaghetti, or other long pasta
1 stick unsalted butter
1 tablespoon fresh chopped oregano
2 teaspoons fresh basil
½ teaspoon red pepper flakes
4 sprigs Italian flat parsley

1. Wash the tomatoes and chop (do not peel or remove the seeds). Remove the pits from the olives and cut in half. Rinse the capers. Drain the oil from the anchovies and separate. Smash, peel, and mince the garlic.
2. Fill a large saucepan with just enough salted water to cover the pasta. Bring to a boil. Add the pasta and cook, uncovered, until al dente (10 to 15 minutes). Drain the pasta thoroughly.
3. Melt the unsalted butter in a frying pan. Add the garlic. Cook over low heat for 1 minute, then add the anchovies. Continue cooking over low heat, gently mashing the anchovies and mixing with the garlic. Add the tomatoes, olives, capers, oregano, basil, and the red pepper flakes. Turn the heat up to medium-low, and cook until the tomatoes have softened. If the sauce is too dry, add 1 tablespoon water or tomato paste.
4. To serve, combine the sauce with the cooked pasta. Garnish with the parsley.

A Bit About Basil

In Greek basil means "regal herb." Italians use basil almost as much as Americans use salt—it's essential to a wide variety of dishes. Deeply fragrant and posessesing a brilliant green color, basil is also exceptional to use as a granish. A simple basil flower can dress up a plate of pasta, especially when it is placed against a rich red sauce. In Italy there are two major varieties of basil: the Genovese type, perfect for pesto sauce, and the minty Neapolitan variety, best for drying. When using fresh basil, you should not chop or slice it with a knife—the leaves will blacken and lose their flavor. Instead, tear the leaves with your fingers.

Chicken in Wine

4 chicken breasts, boneless,
   skinless
¼ cup tomato juice
¼ cup red wine vinegar
3 tablespoons olive oil, divided
2 cloves garlic, crushed
2 tablespoons chopped fresh
   oregano, divided

1 white onion
1 red bell pepper
1 orange bell pepper
2 tomatoes
1 tablespoon freshly chopped
   basil
Salt and pepper, to taste

Serves 4

The marinade does double duty as a sauce in this easy-to-make chicken dish.

1. Rinse the chicken breasts and pat dry with paper towels. Place the chicken breasts in a shallow 9 × 13-inch baking dish. Add the tomato juice, red wine vinegar, 2 tablespoons olive oil, crushed garlic, and 1 tablespoon chopped oregano. Cover and marinate the chicken in the refrigerator for 2 hours.

2. Peel and finely chop the white onion. Cut the bell peppers in half, remove the seeds, and cut into thin strips. Peel the tomatoes, deseed, and cut into 6 wedges.

3. Remove the chicken from the baking dish. Reserve the marinade and place in a small saucepan. Let the marinade boil for 5 minutes. Turn the heat down to low and keep the marinade warm.

4. In a frying pan, heat 1 tablespoon olive oil over medium-high heat. Add the chicken breast halves and cook until the chicken is cooked through and the juices run clear when pierced with a knife. Remove the chicken from the frying pan and drain on paper towels.

5. Add the onion and garlic to the frying pan and cook until the onion is softened. Add the tomato wedges, pressing down on them with a wooden spoon to release their juices. Add the bell peppers. Add the reserved marinade. Return the chicken breasts to the pan, and stir in the chopped basil. Heat through. Taste and season with salt and pepper if desired. Serve over pasta.

Sweet-and-Sour Eggplant Stew

Serves 6

Sicily's most
famous dish,
Caponata is
a popular
Italian appe-
tizer.

2 eggplant
1 large white onion
2 cloves garlic
1 ripe tomato
2 tablespoons capers
5 anchovy fillets

¾ cup olive oil, or as needed
2 cups fresh tomato sauce
½ cup red wine vinegar
½ cup granulated sugar
3 tablespoons chopped fresh
basil

1. Peel and slice the eggplant. Degorge the eggplant by placing slices in a colander and sprinkling with salt. Let the eggplant slices sit for at least 1 hour. Remove from the colander, lay on paper towels, and press down to remove the liquid.

2. Peel and finely chop the onion and garlic. Peel and deseed the tomato, and cut into thin slices. Rinse the capers. Drain and separate the anchovies.

3. In a large frying pan, heat ½ inch of olive oil on medium heat. Add the degorged eggplant. Brown briefly, then cover and simmer on low heat until the eggplant is softened (about 10 minutes). Remove from the pan and clean out the pan.

4. Heat 6 tablespoons of the olive oil over medium heat. Add the chopped onion and garlic. Cook over medium heat for a few minutes, then turn the heat down to low and add the anchovies. Continue cooking on low heat, mashing the anchovies with the back of a spatula and mixing with the softened onion and garlic. Add the tomato and capers, gently pressing down on the back of the tomato to release its juices. Stir in the tomato sauce, red wine vinegar, and sugar.

5. Add the eggplant back into the pan. Turn the heat down to low and cook, stirring occasionally, for 5 more minutes. Sprinkle the fresh basil on top and serve.

Classic Risotto

2 tablespoons olive oil
1 small white onion, minced
½ cup short-grained rice,
    preferably arborio
4 cups chicken stock

1 tablespoon butter
½ cup Parmigiano-Reggiano
    cheese, coarsely grated
1 tablespoon freshly chopped
    basil

Regular boiled rice just can't compare to rich, creamy Italian risotto. One you've mastered the basic recipe, feel free to jazz it up.

1. Heat the olive oil in a medium saucepan. Add the minced onion, and sauté over medium heat until it is soft and translucent. Add the rice, and sauté for 1 to 2 minutes until the grains are shiny and opaque.
2. Stir in ¼ cup of the chicken stock. Continue slowly adding the broth, ¼ cup at a time, and stirring until it is absorbed. The texture of the rice should be rich and creamy.
3. Remove the saucepan from the heat and stir in the butter, Parmigiano-Reggiano cheese, and the chopped basil. Serve immediately.

Tiramisu

4 eggs, separated
¼ cup confectioners' sugar
½ teaspoon vanilla extract
1 pound mascarpone
2 tablespoons Marsala wine
½ cup strong, fresh brewed espresso

2 tablespoons coffee liqueur, such
    as Kahlúa
24 ladyfingers
2 tablespoons powdered hot
    chocolate

This classic Italian dessert is made with rich mascarpone cheese.

1. Beat the egg whites until they begin to form peaks but are not dry. Beat in the confectioners' sugar.
2. Beat the egg yolks until light and fluffy. Beat in the vanilla extract. Vigorously whisk the mascarpone cheese and Marsala wine into the egg yolks. Carefully fold the egg yolks into the egg white mixture.
3. In a small bowl, combine the espresso with the coffee liqueur. Dip the ladyfingers into the espresso. Line a deep 8 × 10-inch serving dish with the dipped ladyfingers. Carefully spread the mascarpone mixture over top. Cover and chill for at least 2 hours. Dust with the powdered chocolate just before serving.

Panna Cotta

Serves 6–8

The Italian version of vanilla ice cream, panna cotta tastes delicious served with fresh fruit in season. Using a vanilla bean instead of vanilla extract gives this dish extra flavor.

¼ cup warm water
1 envelope unflavored gelatin, such as Knox
1 vanilla bean

2¼ cups whipping cream or heavy cream
⅓ cup granulated sugar

1. Pour the warm water into a small bowl. Pour the gelatin over the water and let it stand for 5 minutes to soften. Cut the vanilla bean in half and remove the seeds.
2. In a medium saucepan, heat the whipping cream, vanilla bean and seeds, and the sugar over medium-low heat, stirring continuously to dissolve the sugar. Do not let the cream boil. Continue cooking for 2 to 3 minutes. Remove the vanilla bean.
3. Remove the saucepan from the stove element and stir in the softened gelatin. Continue stirring until the gelatin is completely dissolved. Pour the mixture into a bowl and set the bowl inside a larger bowl of ice water. Cool for 15 minutes, stirring continuously. Pour the liquid into 4-ounce ramekins or custard cups and refrigerate overnight.

An Eating Style Is Born

It was during the Renaissance that the first menus and rules for courses were printed. Table manners started to improve, albeit very slowly. The Italians were the educators of Europe and the famous Galateo by Monsignor della Casa was quickly translated and distributed abroad. The main innovation? The use of individual cutlery for various courses.

Bliss's Gnocchi

Serves 8–10

4 large Yukon gold potatoes
1 teaspoon kosher salt
1 cup all-purpose flour, sifted

1 egg, lightly beaten
1 teaspoon olive oil

Francesco Martorella, owner and chef of Bliss, located in Philadelphia, learned this recipe from his mother. Serve this with their Fresh Plum Tomato and Basil Sauce (page 84).

1. Place the potatoes in a large saucepan. Add enough cold water to cover and sprinkle in the salt. Bring to a boil over medium-high heat. Cook until tender, approximately 30 minutes. Drain, peel the potatoes, and set aside to dry slightly.
2. Mash the potatoes in a food mill or potato ricer and transfer to a large bowl. Add the flour, egg, and oil, and mix well with a rubber spatula to form smooth dough. Turn the dough onto a lightly floured work surface and roll into half-inch-thick tubes. Using a sharp knife, cut the tubes vertically to form the gnocchi, and set aside.
3. Bring a large saucepan filled with salted water to a boil, add the gnocchi, and cook until they rise to the top. Strain, and toss with the olive oil. Serve with tomato sauce.

The Origin of Pizza

In about 1522, tomatoes were brought back to Europe from the New World. They were originally thought to be poisonous. Later the poorer people of Naples added the fruits to their yeast dough and created the first simple pizza. They usually had only flour, olive oil, lard, cheese, and herbs with which to feed their families. All of Italy proclaimed the Neapolitan pies to be the best. At that time, the Tavern of the Cerriglio was a hangout for the Spanish soldiers of the Viceroy, and it is said that the people flocked there to feast on the specialty of the house—pizza.

Bliss's Fresh Plum Tomato and Basil Sauce

Serves 8–10

This goes great over any pasta. Pair it with the Gnocchi (page 83) for a real treat.

24 ripe plum tomatoes
6 ounces extra-virgin olive oil
6 cloves garlic
1 Thai chili or other hot pepper of your choice

¼ cup fresh basil leaves, chopped
Salt and freshly ground black pepper, to taste

1. Bring 4 quarts water to a boil. Score the end of each tomato in a criss-cross motion, just deep enough to cut the skin. Blanch the tomatoes in the boiling water for 20 to 30 seconds to loosen the skin. Shock the tomatoes in ice water. Peel off the skin and slice the tomatoes in half. Remove and discard the seeds, and dice the tomatoes.
2. In a medium-sized pot, heat the olive oil on medium. Add the garlic and hot pepper, and cook for 1 minute. Add the basil and cook for 1 more minute. Add the tomatoes and season with salt and pepper. Reduce heat to medium-low and cook for 10 to 12 minutes. Serve over pasta.

Tournento Rossini

Gioacchino Rossini, the famed Italian composer of the opera The Barber of Seville, was born in Italy in 1792 and died in Paris in 1868. The musical genius also loved fine foods, including truffles and goose liver (foie gras). His famous creation was the "Tournento Rossini," a slice of beef fillet covered with a thin layer of lard. When cooked it is placed on fried or baked bread, with a slice of goose liver on top, and garnished with finely chopped truffles.

Spain: Dining after 10 p.m.

Pan-Fried Flounder with Toasted Almonds

Serves 4

Toasted almonds lend flavor to this simple dish. Be sure to turn the almonds frequently during toasting so that they don't burn.

2 zucchini
2 tomatoes
6 shallots
2 cloves garlic
4 large, fresh flounder fillets, skinned
½ teaspoon salt, or as needed
½ teaspoon black pepper, or as needed

6 tablespoons olive oil, divided
1 tablespoon white wine vinegar
2 teaspoons fresh rosemary
¼ cup whole blanched almonds
¼ teaspoon paprika
2 lemons, cut into wedges
8 rosemary sprigs, to garnish

1. Peel the zucchini and cut into 1½-inch slices. Peel the tomatoes, remove the seeds, and cut into wedges. Peel and chop the shallots and garlic.
2. Season the flounder fillets with the salt and pepper. Lay the flounder out in a 9 × 13-inch shallow baking dish. In a small bowl, combine ¼ cup olive oil, white wine vinegar, fresh rosemary, and the chopped garlic. Pour the marinade over. Cover and marinate the fish in the refrigerator for 2 hours.
3. Twenty minutes before the fish has finished marinating, begin preparing the toasted almonds. Heat the oven to 325°. Spread the almonds on a baking sheet and bake, stirring occasionally, until they are golden brown (about 15 minutes). Remove from the oven.
4. Heat the remaining 2 tablespoons olive oil in a frying pan. Add the shallots and cook until softened. Stir in the paprika. Add the tomatoes, pressing down gently with the back of a spoon to release their juices. Add the zucchini. Cook briefly, then push to the side of the pan. Add the flounder. Cook the fillets until they turn golden brown (about 5–10 minutes). Turn over and cook the other side. Sprinkle the flounder with the toasted nuts and garnish with the lemon wedges and rosemary sprigs.

Pork Chops with Prunes

4 pork loin chops
¼ teaspoon black pepper
⅛ teaspoon paprika, or to taste
¾ pound unpitted prunes
1 tablespoon olive oil

½ cup dry red wine, divided
½ cup apple juice or cider
2-inch cinnamon stick
2 teaspoons brown sugar
¼ cup sour cream

Serves 6

Sweet prunes make a wonderful combination with savory pork. Feel free to enhance the fruity flavors of this dish by adding apples, apricots, or other fruit as desired.

1. Season the pork chops with the black pepper and paprika. Cut each of the prunes in half with a knife and remove the pit.
2. Heat the olive oil over medium-high heat. Add the pork chops and cook until browned, turning over once during cooking. Remove the pork chops. Deglaze the pan with ¼ cup of red wine, bringing the wine to a boil and use a spatula to stir up any browned bits at the bottom of the pan.
3. Add the prunes, the remaining red wine, the apple juice, and the cinnamon stick. Stir in the brown sugar. Add the pork back into the pan. Reduce the heat and simmer, covered, until the pork chops are tender (about 30 minutes). Remove the pork chops and the cinnamon stick from the pan.
4. Add the sour cream into the pan. Bring the prune and sour cream mixture to a boil, stirring to thicken. Pour the sauce over the pork chops and serve immediately.

La Sauce Mahonnaise

Though mayonnaise was invented in Spain, the inventor was actually French. In the early eighteenth century, Louis XIV sent his favorite general, the Duc de Richelieu, to Menorca to deal with some pesky Englishmen who were holed up in the fort near the Mahon harbor. During the long siege, the duke's cook had trouble keeping his master (accustomed to lavish Versailles banquets) happy with his dinners. He figured an interesting sauce might do the trick, but all he could find on the island were eggs and olive oil. He started beating, and soon produced what was christened on the spot as "la sauce mahonnaise."

Radicchio Salad

Serves 6–8

Spanish Cabrales cheese makes an interesting contrast to the slightly bitter taste of radicchio lettuce and endives in this recipe.

2 heads radicchio
2 endives
¼ cup pine nuts
2 tablespoons balsamic vinegar
2 tablespoons extra-virgin olive oil
1 teaspoon sugar
1 teaspoon Dijon mustard
8 ounces Cabrales cheese

1. Wash the radicchio lettuce, pat dry, and tear into bite-sized pieces. Remove the stem from each endive, cut in half, and cut into strips. Chop the pine nuts into thin slivers.
2. In a small bowl, whisk the balsamic vinegar, olive oil, sugar, and Dijon mustard.
3. In a large salad bowl, combine the radicchio and endives and crumble the Cabrales cheese over top. Drizzle with the vinaigrette. Sprinkle the pine nuts over and serve immediately.

Gourmet Tuna Sandwich Spread

Serves 6

Use this spicy spread on crusty French or Italian bread, or on a soft tortilla wrap. For best results, use tuna that is packed in olive oil.

8 capers
2 kalamata olives, pitted
2 (6-ounce) cans tuna
2 tablespoons Dijon mustard
¾ cup mayonnaise
¼ cup extra virgin olive oil
½ teaspoon ground cumin
1 teaspoon cayenne pepper
1 tablespoon chopped pimiento
2 teaspoons chopped fresh parsley
1 teaspoon granulated sugar, optional

1. Rinse the capers and cut in half. Finely chop the olives.
2. In a medium bowl, combine the capers, chopped olives, tuna, Dijon mustard, mayonnaise, olive oil, ground cumin, cayenne pepper, pimiento, and fresh parsley. Taste and add the sugar if desired. Chill until ready to use.

Spanish Frittata

1 tablespoon capers
½ red bell pepper
½ green bell pepper
4 russet potatoes
1 medium Spanish onion
2 cloves garlic
1 tomato
6 medium eggs
⅛ teaspoon cayenne pepper, or
    to taste

¼ cup olive oil, divided
¼ teaspoon salt
¼ teaspoon freshly ground black
    pepper
¼ cup water
½ cup grated Parmesan cheese
2 tablespoons chopped fresh
    parsley

Serves 4

Made with potato, the Spanish version of an Italian frittata is called a tortilla in Spain. Serve it warm or at room temperature for breakfast or at brunch.

1. Rinse the capers and cut in half. Cut the red and green bell peppers into thin strips. Peel the potatoes and cut into thin slices. Peel and chop the onion and garlic. Peel the tomato, cut into 6 slices, and remove the seeds. In a small bowl, lightly beat the eggs. Stir in the cayenne pepper.
2. Heat 2 tablespoons of the oil in a 10-inch frying pan over medium heat. Add the onion, garlic, sliced potato, and the bell peppers. Sprinkle the salt and pepper over. Add the water. Reduce the heat and simmer, covered, until the potatoes are tender when pierced with a fork (10 to 15 minutes). Remove the vegetables from the pan and clean out the pan.
3. In a large bowl, combine the vegetables with the beaten egg. Heat 1 tablespoon olive oil in the frying pan on low-medium heat, making sure that all the pan is covered with the oil. Pour the egg mixture into the pan.
4. When the top of the frittata is firm but still moist, cover the frying pan with a plate. Turn the frying pan over so that the frittata falls on the plate. Clean out the pan and heat the remaining 1 tablespoon olive oil. Carefully slide the frittata back into the pan, so that the bottom is now on top. Sprinkle the cheese, capers and chopped parsley on top. To serve, cut the frittata into wedges.

Poached Shrimp and Avocado Appetizer

Serves 6

You can tell shrimp are cooked when they turn a bright pink color. Be sure not to over-cook them.

3 large ripe avocados
¼ red onion
2 cloves garlic
2 tablespoons capers
6 kalamata black olives, pitted
1½ pounds shrimp, shelled and deveined
7 cups water

1 teaspoon salt
1 bay leaf
2 tablespoons white wine vinegar
2 tablespoons freshly squeezed lemon juice
Zest of 1 lemon
½ teaspoon cayenne powder, or to taste

1. Cut each avocado in half around the pit and remove the pit. Refrigerate the avocado halves until needed. Peel and finely chop the red onion and garlic cloves. Rinse the capers and chop in half. Finely chop the black olives.
2. Rinse the shrimp and pat dry with paper towels. In a large saucepan, bring 6 cups water to a boil, with the salt, chopped onion and garlic cloves, bay leaf, white wine vinegar, lemon juice, and the grated lemon zest. Cover and simmer for 10 minutes. Add the shrimp and simmer, partially covered, until the shrimp turn pink and are cooked through (about 5 minutes). Remove the shrimp from the saucepan and drain. Chill if not serving immediately.
3. Toss the shrimp with the cayenne pepper. Spoon approximately ¼ tablespoon of the shrimp mixture onto each avocado half. Top with a few capers and about 1 teaspoon of the chopped olive. Serve immediately.

Dining on Tapas

Few small Spanish towns have proper restaurants—when people want to eat out, they order tapas. Tapas are the tasty tidbits you are served with drinks. When you want to have a meal, you simply take a table and order a ración of the various tapas. Usually a few raciónes plus a dish of salad and bread will sate a hungry couple. The custom in Spain is for everyone to eat from the same dishes, but if you ask for individual plates they'll be brought to you. Tapas bars are becoming increasingly popular in the States, especially as gathering spots for large groups of friends.

Baked Plantains with Calvados

6 cups lightly salted water
4 ripe plantains, unpeeled
2 tablespoons freshly squeezed
  lime juice
2 tablespoons brown sugar

3 tablespoons Calvados brandy
¼ cup balsamic vinegar
3 tablespoons chopped cilantro
  leaves

Make sure to use ripe yellow plantains. Immature green plantains have a bitter taste when cooked at high temperatures.

1. Preheat the oven to 350°. Grease a 9 × 13-inch glass baking dish.
2. In a large saucepan, bring the water to a boil. Add the plantains. Reduce the heat and simmer, covered, until the skin of the plantain is tender. Remove the plantains from the water and drain. Peel and cut the skin on the diagonal into 2-inch-thick slices.
3. Place the sliced plantain in the baking dish and sprinkle with the lime juice and brown sugar. Pour the Calvados and balsamic vinegar over. Cover the plantains with aluminum foil and bake until they are tender (about 1 hour). Turn the plantains over halfway through cooking. Garnish with the chopped cilantro before serving.

Not Quite a Banana

Plantains are extremely popular in Latin American countries as well as parts of Africa, Asia, and India. They are closely related to the banana, but are longer, have thicker skins, and are usually consumed cooked, not raw. While green, the plantain is considered a starch; later, when it is ripe and its skin turns to a brownish black, it is considered a fruit.

Squid Ink Risotto

Serves 2

Gourmet chefs have used the squid's black ink sac to add an exotic flavor and color to every-thing from pasta to ice cream.

1 small white onion
2 cloves garlic
1 red bell pepper
6 tablespoons olive oil, divided
1¼ pounds baby squid, cleaned
⅛ teaspoon salt
¼ teaspoon cayenne pepper, or to taste

1 cup short-grained rice, preferably arborio
3½ cups chicken broth, or as needed
1 squid ink sachet
3 tablespoons butter
¼ cup chopped flat-leaf parsley

1. Peel and finely chop the onion and garlic cloves. Cut the red bell pepper in half, remove the seeds, and dice.
2. Heat 4 tablespoons olive oil in a large frying pan. Add the onion and garlic and cook over medium heat until softened (5 to 7 minutes). Add the squid pieces and sprinkle with the salt and cayenne pepper. Cook over medium-high heat until browned (about 2 minutes). Add the red pepper and cook for 1 more minute.
3. Push the squid to the side of the pan. Heat 2 tablespoons olive oil over medium heat. Add the rice in batches, stirring until the grains are shiny and opaque. Add ¼ cup of the chicken stock and stir until it is absorbed. Add the ink from the squid sac and stir until absorbed. Continue slowly adding the broth, ¼ cup at a time, until it is entirely absorbed and the rice has a rich, creamy texture.
4. Remove the saucepan from the heat and stir in the butter and the chopped parsley. Serve immediately.

Harvesting Squid Ink

Squid ink can be expensive to buy. But you can avoid this cost if you harvest your own. To clean squid yourself, simply take the squid, grip the head in one hand, the body in the other, and pull them apart. The ink sac, which is thin and silvery, will be in the innards. Puncture the ink sac and squeeze the contents into a small bowl.

Rabbit in Wine

2½-pound rabbit, cut into
   8 pieces
2 teaspoons salt
2 teaspoons pepper
1 small white onion
2 cloves garlic
3 ripe tomatoes

4 carrots
3 tablespoons olive oil
½ teaspoon ground cinnamon
1 tablespoon chopped pimiento
¾ cup dry white wine
½ cup sherry vinegar

Serves 4

Serve this dish with boiled potatoes or over rice, with fresh herbs for garnish.

1. Bring a large pot of heavily salted water to boil. Add the prepared rabbit pieces. Turn the heat down and simmer the rabbit, covered for 1 hour to tenderize it. Remove the parboiled rabbit pieces from the pot and pat dry with paper towels. Season with the salt and pepper. Set aside.
2. Peel and finely chop the onion and garlic. Deseed the tomatoes and cut into thin slices. Peel the carrots and cut on the diagonal into thin slices.
3. In a large saucepan, heat the olive oil over medium heat. Add the onion and garlic. Cook until the onion is softened and translucent (5 to 7 minutes). Add the carrots. Brown for a minute, then add the tomatoes. Cook for another minute, pressing the back of the tomatoes gently with a spoon to release their juices. Stir in the ground cinnamon and the pimiento.
4. Add the wine and sherry vinegar to the pan. Bring to a boil, and add the rabbit pieces. Reduce the heat, cover, and simmer until the liquid has been reduced by half (20 to 30 minutes). Serve immediately.

Roasting a Chicken—Spanish Style

Try this next time you are craving comfort food, but want something new: take a (preferably free-range) chicken and rub it all over—inside and out—with sherry. Then stuff it with some chopped onion, herbs, and a small piece of chorizo sausage. Coat the bird with olive oil and as it cooks, baste it with the drippings. This gives it a wonderful orange color and a spicy kick. After the chicken is cooked, you can chop up the chorizo and add it to a stuffing.

Chorizo in Wine

Serves 4

Fruity red wine makes an interesting pairing with spicy chorizo sausage in this popular Spanish appetizer.

8 ounces chorizo sausage
2 cloves garlic
4 shallots
1 tablespoon olive oil
1 teaspoon paprika
⅓ cup dry red wine
1 bay leaf
2-inch cinnamon stick
1 tablespoon freshly squeezed lemon juice
¼ teaspoon ground nutmeg
½ loaf French or Italian bread, cut into cubes

1. Remove the chorizo sausage from its casing and cut on the diagonal into ¼-inch slices. Peel and chop the garlic cloves and shallots.
2. Heat the olive oil in a saucepan over medium heat. Add the chorizo and cook gently over medium heat until browned (about 2 minutes). Add the garlic and shallots. Stir in the paprika. Cook for 1 to 2 minutes more, until the chorizo is crisp.
3. Add the red wine and bring to a boil. Add the bay leaf and the cinnamon stick. Stir in the lemon juice and ground nutmeg. Reduce the heat and simmer, covered, until the wine has been absorbed (about 15 minutes). Remove the chorizo from the saucepan.
4. Cut the bread into squares. Fasten each slice of chorizo to a piece of bread with a toothpick. Serve immediately. Serve with the bread.

Pigging Out in Spain

Some say Spanish pork rivals prosciutto, but whichever you prefer, there is no denying that Spanish pork products are among the world's best. The Spanish do not eat large portions of pork, mostly because of their intense flavors—these products can be nibbled, rather than feasted upon. Some of the best known include air-dried serrano ham, found in most tapas bars and home kitchens, as well as the paper-thin Iberia ham made from native black-hooved, free-range pigs that eat only acorns. In terms of sausage, chorizo is the leader, while salchichon—a hard, garlicky sausage similar to salami—is also very popular.

Spinach with Raisins and Pine Nuts

3 tablespoons golden raisins
¼ cup apple cider
¾ pound fresh spinach leaves
¾ cup canned chickpeas
2 tablespoons pine nuts
1½ tablespoons olive oil

2 tablespoons chopped red onion
2 cloves garlic, finely chopped
¼ teaspoon salt
¼ teaspoon granulated sugar
⅛ teaspoon paprika, or to taste
¼ cup chopped cilantro leaves

Serves 6

This recipe will even win over those who don't care for spinach. For best results, use tender young spinach leaves.

1. Plump up the raisins by placing them in a small bowl and covering with the cider. Let the raisins sit in the cider for 30 minutes. Drain.
2. Remove the spinach stems. Wash and drain the leaves, and tear into shreds. Rinse the chickpeas and drain in a colander.
3. Toast the pine nuts by heating them in a large frying pan, shaking continuously, until the nuts are browned (about 3 minutes). Remove from the pan and cool.
4. Heat the olive oil in the frying pan over medium heat. Add the onion and garlic and cook over medium heat until the onion is softened and the garlic is browned (5 to 7 minutes). Add the spinach leaves. Sprinkle the leaves with the salt and sugar. Add 2 tablespoons water, cover the pan, and cook until the spinach leaves turn bright green and wilt (about 2 minutes).
5. Add the chickpeas and the softened raisins. Stir in the paprika, chopped cilantro, and pine nuts. Heat through and serve hot.

Olive Oil

You may be surprised to learn that Spain is the world's largest producer of olive oil and olives. Olive oil is used in all manner of cooking, from deep-frying fish, to sautéing vegetables, to drizzling over salads, or whisking into baked goods and desserts—even ice cream! The oils range dramtically in color and flavor, from green to golden, and they have subtle distinguishing flavors.

Marinated Salmon with
Roasted Red Peppers

Serves 8–10

This tastes delicious served over saffron rice.

4 salmon fillets, 8-ounces each
½ cup olive oil
2 tablespoons sherry vinegar
1 tablespoon chopped fresh
  rosemary
½ teaspoon salt, or as needed

½ teaspoon black pepper, or as
  needed
3 large red bell peppers
1 tablespoon red wine vinegar
4 ounces Cabrales cheese
1 jar pitted kalamata olives,
  drained

1. Place the salmon in a shallow 9 × 13-inch glass baking dish. In a small bowl, whisk the olive oil, sherry vinegar, rosemary, salt, and pepper. Marinate the salmon in the refrigerator, covered, for at least 2 hours.

2. Heat the broiler. Wash the red bell peppers. Place the peppers on a broiling pan and brush with the red wine vinegar. Broil the peppers until the skins are blackened and blistered. Immediately remove the peppers from the broiler. Place each pepper in a sealed plastic bag. Wait 15 minutes, then remove the pepper from the bag and peel off the skins. Cut the peppers into thin strips, removing the stems and seeds as you do so.

3. Remove the salmon steaks from the baking dish, reserving the marinade. Place the steaks in the broiler. Broil until the salmon is golden brown (6 to 7 minutes). While broiling, brush the salmon frequently with the marinade.

4. Sprinkle the Cabrales cheese over the roasted red pepper strips. Serve the salmon steaks with the roasted red pepper and the olives.

Squid in Sherry

½ red onion
1 clove garlic
1 pound cleaned squid
4 cups water
4 tablespoons olive oil

⅓ cup sherry vinegar
¼ teaspoon paprika, or to taste
2 tablespoons fresh chopped
   parsley

Serves 4

Strong sherry vinegar makes a frequent appearance in Spanish dishes. If unavailable, white wine vinegar can be used as a substitute.

1. Peel and finely chop the onion and garlic clove. Slice the squid crosswise into thin rings that are no more than ¼-inch thick.
2. In a large saucepan, bring 4 cups water to a boil. Add the squid and cook, uncovered, in the boiling water for 30 seconds. Remove the squid rings and drain on paper towels. Reserve the boiling liquid.
3. In a large frying pan, heat the olive oil over medium heat. Add the red onion and garlic and cook until softened (5 to 7 minutes).
4. Remove the frying pan from the heat and add the sherry vinegar and water. Stir in the paprika.
5. Return the frying pan to the stove element and turn the heat up to high. Add the boiled squid pieces. Cook, covered, over high heat, until the sherry vinegar has been completely absorbed. Stir in the chopped fresh parsley. Serve immediately.

The Moorish Influence—Nuts and Spices

Spanish cuisine is rooted in the common use of five main ingredients: pork, olive oil, garlic, paprika, and saffron. With influences from both Italy and Provence, there is another player that helps define the distinct quality of Spanish cooking, setting it apart from its Mediterranean neighbors: the Moors. Having ruled Spain for almost 800 years, the Moors contributed an array of nuts and spices to Spanish cooking—including almonds, walnuts, saffron, cinnamon, nutmeg, and sesame—used in both savory and sweet dishes. But there are differences. For example, Spanish cooking uses a significant amount of pork, ham, and sausage, which are forbidden in the Muslim diet.

Broiled Oysters on the Half Shell

Serves 4–6

Covering the oysters with a crumb coating protects them from the broiler's intense heat. For an added touch, sprinkle a few crumbs of Cabrales cheese over the broiled oysters before serving.

24 live oysters
¾ cup coarse breadcrumbs
1 small clove garlic, finely chopped
3 tablespoons lemon juice

3 tablespoons olive oil
¾ teaspoon paprika, or to taste
¼ teaspoon ground cumin
¼ cup freshly chopped parsley
4 lemons, cut into wedges

1. Scrub the outside of the oyster shells to remove any dirt or grit. To open the oysters, carefully insert a knife into the back hinge of the oyster between the top and bottom shell. Move back and forth with the knife, cutting the muscle, until you are able to open the shells. Remove the top shell, being careful not to drain off the oyster juice.
2. Preheat the broiler to medium.
3. In a blender or food processor, combine the breadcrumbs, chopped garlic, lemon juice, olive oil, paprika, and ground cumin, and process until the mixture has a crumb-like consistency (about 15 seconds).
4. Spread 1½ teaspoons of the breadcrumb mixture on top of the oysters. Place the oysters on the broiler and broil until the crumbs turn golden brown and the oysters are just cooked (2 to 3 minutes). Lightly garnish each broiled oyster with the chopped parsley and serve with the lemon wedges.

Chocolate Hits Spain, Then Travels Through Europe

Introduced into Spain in 1519 as a beverage, the term *chocolate* originally referred to a drink similar to today's hot chocolate. The Spanish conquistador Hernando Cortés brought the elixer back to Spain after returning from his Mexican expedition, where he was given a taste by the Aztec king Montezuma II. Gradually spreading from Spain throughout Europe, the chocolate drink gained popularity. In 1528 Cortez brought chocolate back from Mexico to the royal court of King Charles V, and monks, hidden away in Spanish monasteries, processed the cocoa beans, keeping chocolate a secret for nearly 100 years.

Braised Beef in Barolo

4 carrots
½ red onion
2 stalks celery
1 clove garlic
2½-pound beef chuck roast
4½ cups Barolo wine
2 slices bacon, chopped
2 teaspoons olive oil, if needed
2 tablespoons tomato paste

2 teaspoons freshly chopped
  thyme
1 tablespoon freshly chopped
  rosemary
Salt and freshly ground black
  pepper, to taste
1 cup beef broth
2 whole cloves
3-inch cinnamon stick

Serves 4

Made from Nebbiolo grapes, Barolo is often called the "King of Italian Wines." Here it lends flavor to a simple beef and vegetable dish.

1. Peel and chop the carrots and onion. String the celery and cut into thin pieces on the diagonal. Cut the garlic clove in half and rub over the beef. Place the beef in a casserole dish and pour 1 cup of the Barolo over. Cover the beef and marinate overnight in the refrigerator.

2. Remove the meat from the refrigerator, reserving the marinade. In a small saucepan, bring the marinade to a boil, and boil for 5 minutes.

3. In a large saucepan or Dutch oven, add the chopped bacon. Cook over medium heat until crispy. Remove the bacon from the pan, but do not clean out the pan.

4. Add the marinated beef to the saucepan and brown on medium-high heat, adding up to 2 teaspoons olive oil if necessary. Remove the beef from the pan. Add the onion, carrots, and celery. Brown briefly, then stir in the tomato paste. Cook for 1 minute, then stir in the thyme, rosemary, salt, and pepper.

5. Add the beef and bacon back into the pan with the marinade and beef broth. Add the cloves and the cinnamon stick. Cook, covered, over medium-low heat until the beef is tender (about 2½ hours). To serve, remove the beef from the pan and cut into thin slices.

Bacalao Español

Serves 4

Make sure
to check
the codfish
and remove
any small
bones before
cooking.

2 large sweet potatoes
1-pound cod fillet
½ red onion
2 cloves garlic
3 ripe tomatoes

3 tablespoons olive oil
⅛ teaspoon cayenne pepper
¼ teaspoon salt
1 tablespoon sherry vinegar

1. Peel the sweet potatoes and cut into chunks. In a large saucepan, add the sweet potatoes with enough salted water to cover them and bring to a boil. Reduce the heat to low, cover, and let simmer until the potatoes are tender when pierced with a fork (about 20 minutes). Remove the potatoes from the saucepan and drain. Cut into large chunks to serve.
2. Chop the codfish into bite-sized chunks. Peel and finely chop the onion and garlic. Peel the tomatoes, remove the seeds, and cut into wedges.
3. Heat the olive oil in a large frying pan over medium heat. Add the onion and garlic, and cook until softened and the onion is translucent (5 to 7 minutes). Add the tomatoes. Cook for 1 minute, pressing gently on the tomatoes with the back of a spatula to release their juices. Stir in the cayenne pepper and salt.
4. Add the cod pieces and the sherry vinegar. Turn the heat down to low. Cook, stirring occasionally, until the cod is opaque (about 15 minutes). Serve immediately with the sweet potatoes.

Saffron

Coming from the Crocus sativus flower, saffron is actually the three stigmas from each blossom. Delicate, orange-yellow filaments, they must be plucked by hand. Spain is the leading producer of saffron, or what they call "Spanish gold," in the world. They use this exotic spice in plenty of stews, sauces, and even in the broth for rice. Most importantly, it's the famous seasoner of paella and bacalao vizcaina, both famed Spanish dishes. Why is saffron so expensive? It takes 225,000 stigmas to yield just 1 pound of saffron. When buying saffron, be careful not to get cheated—many sell look-alikes that are actually dried marigold and safflower petals, which offer almost no color or flavor.

CHAPTER 8
Scandinavia: Straight from the Sea

Grilled Whitefish

**Serves 2
(as an appetizer)**

The secret
to preparing
whitefish is not
to overcook it.
Sear the fish
on the skin
side only, just
long enough to
make the skin
crispy.

*6-ounce fresh whitefish fillet, skin
on*
⅓ cup orange juice
1 tablespoon sea salt

¼ teaspoon white pepper
1 teaspoon granulated sugar
1 tablespoon fresh dill
1 tablespoon olive oil

1. Remove all the bones from the fillet, and cut into 4 equal pieces.
2. In a small bowl, whisk the orange juice, sea salt, white pepper, sugar, and fresh dill. Place the whitefish pieces in a shallow glass baking dish and pour the marinade over. Cover and marinate in the refrigerator for 1 hour.
3. Remove the fish from the refrigerator and discard the marinade. In a heavy frying pan, heat the oil over medium heat. Add the fish pieces, skin-side down. Cook briefly, searing the fish on the skin side only. Serve the whitefish appetizer with Crispy Salad of Vendace Roe (page 103).

Gravlax

Serves 8–10

This tastes
delicious
served on
Norwegian
rye bread,
with mustard
for spreading.

*2 salmon fillets, about 1½
pounds each*
2 tablespoons capers

6 tablespoons granulated sugar
6 tablespoons salt

1. Rinse the salmon fillets and pat dry with paper towels. Check over the fillets for any small bones and remove them with tweezers. Rinse the capers and cut in half.
2. In a small bowl, combine the sugar and salt. Lay the salmon so that the fleshy side is on the bottom. Season the top half of the fillets with the sugar and salt mixture, using your fingers to rub it in. Wrap each of the fillets in aluminum foil and place in a resealable plastic bag. Seal the bag, place the fillets in the refrigerator and leave for 2 days.
3. To serve, unwrap the aluminum foil and drain off any excess water. Cut the fillets into thin pieces. Sprinkle the capers over top.

Crispy Salad of Vendace Roe

2 tablespoons mayonnaise
2 tablespoons sour cream
1 tablespoon olive oil
2 tablespoons red wine vinegar
½ teaspoon sugar
¼ teaspoon salt, or to taste

⅛ teaspoon freshly ground black
  pepper
2 cups mixed salad greens
2 tablespoons finely chopped red
  onion
1 slice dark Finn Crisp bread
2 ounces vendace roe

**Serves 2
(as an appetizer)**

If you cannot find vendace roe, you can substitute another caviar. Toasted rye bread can be used instead of the Finnish dark bread.

1. In a medium bowl, combine the mayonnaise, sour cream, olive oil, red wine vinegar, sugar, salt, and pepper.
2. Wash the mixed salad greens and drain thoroughly. Shred the leaves. Combine the salad greens with the chopped red onion. Toss the salad with the mayonnaise dressing mixture. Crush the bread and mix into the salad. Spread the roe over top. Serve immediately.

Finland's Answer to Caviar

King of all Finnish roes, vendace roe is often compared to caviar. Roe is commonly eaten with toast, rye, or white bread. A Russian specialty, blinis are also often served with roe. At Restaurant Lasipalatsi, there are blini theme weeks every January and February, when a variety of blinis are served with different garnishes, vendace roe being the most popular blini garnish.

Horn of Plenty Mushroom Soup

Serves 2
(as an appetizer)

The nutty flavor of these delicate mushrooms makes them a popular addition to soups and stews. Here they are enjoyed alone as an appetizer.

6 ounces horn of plenty mushrooms
1 parsnip
1 carrot
1 clove garlic
3 tablespoons butter

½ cup chicken stock
½ cup dry white wine
1 cup light cream
¼ teaspoon nutmeg
1 teaspoon chopped fresh thyme
Salt and black pepper, to taste

1. Wipe the mushrooms with a damp cloth and chop. Peel and dice the parsnip and carrot. Peel and mince the garlic.
2. Melt the butter over medium heat in a medium-sized saucepan. Add the garlic and cook until browned. Add the carrot, parsnip, and ½ of the mushrooms.
3. Add the chicken stock, white wine, and cream to the pan. Bring to a boil. Stir in the nutmeg and the thyme. Reduce the heat to low and simmer gently, covered, until the vegetables are tender (30 to 35 minutes).
4. In a blender or food processor, purée the soup. Taste and season with salt and pepper if desired.
5. In the saucepan, heat 1 tablespoon butter over medium heat. Sauté the remainder of the chopped mushrooms until they are softened. Sprinkle over the soup and serve.

Trumpet of Death

In Finland's forests you can find many mushrooms—so much so that each year they name a "mushroom of the year." In 2004 it was the horn of plenty mushroom, also known as the "trumpet of death." Despite its off-putting name, it is a true delicacy. A kind of chanterelle, the horn of plenty is actually black and hollow, but chanterelles are a fine substitute.

Blueberry Soufflé

Serves 4

1 cup blueberries
1 tablespoon lemon juice
4 eggs, separated
¼ teaspoon cream of tartar

6 tablespoons granulated sugar,
  divided
2½ ounces fromage blanc
8 fresh mint leaves, for garnish

Made from whole milk, fromage blanc has a texture similar to cream cheese. If unavailable, yogurt made from whole milk can be used as a substitute.

1. Preheat the oven to 375°. Prepare 4 individual soufflé molds.
2. Rinse the blueberries and drain. In a food processor or blender, purée the blueberries with the lemon juice.
3. Use a blender to beat the egg whites until they begin to stiffen. Beat in the cream of tartar. Beat in 4 tablespoons sugar.
4. Stir the fromage blanc into the blueberries. Carefully fold the blueberry mixture into the egg whites. Spoon the mixture into the soufflé dishes. Bake the soufflés until they are golden and firm (about 15 minutes). Dust with the remaining 2 tablespoons of sugar. Garnish each dish with 2 fresh mint leaves.

Cloudberry Parfait

Serves 2–4

4 cups cloudberries
¼ cup granulated sugar

2 cups heavy (whipping) cream
1 teaspoon almond extract

This is a great dessert to serve when you're in a hurry. Feel free to substitute cloudberries with fresh raspberries if needed.

1. In a small saucepan, combine the cloudberries with the sugar.
2. In a medium bowl, use an electric mixer to beat the whipping cream into stiff peaks. Beat in the almond extract.
3. Set out 4 tall parfait glasses. Spoon ¼ cup of the whipping cream into a glass. Add ¼ cup of the berries on top. Add another layer of whipping cream and berries. Continue with the remainder of the whipping cream and berries. Chill briefly and serve.

Norwegian Salmon Salad

Serves 4

Not only is Norwegian salmon famous for its rich taste and texture, it is high in heart-healthy omega-3 fatty acids.

1 carrot
2 plum tomatoes
2 Seville oranges
½ fennel bulb
3 tablespoons extra-virgin olive oil

3 tablespoons red wine vinegar
2 tablespoons orange juice
¼ teaspoon red pepper flakes
8 ounces Norwegian salmon,
2 tablespoons chopped fresh dill leaves

1. Wash the vegetables. Peel and grate the carrot. Dice the tomatoes. Peel and cut the white pith from the oranges. Cut the oranges into sections, reserving 2 tablespoons of the juice. Thinly slice the fennel bulb.
2. In a small bowl, whisk together the olive oil, red wine vinegar, orange juice, and red pepper flakes.
3. Cut the salmon into chunks. Arrange the salmon in a salad bowl with the tomatoes, oranges, fennel, and grated carrot. Drizzle the dressing over top. Refrigerate until ready to serve. Garnish with the fresh dill before serving.

Hearty Fare

Fermented fish (rakfisk), sour milk cheese (gammelost), and cured leg of mutton (fenålår) probably do not sound particularly gourmet. Norway had no history of aristocratic and bourgeois classes to help raise the culinary bar, as did France. Norway's cuisine was rooted in using the country's bounty of fresh ingredients such as cod, mutton, and cabbage. What makes some of today's Norwegian cuisine "gourmet" is the adoption of foreign, usually French, culinary practices, used to highlight their native culinary resources.

Bergen Fish Soup

2 carrots
1 large celeriac
1 parsnip
½ yellow onion
1 large red potato
¾ pound halibut fillets
¾ pound cod fillets
2 tablespoons freshly squeezed
   lemon juice

1 tablespoon butter
8 cups fish stock
½ teaspoon sea salt, or to taste
½ teaspoon black pepper, or to
   taste
½ cup heavy (whipping) cream
½ cup sour cream
2 tablespoons chopped fresh
   parsley

Serves 10

To make your own fish stock for this dish, boil 3 pounds of fish heads and bones with 8 cups of water. Add a few vegetables such as carrots and potato, and seasonings, and simmer until the stock is flavorful. Strain through a metal sieve and use in the recipe.

1. Peel the carrots, celeriac, and parsnip, and cut into thin matchsticks. Peel and chop the onion and potato. Rinse the fillets, pat dry, and season with the lemon juice. Cut the fillets into chunks.
2. In a large saucepan, add the butter and heat over medium heat. Add the chopped onion and cook until it is soft and translucent. Add the fish stock. Bring to a boil. Add the carrots, parsnip, potato, and celeriac. Stir in the sea salt and black pepper. Reduce the heat to low and cook for 5 minutes. Add the fish and cook for another 10 minutes, or until the vegetables are tender and the fish is cooked through.
3. In a small bowl, whisk together the heavy cream and the sour cream. Remove the soup from the stove element. Whisk the cream mixture into the soup. Stir in the chopped parsley. Serve immediately.

Vodka-Marinated Sirloin

Serves 8

Make sure to turn the bag several times so that the meat is evenly coated with the marinade. If necessary, white vermouth can be used instead of vodka.

½ cup vodka
2 tablespoons olive oil
1 teaspoon crushed black
   peppercorns
1 teaspoon dried thyme
1 teaspoon mustard seed

1 tablespoon finely chopped fresh
   parsley
2 cloves garlic, crushed
3 pound boneless sirloin roast or
   beef tenderloin roast
6 parsley sprigs

1. In a large resealable bag, combine the vodka, olive oil, crushed peppercorns, dried thyme, mustard seed, chopped parsley, and the crushed garlic. Add the roast. Place in the refrigerator and marinate, covered, for at least 8 hours or overnight. Turn the bag occasionally to make sure the roast is completely coated in the marinade.
2. Preheat the oven to 425°. Remove the meat from the bag, and reserve the marinade.
3. In a small saucepan, bring the marinade to a boil over medium-high heat. Reduce the heat to medium and let the marinade boil for 5 minutes. Remove from the heat.
4. Place the roast on a rack in the roasting pan. Insert a meat thermometer into the thickest section of the roast. Roast until the internal temperature of the roast reaches at least 140° (about 1 hour). Brush the roast frequently with the marinade during cooking. Transfer the cooked roast to a cutting board and let stand for 5 minutes before cutting. Serve immediately, garnished with the parsley sprigs.

A Cure for Meat

With such dramatically long winters, Norway's food often did not last. Cows could only go out to pasture for a few short months, and the people relied heavily on cured meats to get them through these winters. Thus began a long tradition of curing, smoking, salting, and pickling.

Lemony Baked Parsnips with Salmon Roe

4 parsnips
¼ cup unsalted butter, melted
4 tablespoons lemon juice

1 tablespoon ground cumin
2 teaspoons ground turmeric
½ cup salmon roe

1. Preheat the oven to 350°. Grease a shallow glass baking dish.
2. Wash the parsnips, peel and cut in half. Cut each half lengthwise, so that you have 4 pieces.
3. Place the parsnips in the baking dish. Brush with the melted butter. Sprinkle with the lemon juice, ground cumin, and the turmeric. Cover with foil and bake until the parsnips are tender (about 30 minutes). To serve, spoon a heaping tablespoon of the salmon roe over each parsnip slice.

Sometimes called red caviar, salmon roe has a flavor similar to beluga caviar but without the hefty price tag.

Cloudberry Cream Dessert

1 cup fresh cloudberries
3 tablespoons granulated sugar,
*   or as needed*
1½ cups whipping cream

1 teaspoon pure vanilla extract
1 teaspoon freshly squeezed lime
*   juice*

Serves 4

1. Toss the cloudberries with the sugar. If desired, add up to 1 more tablespoon sugar so that they are sweet, but still a bit tart.
2. In a medium bowl, beat the whipping cream with an electric mixer until it forms stiff peaks. Beat in the vanilla extract.
3. Dish ¾ cup of the whipping cream into a dessert bowl. Top with ¼ cup of the cloudberries. Sprinkle with a few drops of lime juice. Repeat with the remainder of the whipping cream and berries.

Similar to raspberries in appearance, cloudberries grow only in Arctic regions. If cloudberries are not available, substitute fresh raspberries.

Danish Apple Soup

For best results, be sure to use tart apples such as McIntosh. Feel free to use mild or hot curry powder, according to your own preferences.

2 large McIntosh apples
4 shallots
4 tablespoons butter
2 tablespoons brown sugar
1 teaspoon curry powder
1 cup dry white wine
3 cups plus 2 tablespoons water, divided

2 whole cloves
1 teaspoon grated orange peel
3-inch cinnamon stick
2 teaspoons cornstarch
½ cup light cream
Fresh mint leaves, as garnish

1. Peel the apples, remove the core, and chop. Peel and chop the shallots. In a large saucepan, heat the butter over medium heat. Add the shallots. Cook for 2 to 3 minutes, then add the apples and brown sugar. Cook, stirring occasionally, until the apples are tender (about 5 minutes). Stir in the curry powder.
2. Add the wine and 3 cups water and bring to a boil. Add the cloves, grated orange peel, and cinnamon stick. Turn down the heat and simmer, uncovered, for 10 minutes. Remove the cinnamon stick.
3. In a small saucepan, dissolve the cornstarch in 2 tablespoons water. Add the cream. Bring to a boil, stirring to thicken. Remove the soup from the heat and allow to cool. Use a blender or food processor to purée the soup until it is smooth. Chill the puréed soup for at least 2 hours before serving.

Sitting Down to a Smorgasbord

Though smorgasbords vary from country to country, even from region to region, you will generally find a few items in common: lobster, smoked or dill-cured salmon, smoked trout, prawns, shrimps, pickled or cured herring, smoked eel, roast beef, veal, pork, smoked reindeer meat, reindeer tongue, ham, liver pastes, tomatoes, onion rings, eggs, pickled cucumber, gherkins, beet root, and many preserves such as cranberry or red whortleberry. Cheeses include local varieties of Danish blue, sweet goat cheese, and (be warned—this one is powerful) the exceedingly strong Norwegian gamalost.

Danish Stuffed Cabbage

1 large head green cabbage
1 pound lean hamburger
½ yellow onion, finely chopped
1 egg, lightly beaten
1½ cups tomato sauce
1 cup crushed breadcrumbs

3 tablespoons white vinegar
1 tablespoon granulated sugar
¼ teaspoon ground nutmeg
1 recipe Rich Cream Sauce (page 112)

Serves 6

The entire cabbage, and not just the leaves, is stuffed in this Danish dish. For an added touch, sprinkle grated Jarslberg cheese over the cream sauce.

1. Preheat the oven to 350°. Grease a shallow 9 × 13-inch glass baking dish.
2. Core the cabbage. Remove the outer leaves, reserving a few. Use a knife to carefully hollow out the cabbage, leaving a shell ½ to 1 inch thick. In a large saucepan, add enough salted water to cover the cabbage. Heat to boiling. Add the cabbage. Turn off the heat and let the cabbage stand in the boiling salted water for 15 minutes. Remove and drain.
3. In a medium bowl, combine the hamburger, chopped onion, egg, tomato sauce, breadcrumbs, vinegar, sugar, and nutmeg. Carefully fill the shell of the cabbage with the hamburger mixture. Lay the reserved leaves over the top and bottom holes and secure with toothpicks.
4. Fill an ovenproof saucepan with 4 cups of water. Stand the cabbage in the pot. Cover and bake the cabbage for 1 hour, or until the filling is cooked through.
5. When the cabbage has nearly finished baking, prepare the cream sauce. To serve, cut the cabbage into wedges and pour the sauce over.

Rich Cream Sauce

Yields 2 cups

This flavorful sauce makes the perfect topping for Danish Stuffed Cabbage (page 111).

2 yellow onions
6 whole cloves
4 tablespoons butter
3 tablespoons all-purpose flour
2 cups light cream

¼ teaspoon celery salt, or to taste
¼ teaspoon grated nutmeg
Salt and pepper, to taste

1. Peel the onions. Stud each onion with 3 cloves, stuffing each clove in different parts of the onion.
2. In a medium saucepan, melt the butter over low heat. Make a roux by adding the flour, whisking continuously, until the flour is fully incorporated into the butter (2 to 3 minutes). Slowly add the cream and bring to a boil. Remove from the heat and add the studded onions. Stir in the celery salt.
3. Cook over low heat until the sauce has thickened (about 20 minutes). Remove the onions. Sprinkle the nutmeg over top. Season with salt and pepper if desired. Use as called for in a recipe.

Three Main Types of Finnish Cuisine

Finnish cuisine can be divided into three main categories. Starting in the north, you will find Lappish cuisine that includes such "wilderness" dishes as reindeer, salmon, trout, arctic berries, mushrooms, and willow grouse. Cooking styles and methods tend to be simple, and food is often prepared on an open fire. But Finnish cuisine is also a product of historical influences. Two centuries ago, Finland was part of Sweden, then the Russian Empire. Thus, many dishes on the west coast have strong Swedish influences, while in the east in places like Carelia you will taste Russian influences.

Danish Rum Raisin Muffins

1 cup raisins
1¼ cups dark rum
1½ cups all-purpose flour
1½ teaspoons baking powder
½ teaspoon baking soda
½ cup granulated sugar
¼ cup brown sugar

¼ teaspoon salt
¼ teaspoon ground nutmeg
⅛ teaspoon ground allspice
1 stick unsalted butter
2 eggs
¾ teaspoon vanilla extract
1 cup sour cream

Yields 18

For an extra touch, add a dollop of whipped cream to the muffins before serving.

1. Soak the raisins in the rum for 2 hours. Drain the raisins. Reserve 2 table-spoons of the rum.
2. Preheat the oven to 375°. Grease a muffin pan.
3. In a large bowl, combine the flour, baking powder, baking soda, granulated sugar, brown sugar, salt, nutmeg, and allspice. Cut in the butter and mix with your hands so that it forms coarse crumbs.
4. Lightly beat the eggs. Stir in the vanilla extract and the sour cream. Make a well in the middle of the flour and add the sour cream mixture. Stir the sour cream mixture into the flour to form a lumpy batter similar to pancake batter (do not overmix the batter). Stir in the raisins and up to 2 tablespoons rum as desired.
5. Spoon the mixture into the muffin tins, filling them approximately ¾ full. Bake until the muffins are browned and a toothpick inserted in the middle comes out clean (20 to 25 minutes). Cool on a wire rack before serving.

Danish Christmas Goose
with Apples and Prunes

Serves 8–10

For an authentic Danish Christmas meal, serve this goose dish at your holiday table. The cooking time for goose is 20 to 25 minutes per pound, so adjust the cooking time according to the size of your bird.

1 pound prunes
3 cups dry white wine
3 tart red apples

1 yellow onion
8- to 10-pound young goose
1 lemon, cut in half

1. Soak the prunes overnight in the wine to soften.
2. Preheat the oven to 350°.
3. Drain and chop the prunes. Peel the apple, remove the core, and cut into thin slices. Peel the onion and cut into quarters.
4. Remove the giblets and neck from inside the goose. Rinse the goose under cold running water, and pat dry with paper towels. Rub the outer skin of the goose with the lemon. Lightly stuff the inside of the goose with the sliced apples, chopped prunes, and onion. Place the goose, breast-side up, on a large roasting pan. Prick the skin in several places to drain off the fat. Use string to tie the legs and and tail of the goose together. Use skewers to close the stuffing cavity. Insert a meat thermometer into the thickest part of the thigh.
5. Roast the stuffed goose for 2½ hours. Cover the goose with aluminum foil, and roast for another 30 minutes, or until the internal temperature reaches 180°. Let the goose stand for 10 minutes before carving. Remove the stuffing and serve on the side.

Finnish Sauerkraut Soup

1 pound stewing beef
¼ cup smoked ham
½ white onion
2 carrots
2 tablespoons vegetable oil
8 cups beef broth

3½ cups sauerkraut
½ teaspoon caraway seeds
1 tablespoon brown sugar
½ teaspoon paprika
Salt and pepper, to taste
¼ cup sour cream

Serves 4

Feel free to substitute the smoked ham with a ham bone.

1. Cut the beef into thin cubes. Dice the smoked ham slices. Peel and chop the onion. Peel and dice the carrots.
2. In a frying pan, heat the oil over medium heat. Add the onion and cook until soft and translucent (5 to 7 minutes). Add the beef and cook until browned. Cook the beef in 2 batches if necessary.
3. In a large saucepan, heat 4 cups of the beef broth to a boil. Add the sauerkraut. Cook, uncovered, for 20 minutes, or until the sauerkraut is tender.
4. Add the onion, browned beef, diced ham, and carrots. Add the remaining 4 cups of broth. Heat to boiling. Stir in the caraway seeds, brown sugar, and paprika. Reduce the heat and simmer, uncovered, for 30 minutes. Taste and season with salt and pepper, if desired. Remove from the heat and stir in the sour cream. Serve immediately.

'Tis the Season

With such starkly defined seasons, the Finnish put tremendous value on seasonal dishes. In early spring, when the lakes and seas are still covered with ice, the specialty is "turbot," eaten with its roe and liver. As Finland enters warmer seasons, new potatoes appear, and are eaten boiled with butter, dill, and marinated herring. June 21 marks the start of crayfish season, when crayfish parties are all the rage. Boiled in salty water with lots of dill, the crayfish are then eaten cold with toast, butter, and chopped fresh dill. Wild mushrooms and berry season starts in June, with chanterelles and blueberries. When the first snow arrives, the Finnish focus on root vegetables, and everything they gathered—now stored in their freezers—during summer and autumn.

Swedish Apricot and Prune Pork Loin

Serves 6–8

Apricot and pork make a great combination. If desired, feel free to thicken the sauce by adding a "cornstarch slurry" made by dissolving 1 tablespoon cornstarch in 2 tablespoons of water.

3½ cups water, divided
¼ teaspoon ground allspice
20 dried apricots, pitted
3-pound pork loin, visible fat removed
1 teaspoon salt
¼ teaspoon freshly ground black pepper

1 teaspoon dried thyme
1 cup chicken broth
1 cup dry white wine
2 teaspoons brown sugar
1½ tablespoons orange marmalade

1. In a medium bowl, bring 2½ cups water to a boil over medium heat. Stir in the ground allspice. Add the dried apricots. Simmer uncovered, stirring occasionally, until the apricots have softened (about 5 minutes). Remove the apricots with a slotted spoon. Reserve the juice.
2. Preheat the oven to 325°.
3. With a sharp knife, make 10 slits across the pork loin. Rub the roast with salt, pepper, and dried thyme. Insert 1 cooked apricot in each slit.
4. Place the pork in a large roasting pan, with a meat thermometer inserted in the center. Place 1 cup water and the chicken broth in the bottom of the pan. Roast the pork for 1½ hours, or until the temperature on the meat thermometer reaches 155°. Remove the roast and let it stand for 15 minutes.
5. While the cooked roast is standing, prepare the sauce. Finely chop the remaining 10 apricots. In a small saucepan, bring the chopped apricots, wine, brown sugar, and orange marmalade to a boil. Reduce the heat and simmer until thickened (about 5 minutes). Purée in a blender or food processor until smooth. Reheat and serve with the pork.

Swedish Apple Cake

Serves 6–8

7 Granny Smith apples
2 cups water
2 teaspoons ground cinnamon, divided
½ teaspoon ground nutmeg
½ cup butter, softened

2 cups unseasoned dry bread-crumbs
¼ cup granulated sugar
Vanilla Sour Cream Sauce (page 118)

Homemade applesauce adds extra flavor to this simple apple cake recipe. It can also be served with vanilla ice cream instead of the sour cream sauce.

1. Peel the apples, remove the core, and chop. In a medium saucepan, bring the apples and water to a boil. Stir in 1 teaspoon cinnamon and the nutmeg. Reduce the heat to medium-low and simmer the apples, covered, until they are softened (about 25 minutes). Stir the mixture occasionally and add more water if it gets too dry. Remove and cool. Mash the apples into a sauce.
2. Preheat the oven to 350°. Grease the bottom of a 9-inch square cake pan.
3. In a medium saucepan, melt the butter over low heat. Stir in the bread-crumbs, sugar, and 1 teaspoon cinnamon.
4. Spread half the crumb mixture in the bottom of the pan, pressing down firmly into the pan. Add the applesauce. Top with the remaining crumb mixture.
5. Bake the cake for 30 minutes, or until browned. Let cool on a wire rack for 15 minutes. To serve, top with the sour cream sauce.

Glogg, Glogg, Glogg

A traditional drink of the Swedish and Finnish Advent season (the six weeks leading up to Christmas), glogg is made from red wine and is served in a glass containing a few almonds and raisins. Glogg's origins date back to the medieval days of mulled wine (wine heated with spices). But glogg tends to be much sweeter than its mulled counterpart, and generally has a higher alcohol content. A few key treats such as gin-gersnaps, gingerbread, and cinnamon rolls are served with glogg.

Vanilla Sour Cream Sauce

**Yields about
2 cups**

This simple
sauce adds
the crowning
touch to
Swedish Apple
Cake (page
117) It also
tastes delicious
served over
fresh fruit.

1½ cups sour cream
½ cup plain yogurt
2 tablespoons brown sugar
2 tablespoons granulated sugar

Juice from 2 lemons
1 tablespoon apple brandy
    liqueur, optional

In a small bowl, combine the sour cream, yogurt, sugars, and lemon juice. Add the liqueur if using. Chill until ready to use.

Lingonberry Sherbet for Adults

Serves 2–4

Don't have
an ice cream
maker? Purée
the frozen
berry mixture
in the blender.

¾ cup lingonberries
2 tablespoons lemon juice
⅔ cup water

½ cup granulated sugar
2 tablespoons vodka

1. Combine the berries, lemon juice, water, and sugar in a saucepan over medium-high heat. Bring to a boil and cook for 5 minutes, stirring continuously, until the mixture has thickened.
2. Strain the mixture through a mesh strainer into a bowl. Let cool. Stir the vodka into the berry mixture. Place the mixture in an ice cream maker and freeze according to the manufacturer's directions. Keep the sherbet frozen until ready to serve.

Crayfish Quiche

2 tablespoons butter
2 tablespoons minced shallots
2 tablespoons minced celery
1 cup peeled crayfish tails
¼ teaspoon salt, or to taste
⅛ teaspoon black pepper, or to
    taste
½ cup sliced plum tomatoes
3 large eggs

1 cup light cream
¼ teaspoon ground nutmeg
¼ teaspoon cayenne pepper
2 tablespoons chopped fresh dill
1 tablespoon Worcestershire
    sauce
1½ cups Jarlsberg cheese, grated
1 (9-inch) baked pie shell

1. Preheat the oven to 350°.
2. Melt the butter in a pan over medium heat. Add the shallots and the celery. and sauté until tender. Stir in the crayfish tails, and the salt and pepper. Add the tomatoes and cook until the tomatoes are softened.
3. In a medium bowl, whisk the eggs with the cream, nutmeg, cayenne pepper, chopped dill, and the Worcestershire sauce.
4. Lay ¾ cup of the Jarlsberg cheese over the pie shell. Top with the cooked crayfish and tomato mixture. Pour the beaten egg over. Sprinkle the remaining ¾ cup cheese over top.
5. Bake until the quiche has set, and a toothpick inserted in the middle comes out clean (about 35 to 40 minutes).

Citrus Crème Fraîche

The crayfish quiche goes great with a dollop of this. To prepare homemade crème fraîche, combine ¼ cup heavy cream with 1½ teaspoons buttermilk and refrigerate for 24 hours. The day you want to make the quiche, simply add the juice from 1 orange and 1 lemon to the crème fraîche, along with 1 teaspoon dried chervil. Season with salt and pepper as desired.

Swedish Potato Dumplings

Yields 16–20 dumplings

Good filling choices for these dumplings include crisp cooked bacon, smoked ham, or caramelized pearl onions.

2 pounds russet potatoes
¼ cup butter or margarine
3 tablespoons milk

2 eggs, lightly beaten
¾ cup all-purpose flour
¼ teaspoon salt

1. Peel the potatoes and cut into quarters. Fill a large saucepan with enough salted water to cover the potatoes. Boil the potatoes until they are tender when pierced with a fork (about 20 minutes). Drain the potatoes.
2. In a large bowl, mash the potatoes with the butter and milk. Stir in the eggs, flour, and salt. Allow the mixture to cool.
3. Use your hands to form the dough into 16 to 20 balls. With your thumb, make an indentation in the top of each dumpling. Fill the hole with the filling mixture of your choice and pinch the hole closed. Press down lightly on each dumpling so that it has a flat surface.
4. Bring a large saucepan of lightly salted water to boil. Add the dumplings, a few at a time. Bring the water back to a near-boil, and cook the dumplings in the simmering water until they float to the surface (10 to 15 minutes). Serve immediately.

Swedish Sour Baltic Herring

Caught in the months of May and June, processors immerse the herring for 24 hours in brine, then remove its head and clean it. The next step is to stack the herring in barrels, leaving them in the sun for a day, jump-starting the fermentation process. Next the herring is placed in a cool storage room and fermented, and the aroma grows stronger. Gifted canners determine the precise point at which they are ready for canning. Swedes eat ripe sour Baltic herring with thin, hard bread and boiled potatoes. Sometimes they eat it with milk, though a more common accompanying beverage is beer or aquavit. Intrepid eaters devour the herring without pause, while others first rinse it in soda water.

Twice-Baked Lobster Soufflé

Serves 6

This delicious signature dish of the West Arms Hotel, Llanarmon DC, North Wales, by Chef Grant Williams, combines the rich sweetness of lobster with the effervescence of champagne.

2 tablespoons butter
½ cup Parmesan, grated
2 tablespoons self-rising flour
½ cup whole milk
½ onion, peeled
1 bay leaf
2 peppercorns

2 egg yolks, lightly beaten
2 ounces lobster meat, cooked
1 tablespoon snipped fresh chives
3 egg whites
1 recipe Glazed Champagne and
   Oyster Sauce (page 123)

1. Brush 6 small ramekins with butter and sprinkle with a little of the Parmesan cheese.
2. Melt the butter in a saucepan over medium heat. Add the flour and whisk constantly to form a roux. In another saucepan, heat the milk on medium with the onion, bay leaf, and peppercorns. Strain the milk, discarding the solids, and add it to the roux. Stirring constantly, cook until the sauce thickens. Remove from heat and let cool slightly. Add the egg yolks, lobster, remaining Parmesan, and chives.
3. Preheat the oven to 320°.
4. Whisk the egg whites until stiff and carefully fold into the lobster mixture. Bake in a bain-marie for 15 to 20 minutes. Let cool, then remove from the ramekins and place on wax or parchment paper. (The soufflés can be kept in the refrigerator for up to 4 days.)
5. When you're ready to serve, put the soufflés back into a preheated oven for 10 minutes until well risen. Serve over the oyster sauce.

Lady Lobsters Only

Lobsters can grow all the way to 10 pounds but are best eaten when they are between 1 and 3 pounds. "When choosing a lobster," warns Chef Graham Tinsley of Castle Hotel, Conway, "always buy a female because their flesh has a more subtle flavor, whereas the male lobster has a dense, meatier flesh." There are two ways to identify female lobsters. First, the tail of the female is much broader and straighter than that of the male, which tapers slightly. Second, if the first two legs closest to the body are very spindly compared to the others, it is a female.

Glazed Champagne and Oyster Sauce

18 oysters
⅓ cup total small-diced
   vegetables (such as carrot,
   celery, leek, and shallots)
¾ cup champagne
1 cup fish stock

1¾ cups heavy cream (or double
   cream, if available)
3 egg yolks
Salt and freshly ground pepper,
   to taste

Serves 6

Serve this
with the
Twice-Baked
Lobster
Soufflé (page
122).

1. Open the oysters and reserve all the juices. Bring the oyster juice to the boil, plunge in the oysters for 30 seconds, then remove with a slotted spoon and keep warm.
2. Combine the oyster juice, vegetables, champagne, and fish stock in a pan and simmer over medium heat until reduced to a syrupy consistency. Add 1¼ cups of the cream and cook until thickened, about 2 or 3 minutes.
3. Whip the remaining cream, remove the sauce from the heat, and fold in the egg yolks and the whipped cream. Season with salt and pepper.
4. To serve the dish: Place 3 oysters on each plate, cover with the sauce, and place under a very hot grill until the sauce is golden brown. Put a soufflé in the center of each plate and serve immediately.

Rags to Riches for the Oyster

Once a staple food of the poor in England, oysters are now considered a luxury, or "gourmet," food. Oysters are best eaten raw, straight from the shell with just a squeeze of lemon or a touch of shallot vinegar. Oysters, like all shellfish, should be bought live, and their shells should be tightly closed. Traditionally, fresh oysters should be bought only during the months with an *r* in them.

Chicory and Orange Salad

Lamb's lettuce leaves add a nutty flavor to this salad recipe. For an added touch, garnish the salad with radish "roses" before serving.

1 head chicory
1 bunch lamb's lettuce
2 seedless oranges
2 tablesoons fresh red currants
2 tablespoons freshly squeezed lemon juice

2 teaspoons olive oil
2 tablespoons Perrier or other mineral water
⅛ teaspoon fleur de sel (French sea salt)

1. Wash the chicory, drain thoroughly, and shred. If using fresh lamb's lettuce, carefully rinse it under running water and drain. (If using prepackaged lamb's lettuce, there is no need to clean it.) Peel the oranges and separate into segments. Rinse the currants and pat dry with paper towels.
2. Whisk together the lemon juice, olive oil, mineral water, and fleur de sel.
3. Combine all the salad ingredients. Drizzle the dressing over top. Serve immediately or refrigerate until ready to serve.

Apple and Onion Purée

Serves 4 (as an accompaniment to meat)

This simple combination blends two distinct types of sweetness and is delicious served alongside almost any meat.

2 green apples, peeled and diced

½ onion, peeled and diced
2 tablespoons olive oil

Combine the apples and onion. Sauté in pan with olive oil for 5 minutes. Transfer to a blender or food processor and purée until smooth.

The Hearty British Breakfast

Once upon a time the British used to sit down to a monster-sized breakfast including ham, deviled kidneys, bacon rolls, scrambled eggs, sausage, black pudding, pheasant, pie, hot toast, rolls, sweet butter, marmalades, jams, and fruit. In the twentieth century, war rations led to downsizing the hearty meal, and today it is modest by comparison, usually made up of cereal, eggs, and bacon, toast, marmalade, and tea or coffee.

Braised Conway Mussels

4½ pounds mussels
2 large shallots
1 clove garlic
½ cup dry white wine
1 cup heavy cream (or double
   cream, if available)

2 tablespoons chopped fresh
   parsley
Freshly ground black pepper, to
   taste

Chef Graham Tinsley says, "I never use any other mussels, and I'm sure if you have the chance to try them for yourself, you will agree they are the best." Discard any mussels that are damaged or that are fully open and don't close if you give them a squeeze.

1. Clean the mussels by removing all the barnacles and the beards from the outside of the shells in plenty of cold running water.
2. Peel and finely chop the shallots and garlic.
3. Heat a heavy-bottomed saucepan that has a tight-fitting lid. Add the mussels, shallots, garlic, and white wine to the pan, cover with the lid, and cook until the mussels open (this should take only 2 to 3 minutes). When the mussels are open, remove from the pan with a slotted spoon.
4. Simmer the cooking liquid over medium heat until it is reduced by half, then add the double cream. Bring the sauce to a boil and add the parsley.
5. Return the mussels to the pan with the sauce to reheat. Season with freshly ground black pepper and serve.

Le Moule Est Arrivé!

At one minute past midnight on the third Thursday of each November, over 1 million cases of Beaujolais Nouveau are shipped, and met with almost fanatical worldwide expectation. But in Conway, they have a variation on the theme: "Le moule est arrivé!" (The mussels have arrived!). Once upon a time collected for their pearls, today Conway mussels adorn plates, not earlobes.

Bread and Butter Pudding

Serves 4–6

To dress up this dish, add a touch of vanilla-scented whipped cream and a few sautéed apricots.

About 4 tablespoons butter
4 slices thick white bread
2 ounces sultanas
2¼ cups whole milk
2¼ cups heavy cream (or double cream, if available)

1 vanilla pod, split
8 eggs
½ cup caster (or "superfine") sugar
¼ cup apricot jam
6 fresh apricots, sautéed in butter

1. Preheat the oven to 300°.
2. Butter the bread, cut off the crusts, and cut each slice into 4 triangles. Sprinkle the bottom of an earthenware dish with the sultanas and arrange the bread over the top.
3. In a saucepan over medium heat, combine the milk, cream, and vanilla pod. In a bowl, whisk together the eggs and the sugar. When the milk mixture comes to a boil, pour over the egg mixture, whisking to form a custard. Pour over the bread and place the dish in a bain-marie. Bake for 45 to 50 minutes, until the custard feels firm.
4. Heat the apricot jam in a saucepan with a little water and brush over the surface of the pudding. Garnish each with a sautéed apricot and serve at room temperature.

The Origin of Eggnog

Eggnog is an English creation, descending from a hot British drink called posset, made of eggs, milk, and wine or ale. The second half of its name ("nog") is a British word for strong ale, made from eggs beaten with sugar, milk or cream, and some kind of spirit. Eggnog has made its way into kitchens across the world: in the American South, for example, it is served with bourbon, not ale. People in New Orleans also drink plenty of eggnog, and during the holidays it is served alongside syllabub (an equally rich, but less potent mixture, made with milk, sugar, and wine).

Seared Scallops with Saffron Mash

Serves 4
_____

This is a favorite recipe of Chef Glen Watson of London's restaurant Brasserie Roux, at the Sofitel St. James.

12 diver scallops
Pinch saffron
1¼ cups mashed potatoes
Pinch salt

1¼ cups Citrus and Shallot
   Dressing
1 teaspoon chervil

1. Prepare a grill to medium-high heat. Grill the scallops for 1½ minutes on each side.
2. Line a strainer with cheesecloth and add the saffron and enough water to moisten; then drain the water through. Add the saffron to the mashed potatoes. Heat up the mash, if necessary, and place 3 small mounds on each serving plate. Place a cooked scallop on each mound of mash.
3. Warm the dressing and spoon it down the sides of each plate. Sprinkle with chervil. Serve immediately.

Citrus and Shallot Dressing

Serves 4
_____

This light dressing bursts with citrus flavor from lime and lemon juice. Serve over Seared Scallops with Saffron Mash.

1¼ cups finely chopped shallots
¼ cup olive oil, divided
¾ cup fresh-squeezed lemon
   juice
½ cup fresh-squeezed lime juice
1 teaspoon caster sugar

1 teaspoon chopped fresh dill
1 teaspoon chopped fresh flat-leaf
   parsley
Salt and pepper, to taste
1 cup diced plum tomato

1. Sauté the shallots quickly in 1 tablespoon of the oil over medium heat until just softened.
2. Add the lemon and lime juice, sugar, chopped herbs, salt, and pepper. Add the rest of the oil. Remove from heat and let cool.
3. Add the tomatoes and mix well.

Smoked Salmon Pancakes

Serves 6

Britain is famous for its smoked fish dishes. The next time you're preparing poached or scrambled eggs, try serving them with smoked fish instead of sausage or bacon.

6 ounces smoked salmon
4 boiling potatoes
6 tablespoons butter, divided
⅔ cup light cream, divided
¼ teaspoon salt

½ teaspoon ground nutmeg
2 tablespoons chopped fresh dill
2 large eggs, lightly beaten
½ teaspoon black pepper

1. Finely chop the smoked salmon. Wash and peel the potatoes, and cut into chunks. Fill a large saucepan with enough salted water to cover the potatoes. Bring to a boil. Cook the potatoes in the boiling water until they are tender and can easily be pierced with a fork. Drain.
2. Place the potatoes in a bowl and add ¼ cup butter. Mash, using a fork or a potato masher. Add in 2 tablespoons of the cream as you are mashing, and stir in the salt and nutmeg.
3. Stir in the remainder of the cream, the fresh dill, the beaten egg, and the pepper. In a food processor, process the smoked salmon with the mashed potato mixture until smooth. Process in batches if necessary.
4. Heat 2 tablespoons margarine in a frying pan over medium heat. Drop a heaping tablespoon of the mashed potato and smoked salmon mixture into the frying pan. Cook until golden brown, turning over once. Continue with the remainder of the pancakes. Serve hot.

Fish and Chips

Fish and chips were born in the nineteenth century, served in working-class districts as a cheap meal easily consumed after a hard day's work. The fish was cooked in shallow pans and usually just eaten plain and cold. The evolution continued, with some shops soon serving baked potatoes in addition to fish, before chips took center stage. There is a rivalry in London about who first served them: was it Malin's in the East End in 1868, or John Lees's wooden hut in Mossley, Manchester, in 1863? The real answer may never be known. Today fish and chips dishes are even offered in upscale gourmet restaurants, though the recipes are usually adapted, using expensive fish and a choice of sauces.

Basic Cheese Soufflé

¼ cup unsalted butter
¼ cup all-purpose flour
⅛ teaspoon salt
⅛ teaspoon black pepper

1 cup cold whole milk
4 large eggs, separated
4 ounces Jarlsberg cheese, grated

Serves 4

Feel free to experiment with this basic soufflé recipe by adding toma-toes or other garden veg-etables and fresh herbs as desired.

1. Preheat the oven to 350°. Grease a soufflé dish.
2. To prepare the soufflé base, melt the butter over medium heat in a heavy saucepan. Make a roux by adding the flour, salt, and pepper and stirring continuously for 2 to 3 minutes, until the flour is incorporated. Gradually whisk in the milk, stirring continuously until the mixture thickens. Remove from the heat and whisk in the egg yolks. Stir in the cheese.
3. Beat the egg whites until stiff peaks form. Carefully fold the egg whites into the base mixture.
4. Pour the soufflé mixture into the dish. Bake until soufflé turns a light golden brown and a toothpick inserted in the middle comes out clean. Serve immediately.

Medieval Game

Not chess, checkers, or backgammon. Think partridge, quail, and turtledoves. In medi-eval days, game featured prominently in the diet, especially during winter. Stuffings were created to both flavor the game and make the dishes last longer. Typically stuffings were very rich and could include a multitude of ingredients: saffron, oysters, prunes, cinnamon, oranges and lemons, cloves, etc., mixed together with bread and some sort of fat (bacon was common). The birds were often served with fruit sauces, much like today's use of currants, blackberries, and cranberries in many gourmet sauces.

CHAPTER 10
Central and South America: Road to Rio and Beyond

Brazilian Hot Cocoa

Seves 4

Instant cocoa
mix can't
compare
to this rich
drink, which
gets its flavor
from real
chocolate and
strong coffee.

4 ounces bittersweet chocolate
4 ounces semisweet chocolate
1¾ cups boiling water
3 cups whole milk

1 cup coffee cream
½ cup strongly brewed coffee
1 cup granulated sugar

1. Break the chocolate into pieces. In a medium saucepan, bring the water to a boil. Add the chocolate and melt in the boiling water, stirring continuously. Remove the melted chocolate from the heat and cool.
2. In a large saucepan, heat the milk and coffee cream until nearly boiling. Add the hot coffee and sugar, stirring continuously to dissolve the sugar. Stir in the melted chocolate. Serve hot.

Brazilian Bananas with Rum

Serves 4–6

For best
results, use
underripe
bananas in
this recipe.
Ripe bananas
may fall apart
during baking
or become
"mushy."

1 tablespoon butter
¼ cup firmly packed brown sugar
¼ cup granulated sugar
⅓ cup fresh lemon juice
2 tablespoons pineapple juice

2 tablespoons white rum
4 medium-sized underripe
   bananas
2 tablespoons toasted coconut

1. Preheat the oven to 400°. Grease a shallow glass 9 × 13-inch dish.
2. In a medium bowl, cream the butter with the brown sugar. Stir in the white sugar, lemon juice, pineapple juice, and rum.
3. Peel the bananas and slice in half lengthwise. Lay the bananas in the baking dish, flat-side down. Spread the sugar and juice mixture over. Bake for about 15 minutes, until the bananas are tender but still slightly firm. Baste the bananas with the sugar mixture once or twice during cooking. Cool. Sprinkle with the toasted coconut before serving.

Bahian-Style Shrimp Stew

¾ pound frozen cooked tiger
   shrimp, shelled and deveined
1 small white onion
2 cloves garlic
2 tablespoons olive oil
2 tablespoons tomato paste
1 tablespoon freshly squeezed
   lemon juice
½ teaspoon granulated sugar

¾ cup thin coconut milk
½ cup thick coconut milk
3 tablespoons dende oil
½ teaspoon salt
Freshly ground black pepper, to
   taste
1 tablespoon chopped fresh
   cilantro leaves

Serves 4

A type of palm oil, dende oil's orange color and nutty flavor make it a staple ingredient in Brazilian cooking. Substitute palm oil if dende oil is unavailable.

1. Rinse the frozen shrimp under warm running water until thawed. Pat dry on paper towels. Peel and finely chop the onion and garlic.
2. In a large frying pan, heat the olive oil. Add the chopped onion and garlic. Cook over medium heat until the onion is soft and translucent (5 to 7 minutes). Stir in the tomato paste, lemon juice, and sugar. Cook briefly, then add the coconut milk and dende oil. Bring to a boil. Add the chopped shrimp, salt, and pepper. Stir in the cilantro leaves. Cook over medium heat for 5 more minutes. Serve hot.

Thin Coconut Milk?

For the coconut milk called for in the recipe, buy canned and spoon off the top layer for the thick coconut milk and pour out the liquid underneath for the thin coconut milk. Canned coconut milk naturally separates.

Mined Pork

Can't find Portuguese chourico sausage? Use Mexican chorizo sausage instead. In either case, be sure to remove the sausage from its casing before adding it to the pan.

½ pound smoked chourico
    sausage
2 large tomatoes
1 malagueta pepper (bird chilies)
1 white onion
1 tablespoon olive oil
2 pounds boneless pork, finely
    chopped

2 tablespoons lemon juice
1 tablespoon white vinegar
Salt and freshly ground black
    pepper, to taste
3 hard-boiled eggs, finely
    chopped
2 tablespoons minced fresh
    parsley

1. Remove the chourico sausage from its casing and cut into ¼-inch slices. Blanch the tomatoes, remove the peels, and cut each tomato into thin slices. Cut the malagueta pepper in half, remove the seeds, and mince. Peel and finely chop the onion.
2. Heat the olive oil in a heavy frying pan on medium heat. Add the pork and cook, stirring frequently, until it is browned. Remove the pork from the pan, but do not clean out the pan.
3. Add the chopped onion and cook until the onion is soft and translucent (5 to 7 minutes). Add the tomatoes, and cook over medium-low heat, gently squeezing the tomatoes with the back of a rubber spatula so that they release their juices. Add the malagueta pepper, lemon juice, and white vinegar. Stir in the salt and pepper.
4. Add the pork back into the pan and add just enough water to cover. Simmer, uncovered, over low heat until the pork is tender and the water has been absorbed. Remove the mixture from the pan, place in a large bowl, and toss with the chopped egg. Sprinkle with the fresh parsley. Season with added salt and pepper if desired. Serve immediately.

Paulista Shrimp Cake

2 pounds medium fresh shrimp,
   peeled and deveined
2 tablespoons lemon juice
1 small white onion
1 garlic clove
1 (14-ounce) can palm hearts
1 red bell pepper
1 green onion
2 hard-boiled eggs
1 teaspoon salt

1 cup water
½ teaspoon cornstarch
4 teaspoons tapioca starch
½ cup olive oil, divided
1¼ cups canned tomatoes
Salt and pepper
1 cup green peas
½ cup finely chopped black olives
2 tablespoons chopped fresh
   parsley

Serves 6

A featured dish in the state of São Paulo in Brazil, this is a favorite of Ambassador Rubens Barbosa, whose mother cooked it frequently when he was growing up.

1. Rinse the shrimp under warm running water. Pat dry with paper towels. Place the drained shrimp in a bowl and toss with the lemon juice. Peel and finely chop the onion. Smash, peel, and mince the garlic. Rinse the canned palm hearts and drain in a colander. Cut the red bell pepper in half, remove the seeds, and finely chop. Rinse the green onion and dice. Peel and mash the hard-boiled eggs.

2. Dissolve the salt in the water. Add the cornstarch and the tapioca starch to the water, stirring to dissolve. Let stand for 1 hour.

3. Heat 2 tablespoons olive oil in a frying pan. Cook the onion and garlic over medium heat until the onion is softened (about 5 minutes). Add the shrimp and the chopped pepper. Stir in the canned tomatoes, and the salt and pepper. Bring to a boil. Reduce the heat to low, and stir in the green peas, palm hearts, green onion, olives, and the parsley. Remove the frying pan from the heat. Give the starch and water mixture a quick re-stir and mix it in thoroughly.

4. Place the shrimp mixture in a large bowl. Stir in the hard-boiled egg pieces. Take a heaping tablespoon of the mixture, and flatten between the palms of your hands to form a thin cake. Continue with the remainder of the shrimp mixture.

5. Heat the remaining olive oil in a frying pan. Cook the shrimp cakes over medium heat, until they are golden brown (about 6 minutes). Turn the cakes over once during cooking.

Veal and Vegetable Stew

Serves 6

This stew can be prepared in advance and frozen—just don't add the potatoes until you defrost and reheat.

2 medium white onions
3 cloves garlic, mashed
2 carrots
3 sweet potatoes
1 small acorn squash
2 tablespoons olive oil, divided
2 pounds veal, cubed
2 cups beef broth, or as needed

1 (14-ounce) can crushed
    tomatoes, with juice
½ teaspoon salt
¼ teaspoon black pepper
½ teaspoon dried parsley
½ cup water, or as needed
1 cup canned apricots or peaches

1. Peel and chop the white onions. Smash, peel, and chop the garlic cloves. Wash and peel the carrots and cut into matchsticks. Peel and chop the potatoes and the acorn squash.
2. In a large saucepan or Dutch oven, heat 1 tablespoon olive oil. Add half the veal and cook over medium-high heat until browned. Remove from the pan. Brown the remainder of the veal and remove from the pan. Do not clean out the pan.
3. Heat 1 tablespoon olive oil. Add the carrots. Cook over medium heat for 5 minutes, then add the onion and garlic. Cook over medium heat for 5 more minutes, until the carrots are browned and the onion is softened. Deglaze the pan by adding ½ cup beef broth and bringing to a boil, using a spatula to stir up any browned bits from the bottom of the saucepan.
4. Add the tomatoes and remaining 1½ cups beef broth. Bring to a boil. Stir in the salt, pepper, and dried parsley. Add the veal, chopped potatoes, and squash. Reduce heat to low and simmer, covered, until the veal is cooked and the vegetables are tender (about 45 minutes), adding water as necessary. Add the canned apricots. Heat through and serve hot.

Tasting Ecuador

When in Ecuador, try to sample the following dishes: caldo or sopa (soups, available as a breakfast item in markets); lechón (roasted suckling pig); llapingachos (potato and cheese pancake, often served with small bits of meat); locro, soup (with potatoes, corn, and avocado); parrilla (mixed meat barbequed Argentine style).

Aloo Tikki (Indian Potato Cakes)

**Serves 10
(as an appetizer)**

This recipe
is from
Chef Rajesh
Kattaria of the
Ritz-Carlton,
Dearborn, MI.
Serve with
Fresh Mango
Chutney
(below).

*2 pounds Idaho potato, peeled
2 ounces channa dahl (Indian
   lentils) or chickpeas
Salt, to taste
Red chili powder, to taste
1 egg yolk*

*2 teaspoons finely chopped
   ginger
2 cloves garlic, finely chopped
¼ cup finely chopped cilantro3
   tablespoons olive oil*

1. Boil the potatoes until tender. Drain and let cool. Mash the potatoes.
2. Boil the lentils until softened (about 30 minutes). Let cool.
3. Add the cooled lentils, salt, red chili powder, egg yolk, ginger, garlic, and the cilantro to the mashed potatoes. Combine the lentil and mashed potato mixtures and form into patties.
4. Heat the olive oil over medium-high heat. Pan-fry the patties until golden brown on both sides.

Fresh Mango Chutney

**Yields approxi-
mately 1 cup**

Let the
chutney mari-
nate in the
refrigerator
for 1 or 2
hours before
serving.

*1 medium-sized slightly underripe
   mango
1 fresh jalapeño, sliced into thin
   rings*

*1 tablespoon finely chopped fresh
   cilantro
1 teaspoon salt
⅛ teaspoon ground cayenne
   pepper*

Cut the flesh of the mango away from the large seed inside. Cut the mango into paper-thin slices. Place in a bowl. Add the jalapeño, cilantro, salt, and cayenne, and toss gently.

Lamb Curry with Banana Raita

4 cups plain yogurt, divided

3½ tablespoons garam masala

1 tablespoon lemon juice

3 tablespoons chopped fresh parsley

2 pounds lamb shoulder, cubed

3 large bananas

2 tablespoons tahini (sesame paste)

1 teaspoon ground cardamom

¼ teaspoon chili paste, or to taste

¼ cup chopped coriander (cilantro) leaves

2 tablespoons olive oil

2 onions, finely chopped

2 medium cloves garlic, finely chopped

2 jalapeño chili peppers, deseeded and chopped

1 cup water, or as needed

Serves 6–8

Sweet banana raita makes the perfect side dish for spicy lamb curry.

1. In a shallow glass 9 × 13-inch baking dish, combine 3 cups yogurt, the garam masala spice mixture, lemon juice, and fresh parsley. Add the lamb cubes, turning to make sure all the cubes are coated in the marinade. Cover and refrigerate for 2 hours.

2. To make the Banana Raita, peel the bananas and cut into 4 to 5 pieces. In a food processor, process the chopped banana until smooth. Stir in 1 cup yogurt, tahini, ground cardamom, chili paste, and chopped cilantro. Process again until smooth. Chill the raita while preparing the lamb curry.

3. In a heavy frying pan or Dutch oven, heat the olive oil over medium heat. Add the onion and garlic and cook until the onion is softened. Add the chili peppers and cook until the skin begins to blister and brown.

4. Add the lamb to the pan with the yogurt marinade. Reduce heat and simmer, covered, until the lamb is tender and cooked through (about 2 hours). Add water as is necessary during cooking. Serve the curry over rice, with the banana raita.

Yogurt Sauce

Yields approximately 1½ cups

Feel free to use this sauce with beef or chicken, or as a substitute for margarine in a pita bread sandwich.

1 cup plain yogurt
½ cup sour cream
1 tablespoon lemon juice
⅛ teaspoon ground cumin

1 tablespoon chopped fresh mint
¼ teaspoon chili paste, or as desired
4 mint sprigs, as garnish

In a medium bowl, combine the yogurt, sour cream, lemon juice, ground cumin, chopped mint, and chili paste. Cover and chill for at least 1 hour to give the flavors a chance to blend. Serve chilled, with the mint sprigs as garnish.

Yogurt

Yogurt, though popular for years in Europe, Eastern Europe, the Middle East, and Western Asia, only recently became popular in the United States. We can credit its rise in popularity to the immigration of people from other countries to the United States. Many cultures have their own varieties.

Chilled Cucumber Soup

*1 large cucumber, peeled and
    grated*
1 small garlic clove, crushed
2 cups plain yogurt
2 cups water

Table salt, to taste
1 tablespoon vegetable oil
¼ teaspoon cumin seeds
*1 teaspoon finely chopped fresh
    mint for garnish*

Serves 6

In the swel-
tering heat
of summer,
this soup has
a wonderful
cooling effect.

1. Place the cucumber in a bowl and chill for about 30 minutes. Pour off the cucumber juice that collects in the bowl. Press down on the cucumber to get out as much juice as possible.
2. Combine the cucumber and garlic; then stir in the yogurt and water. Combine thoroughly. Add salt to taste. Set aside.
3. Heat the oil in a small skillet on medium. Add the cumin seeds and sauté for about 1 minute or until the seeds start to crackle and you can smell the aroma. Remove from heat.
4. Stir the cumin into the yogurt soup. Cover and refrigerate for 2 hours.
5. When ready to serve, pour equal portions into 6 shallow bowls and garnish with the mint.

Vegetarianism in India

While many Indians are vegetarian—having been influenced by Buddha (founder of Buddhism) and Mahavir (founder of Jainism)—there are still those who do consume meat. The so-called lower strata of society—namely, the scheduled castes, the scheduled tribes, and the backward castes—fall into this category. Many of them practice the Beast's Day Out, a "selective vegetarianism"; people opt not to eat meat on certain days of the week (e.g., no fish on Mondays). One major factor contributing to the rise of vegetarianism in India was that kings such as Ashoka discouraged the killing of animals.

Quail with Curry

Serves 4

Garam masala rub provides most of the heat in this spicy curry dish.For best results, make sure to get a good garam masala from an international or specialty market, or make your own.

1 tablespoon garam masala spice mixture
½ cup plain yogurt
4 whole quail, deboned
1 white onion
2 cloves garlic
2 tomatoes
4 tablespoons ghee (clarified butter), divided
3-inch cinnamon stick
1 tablespoon chickpea flour (besan)
2 tablespoons water
2 tablespoons garam masala curry paste
¼ cup thick coconut milk
½ teaspoon turmeric

1. In a small bowl, combine the garam masala spice mixture with the yogurt. Clean the quail. Use a knife to make several diagonal cuts in the skin. Rub the spiced yogurt over the quail. Cover and marinate, overnight, in the refrigerator.
2. Preheat the oven to 325°. Peel and chop the onion and garlic. Peel the tomatoes, remove the seeds, and thinly slice. Remove the quail from the refrigerator and place on a large baking sheet (do not clean off the yogurt). Bake until the quail are cooked through (about 1 hour).
3. While the quail is baking, prepare the remainder of the vegetables. In a frying pan, heat 2 tablespoons ghee over medium heat. Add the onion and garlic and cook until soft and translucent (5 to 7 minutes). Add the tomatoes, pressing down gently with a spatula to release their juices. Add the cinnamon stick. Reduce the heat to low and cook gently, stirring occasionally, for 10 minutes. Remove the cinnamon stick.
4. In a small bowl, whisk the chickpea flour into the water. Set aside. In a small saucepan, heat 2 tablespoons ghee over medium-high heat. Stir in the garam masala curry paste. Heat briefly, and then add the chickpea flour and water mixture, stirring quickly to thicken. Slowly whisk in the coconut milk. Stir in the turmeric. Remove from the heat.
5. To serve, place the quail on a large platter, surrounded by the vegetables. Pour the sauce over the quail.

Lobster Korma

2 live lobsters, about 1½ pounds
    each
1 teaspoon saffron strands
1 cup evaporated milk, plus 2
    tablespoons
3 tablespoons ghee (clarified
    butter)
1 ice-cube container garlic purée,
    thawed (see below)

1 tablespoon minced ginger
4 ice-cube containers onion
    purée, thawed (see below)
1 teaspoon turmeric
1 teaspoon garam masala spice
    mixture
⅓ cup plain yogurt
¼ cup chopped fresh coriander
    (cilantro) leaves

Enhance the exotic appearance of this dish by reserving the lobster shells and using them as a "bowl" in which to serve the korma.

1. In a large saucepan, bring at least 8 cups salted water to a boil. Add 1 of the lobsters to the boiling water. Bring the water back to a boil. Reduce the heat and simmer, covered, until the lobster shell turns red and the meat is cooked (about 10 to 12 minutes for a 1½-pound lobster). Use tongs to remove the lobster. Drain the lobster in a colander. Repeat with the other lobster. Remove the cooked lobster meat from the shell, and chop into bite-sized chunks.

2. Place the saffron strands in a small bowl and add 2 tablespoons evaporated milk. Soften for 5 minutes. Remove the saffron strands. Discard the milk.

3. To make the korma mixture, heat the ghee in a large frying pan. Add the garlic purée, ginger, and the onion purée. Cook over medium heat until the onion is softened. Stir in the turmeric and the garam masala spice mixture. Add the yogurt. Heat to boiling, then add the chopped lobster meat. Stir in the saffron strands and chopped cilantro leaves. Heat through. Serve immediately.

Garlic and Onion Purée

Take 30 peeled garlic cloves and purée in a blender, adding no water. Scrape the purée out of the container, divide evenly among 10 ice-cube molds, and freeze. For the onion purée, peel 10 medium-sized Spanish onions. Coarsely chop the onions and place them in boiling water for 3 minutes. Drain, and then purée in a blender processor until very fine in texture. Scrape out of the container, divide evenly among 10 ice-cube molds, and freeze.

Rose-Flavored Yogurt Lassi

Serves 4

If you cannot find rose water, substitute your favorite syrup. Lassi has a short shelf life and is best served fresh.

4 cups plain yogurt
2 tablespoons sugar
1½ tablespoons rose water

½ cup water
5–6 ice cubes
Rose petals, for garnish

1. Line a sieve with several layers of cheesecloth. Place the yogurt in the sieve and suspend over a bowl.
2. Let any liquid drain into the bowl, then discard the liquid. Tie the ends of the cheesecloth to form a pouch. Weigh it down using a few cans in a plastic bag as weight. Let it sit for about 2 hours to allow any remaining liquid to drain out. Remove the cheesecloth.
3. In a blender, combine the yogurt, sugar, rose water, water, and ice cubes; blend well. Add more water if you like a thinner consistency. Serve garnished with rose petals.

Rose Water

Rose water is made, as the name suggests, from roses. Cotton balls doused in chilled rose water make wonderful facial cleansers.

Akhni Stock

Yields 6 cups

8 cups water
2 Spanish onions, chopped
4 ounces garlic purée
    (page 143)
2 teaspoons minced ginger
10 whole green cardamom pods

2 bay leaves
4 whole cloves
¼ cup chopped cilantro
1 teaspoon salt
1 tablespoon unsalted butter
2 (3-inch) cinnamon sticks

1. Bring the water to a boil over medium heat. Add chopped onion, puréed garlic, ginger, cardamom pods, bay leaves, cloves, chopped cilantro, salt, clarified butter, and the cinnamon sticks. Reduce heat and simmer, covered, for 30 minutes.
2. Remove the bay leaves and the cinnamon sticks, and strain the soup through a mesh strainer. Refrigerate or freeze until ready to use as called for in a recipe.

The Art of Drinking in India

Brewing and drinking of various liquors was developed as an art in ancient India. Karnataka is the homeland to a variety of indigenous alcohol and liquors including ones brewed from rice, ragi (sweet barley), palm, and ichala (wild palm), as well as milder ones made with grapes, mangoes, jackfruit, coconut, and dates flavored with flower essences. Sculptures and Kavyas depict drunkards and drinking scenes, suggesting that drinking provided occasional amusement and relief, though abstinence from alcohol was respected and widely practiced.

Follow the directions in "Garlic and Onion Purée" (page 143) to make the garlic purée for this recipe. For a more authentic touch, replace the butter with ghee (clarified butter) if desired.

Curried Lamb Kebabs

Serves 2–4

Zucchini, tomatoes, and fresh mushrooms would all be good choices to cook with the lamb. Thinly cut the vegetables and thread onto the skewers with the lamb, alternating between a meat and a vegetable.

1 papaya
1¼ cups plain yogurt, divided
1½ pounds lamb, cut into 1½-inch cubes
4 cloves garlic
2 tablespoons lemon juice, divided

1 teaspoon cayenne pepper
1 teaspoon ground coriander
1 teaspoon ground cumin
6 cardamom pods, crushed
¼ cup olive oil

1. Peel the papaya and cut into thin slices. In a food processor, purée the papaya with 1 cup yogurt until smooth. Place the lamb cubes in a shallow 9 × 13-inch baking dish. Coat the lamb with the yogurt and papaya mixture. Cover and marinate in the refrigerator overnight.
2. Smash, peel, and mince the garlic. In a blender or food processor, purée the minced garlic with 1 tablespoon lemon juice to form a paste.
3. Preheat the grill.
4. In a large bowl, combine the garlic paste, cayenne pepper, coriander, ground cumin, and crushed cardamom, olive oil, and the remaining 1 tablespoon lemon juice and ¼ cup yogurt. Remove the marinated lamb from the refrigerator and coat with the mixture.
5. Thread the marinated lamb onto skewers. Grill on medium heat until the lamb reaches the desired level of doneness (about 10 minutes for medium rare). Serve immediately.

Not So Hot

Indian dishes use spices most often in an aromatic and subtle way—not necessarily to make a dish hot. Indians consider the ways elements in a recipe interact, and will commonly use cooling as well as warming spices, bland spices together with pungent spices, and sweet spices alongside hot spices. Spices are also used as a simple and effective way to add color and healthful properties.

Shrimp in Coconut Milk

1 bay leaf
1 teaspoon cumin seeds
1 (1-inch) cinnamon stick
2 cloves
4 black peppercorns
1-inch piece fresh gingerroot,
    peeled and sliced
4 garlic cloves
Water, as needed

3 tablespoons vegetable oil
1 large red onion, minced
½ teaspoon turmeric powder
1 pound shrimp, peeled and
    deveined
1 (14-ounce) can light coconut
    milk
Table salt, to taste

Serves 4

A nice varia-
tion is to fry
the shrimp
first. It adds
a nice crisp-
ness. Serve
with steamed
white rice.

1. In a spice grinder, roughly grind the bay leaf, cumin seeds, cinnamon stick, cloves, peppercorns, ginger, and garlic. Add 1 tablespoon of water if needed.
2. In a medium-sized skillet, heat the vegetable oil. Add the ground spice mixture and sauté for about 1 minute. Add the onions and sauté for 7 to 8 minutes or until the onions are well browned.
3. Add the turmeric and mix well. Add the shrimp and sauté for about 2 to 3 minutes, until no longer pink.
4. Add the coconut milk and salt. Simmer for 10 minutes or until the gravy starts to thicken. Remove from heat and serve hot.

Consummate Hosts

If you travel throughout India, you soon realize that they are the consummate hosts. In Sanskrit literature, three famous words, Atithi Devo Bhava ("the guest is truly your god") suggest how Indians feel about hospitality. Indians believe they are honored to share their meal, and even the poorest are anxious to share what they have. An Indian host is typically very proud and would be horrified if a guest were to leave hungry or unhappy. Thus when invited to someone's home in India, it is best to happily agree—and be sure to leave plenty of room to eat.

Salmon in Saffron-Flavored Curry

Serves 4

"The king of the sea marries the queen of spices" is the best way to describe this dish. Serve with naan bread.

4 tablespoons vegetable oil
1 large onion, finely chopped
1 teaspoon ginger-garlic paste (see sidebar below)
½ teaspoon red chili powder
¼ teaspoon turmeric powder
2 teaspoons coriander powder
Table salt, to taste
1 pound salmon, boned and cubed
½ cup plain yogurt, whipped
8 tablespoons whole milk
1 teaspoon saffron threads

1. In a large, nonstick skillet, heat the vegetable oil. Add the onions and sauté for 3 to 4 minutes or until transparent. Add the ginger-garlic paste and sauté for 1 minute.
2. Add the red chili powder, turmeric, coriander, and salt; mix well. Add the salmon and sauté for 3 to 4 minutes. Add the yogurt and lower the heat. Simmer until the salmon has cooked through.
3. Warm the milk over low heat until it is warm to the touch (but not hot).
4. In a dry skillet, dry roast the saffron threads over low heat until fragrant, about 1 minute. Remove from heat. Combine the warm milk and saffron threads, and add to the salmon and mix well. Cook for 1 minute. Serve hot.

Ginger-Garlic Paste

To make the ginger-garlic paste, in a food processor, combine the following: 2 serrano green chilies (stems removed), ½ cup fresh gingerroot (peeled), ½ cup garlic cloves (peeled), and 1 tablespoon cold water. Purée to form a smooth paste. Add no more than 1 tablespoon of water to help form a smooth consistency. Store the paste in an airtight jar in the refrigerator. It will keep for up to two weeks.

Split Lentil Dumplings

1 cup skinned and split black
  gram (also called white
  lentils), rinsed
½ teaspoon fenugreek seeds
4 cups hot water

1-inch piece fresh gingerroot,
  peeled and coarsely chopped
2 serrano green chilies
Table salt, to taste
Vegetable oil for deep-frying

Serves 4

These delightful dumplings can be served as cocktail appetizers.

1. Soak the gram and fenugreek seeds together in the hot water for about 2 hours. Drain.
2. In a food processor, combine the soaked gram, ginger, chilies, and salt. Process to a smooth batter. Add up to 2 tablespoons of water if needed. Transfer to a bowl.
3. Heat the vegetable oil in a deep pan or a deep fryer to 375°. Place a few tablespoons of the mixture, one at a time, into the oil. Make sure you do not overcrowd the pan. Deep-fry the balls until golden brown all over, about 2 to 3 minutes. Remove with a slotted spoon and drain on a paper towel. Let the oil return to temperature between batches. Continue until all the mixture is used. Serve hot.

The Requisite Condiments

You will almost always find a selection of fresh chutneys, dried fruit chutneys, and hot pickles as an accompaniment to an Indian meal. Aimed at heightening and balancing flavors, condiments can make an enormous impact on the taste of a dish. Working on several levels, these items often taste simultaneously sweet, pungent, hot, and sour. Some of the leading chutneys are cilantro, mint, and coconut, while pickle favorites (which are preserved in oil, not vinegar) include lime, mango, and eggplant.

Gooseberry Chutney

Serves 10

This popular chutney makes an excellent accompaniment to game birds. Stored in a covered container in the refrigerator, it will last for up to one week.

3 tablespoons vegetable oil
2 teaspoons minced ginger
1 clove garlic, minced
2 tablespoons finely chopped onion
1¼ cups cider vinegar
1½ cups granulated sugar

4 cups fresh green gooseberries
¼ cup balsamic vinegar
½ teaspoon ground cinnamon
⅛ teaspoon cayenne pepper, or to taste
¼ teaspoon salt

1. In a heavy-bottomed saucepan, heat the oil. Stir in the minced ginger and garlic. Add the chopped onion. Cook over medium heat until the onion is soft and translucent (5 to 7 minutes).
2. Add the cider vinegar and sugar and bring to a boil, stirring to dissolve the sugar. Add the gooseberries, balsamic vinegar, ground cinnamon, cayenne pepper, and salt. Bring back to a boil, stirring continually. Reduce the heat and let the chutney simmer, uncovered, until the gooseberries are softened and the mixture has thickened (about 30 minutes). Cool. Serve immediately, or cover and refrigerate to give the flavors a chance to blend. (The chutney will keep for up to a week.)

Regional Distinctions

There are strong distinctions between regional Indian dishes. In the north and the west, Kashmiri and Mughlai cuisines show strong Central Asian influences. To the east, the Bengali and Assamese resemble the cuisines of East Asia. All coastal kitchens make use of fish and coconuts, while desert cuisines of Rajasthan and Gujarat use an immense variety of dahls and achars (preserves) to substitute for the relative lack of fresh vegetables. All along the northern plain, a variety of flours are used to make chapatis and other breads.

Mango Cheesecake

¼ cup water

1 envelope unflavored gelatin

2 cups Indian cheese (paneer), crumbled

1 cup ricotta cheese

4 tablespoons sweetened mango pulp

2 tablespoons sweetened condensed milk

1 cup heavy cream, whipped

1 (15-ounce) can Alphonso mango slices, drained, or fresh mango slices, coarsely chopped

Sprinkle some toasted coconut on this dessert to bring the tropics home in the middle of winter.

1. Heat the water on low in a small pan, sprinkle the gelatin on top, and heat until the gelatin completely dissolves. Set aside.
2. In a bowl, combine the Indian cheese, ricotta cheese, mango pulp, and condensed milk. Mix well and make sure that there are no lumps. A handheld blender works well for this.
3. Slowly add the gelatin to the cheese mixture; mix well.
4. Fold in the whipped cream, and pour into a lightly buttered 6-cup mold. Chill until firm, about 2 hours.
5. When ready to serve, invert the mold onto a serving platter and top the cheesecake with the Alphonso mango.

Royal Kitchens

It was in large part thanks to Indian royalty, the rajahs, that Indian cuisine reached for culinary heights. Rulers encouraged their personal chefs to create elaborate feasts and unique dishes. Chefs vied with one another to succeed in creating the most exotic dishes, pushing the envelope when it came to innovative combinations and ornate presentation. The result? Centuries of patronage to the art of cooking, and a large repertoire of delicious recipes.

CHAPTER 12
Thailand: Land of Lemongrass, Coconut, and Curry

Tamarind Sauce

Serves 4

This sauce is used to complement many different Thai dishes.

½ cup fish sauce
7 tablespoons tamarind juice

½ cup palm sugar
1 teaspoon red chili oil

Mix together all the ingredients in a pan over medium heat. Cook until the sugar melts, stirring throughout. Remove from heat when slightly caramelized.

Chili Prawns with Tomato Sauce

Serves 4

Tropika Restaurant, in Vancouver, British Columbia, serves Malaysian, Indonesian, and Thai cuisine that appeals to the large number of immigrants living in the city.

1 tablespoon vegetable oil
½ teaspoon minced garlic
1 green onion, cut into 2-inch-long pieces
1 large tomato, cut into 8 pieces
1 pound tiger prawns, peeled, deveined, and cleaned

½ teaspoon chili sauce
1 tablespoon tomato sauce
½ teaspoon salt
2 teaspoons granulated sugar
1 tablespoon coconut milk
1 egg, beaten well

Preheat a wok on high, then add the oil and swirl it around to coat the pan. Add the garlic, green onion, and tomato. Stir-fry for 1 minute. Add the prawns, chili sauce, tomato sauce, salt, and sugar. Stir-fry until the prawns turn golden yellow. Add the coconut milk and egg, reduce heat to medium-low, and keep stirring until the egg is cooked. Serve.

Jungle Curry Paste

2 tablespoons vegetable oil

12 serrano chilies, seeded and chopped

6–8 Thai bird chilies, seeded and chopped

1 tablespoon shrimp paste

1 stalk lemongrass, tough outer leaves removed and discarded, inner core minced

1 (3-inch) piece ginger, peeled and chopped

4 shallots, chopped

1 cup chopped basil

½ cup chopped mint

¼ cup chopped chives

¼ cup chopped arugula

Yields approximately 2 cups

This curry has the look of a pesto. In fact, you can use it in a similar manner, tossing a tablespoon or so to taste with hot pasta.

1. In a medium-sized sauté pan, heat the oil on medium. Add the chilies, shrimp paste, lemongrass, ginger, and shallots, and sauté until the shallots begin to turn translucent and the mixture is very fragrant.

2. Transfer the mixture to a food processor and process until smooth, adding 1 or 2 tablespoons of water to help with the grinding.

3. Add the remaining ingredients and more water if necessary and continue to process until coarsely blended.

Arugula

Arugula is a specialty green with a peppery, somewhat bitter taste. Although we Westerners associate it with Italian cuisine, it was originally cultivated in western Asia. If you can't find it (check in the herb section), you can substitute spinach in this recipe, although with a slightly less flavorful result.

Chicken in Coconut Milk

Serves 2

This is a classic Thai recipe, offered by Banyan Tree Phuket, bordered by the golden sands of the Andaman Sea. This is an excellent dish to pair with rice. Serrano chilies are extremely hot—feel free to substitute a milder chili pepper if desired.

3 cups coconut milk
2 sticks lemongrass
1 small red serrano chili, crushed
2 tablespoons chopped galangal root
1 knob turmeric root
3 kaffir lime leaves
½-pound skinless, boneless chicken breast, thinly sliced

2 tablespoons fresh-squeezed lemon juice
2 tablespoons fish sauce
3 shiitake mushrooms
1 tablespoon chopped green onion
1 tablespoon chili oil
1 tablespoon cilantro leaves

In a pan over low heat, warm the coconut milk with the lemongrass, chili, galangal, turmeric, and lime leaves for about 2 to 3 minutes, until fragrant. Add the chicken, increase heat to medium-low, and simmer, uncovered, until the chicken is cooked through. Add the lemon juice and fish sauce. Add the mushrooms and cook until just tender. Remove the galangal root. Serve in bowls, garnished with the green onion, chili oil, and cilantro leaves.

What Is Galangal?

Galangal is a root that you can find in many Asian specialty markets. Galangal gives a distinctive, lightly acid taste to dishes, and often galangal slices are added to various curries and soups. Some people even crush the bulb, boil it in water, and eat it to cure upset stomachs.

Green Mango and Shrimp Salad

20 medium shrimp, deveined and
   butterflied
3 green mangoes
1 carrot, peeled
2 tablespoons fish sauce
2 tablespoons fresh-squeezed
   lime juice
½ teaspoon granulated sugar

1 clove garlic, finely chopped
½ green onion, chopped
Chopped fresh cilantro, to taste
½ cup coconut cream
Dry shrimp powder
Unsalted roasted peanuts,
   crushed

Serves 4

This original creation by Chef Sean Beaton of Rendezvous Restaurant and Winery in Belize is rooted in Asian culture. You can substitute chayote for the green mango, and jicama for the green papaya.

1. Bring a large saucepan with water to a near boil. Add the shrimp. Poach the shrimp in the just simmering water until they turn pink. Be careful not to overcook. Drain the poached shrimp on paper towels.
2. Finely julienne the mango and carrot, and mix together in a large bowl.
3. In another large bowl, mix together the fish sauce, lime juice, sugar, and garlic until the sugar dissolves. Add the green onion, cilantro, and poached shrimp. Add the coconut cream and stir to mix.
4. Pour the shrimp mixture over the mango and carrot, and toss to mix. Garnish each serving with shrimp powder and crushed peanuts.

Eating Habits in Thailand

Thai people do not use knives and forks, but rather forks and spoons, holding the fork in their left hand to help get the food onto the spoon, held in the right hand. They then eat directly from the spoon. Most Western cultures eat with the fork because they have to cut their food, whereas in Thai food everything is usually precut. But beware: Stuffing your mouth is considered impolite, and you should avoid scraping the utensils against your plate. The Thai people also do not scoop portions onto their plates—instead, they share from a common dish, placed at the center of the table, taking only enough for a bite or two at a time.

Stir-Fried Asparagus, Oyster Mushrooms, and Shrimp in Garlic Sauce

Serves 4

A thin, salty liquid made with anchovies, fish sauce is indispensable in Thai cooking. Feel free to experiment with replacing soy sauce with fish sauce in your favorite Asian recipes.

8 ounces oyster mushrooms
¾ pound fresh medium-sized shrimp
¾ pound asparagus
2 cloves garlic
3 tablespoons vegetable oil

2 teaspoons oyster sauce
2 tablespoons fish sauce
½ teaspoon brown sugar
1 tablespoon chopped fresh cilantro leaves
¼ teaspoon chili paste with garlic

1. Wipe the oyster mushrooms clean with a damp cloth. Cut in half if the caps are very large. Rinse the shrimp in warm water and pat dry with paper towels. Remove the shells from the shrimp, but leave the tails intact. Wash the asparagus and drain thoroughly. Remove the tough ends and cut on the diagonal into 1-inch pieces. Smash, peel, and finely chop the garlic.
2. Heat a wok over high heat. Add the oil, swirling so that the entire surface is coated. When the oil is hot, add the garlic and stir-fry until fragrant (about 30 seconds). Add the shrimp and stir-fry until it turns pink. Add the asparagus pieces. Stir-fry for 1 minute, then add the mushrooms.
3. Stir in the oyster sauce, fish sauce, and brown sugar. Heat through and stir in the cilantro leaves, and chili paste if using. Serve hot.

Crab Spring Rolls

Yields 15 rolls

1 pound crabmeat, picked over
  to remove any shells, and
  shredded
1 tablespoon mayonnaise
¼–½ teaspoon grated lime peel
15 spring roll or egg roll
  wrappers

2 egg yolks, lightly beaten
Canola oil for deep frying
15 small, tender Boston lettuce
  leaves
Mint leaves
Parsley leaves

The key to keeping the fat to a minimum when deep-frying is using clean, hot cooking oil and immediately transferring the rolls to paper towels to absorb excess oil.

1. In a small bowl, mix the crabmeat with the mayonnaise and lime peel.
2. Place 1 tablespoon of the crabmeat mixture in the center of 1 spring roll wrapper. Fold a pointed end of the wrapper over the crabmeat, then fold the opposite point over the top of the folded point. Brush a bit of the egg yolk over the top of the exposed wrapper, then fold the bottom point over the crabmeat and roll to form a tight packet; set aside. Repeat with the remaining crabmeat and wrappers.
3. Heat the oil to 365° in a skillet or deep fryer. Deep-fry the rolls 3 to 4 at a time for 2 minutes or so, until they are a golden brown; drain on paper towels.
4. To serve, wrap each spring roll in a wrapper with a single piece of lettuce, and a sprinkling of mint and parsley. Serve with your favorite dipping sauce.

Defining Thai Cuisine

Like the word Thai (which means "free"), Thai cooks are often flexible in their cooking, not bogged down by exact measurements. Thai food combines the best of several Eastern cuisines: the bite of Szechwan Chinese, the tropical flavor of Malaysian, the coconut creaminess of southern Indian, and the aromatic spices of Arabian food. Thai food is often made hot using chilies, and then toned down with the addition of locally grown roots and aromatic herbs.

Hot and Sour Prawn Soup

Serves 4

For extra flavor, crush the prawn shells with a mortar and pestle and add them to the broth. If using the shells, strain the soup before serving.

1 pound medium-sized fresh prawns, shelled and deveined
15-ounce can straw mushrooms
8-ounce can baby corn
4 hot Thai chilies (prig hang)
1 lemongrass stalk
4 kaffir lime leaves
4 cups water
1 cup chicken or fish stock

1 tablespoon freshly squeezed lemon juice
2 tablespoons freshly squeezed lime juice
1 tablespoon fish sauce
2 tablespoons soy sauce
1 teaspoon brown sugar
2 tablespoons chopped cilantro

1. Soak the prawns in warm salted water for 5 minutes, and pat dry with paper towels. Chop into small pieces. Rinse the mushrooms and baby corn under warm running water and drain. Thinly slice the mushrooms.
2. Cut the chili peppers in half, remove the seeds, and chop thinly. (Wear plastic gloves while working with the chilies and wash your hands afterward.) Bruise the lemongrass by pounding it with a mallet and thinly slice. Finely chop the kaffir leaves.
3. In a medium saucepan, bring the water, stock, and the lemongrass to a boil. Reduce heat and simmer, covered, for 15 minutes, until the water and stock is infused with the lemongrass flavor.
4. Add the kaffir leaves, chilies, lemon juice, lime juice, mushrooms, and baby corn. Simmer for 2 minutes, then stir in the fish sauce, soy sauce, and brown sugar. Add the prawns, heat through. Garnish with the chopped cilantro just before serving.

Bananas in Coconut Milk

6 medium bananas,
  not over-ripe
¾ cup thick coconut milk
¾ cup thin coconut milk

⅓ cup granulated sugar
¼ teaspoon ground cinnamon
3 tablespoons crushed peanuts

Serves 4–6

This is a simple version of a popular Thai treat. For added decadence, top with a dollop of "ice cream" made from coconut milk.

1. Peel the bananas and cut on the diagonal into 2-inch pieces.
2. In a medium saucepan, bring the coconut milk to a boil. Add the sugar, stirring to dissolve. Stir in the ground cinnamon.
3. Add the sliced banana. Reduce the heat and allow the bananas to simmer, uncovered, until the bananas are softened but not mushy (3 to 5 minutes, depending on the ripeness of the banana). To serve, spoon the heated bananas and coconut milk into dessert bowls. Sprinkle the crushed peanuts over top.

History of Thai Cuisine

Thai cuisine, known worldwide for its blend of aromatic herbs, fragrant spices, and colorful presentation, was born out of a centuries-old tradition. The cuisine of Thailand is, like many, the synthesis of styles from different races of people in the country. Thai food ranges from simple home cooking for the family, to the "Royal Cuisine," which, in the past, was prepared only in the inner court's palace and served solely to royal and aristocratic households and their guests.

Tom Ka Kai

Serves 4–6

This soup can be served as is or ladled over mounds of rice in individual serving bowls. It goes great with some cooked noodles thrown in.

2 cups chicken broth
1 teaspoon sliced kaffir lime leaves
1 (2-inch) piece lemongrass, bruised
1 (1-inch) piece ginger, sliced thinly
4 tablespoons fish sauce

2 tablespoons lime juice
1 boneless, skinless chicken breast, cut into bite-sized pieces
5 ounces coconut milk
2–4 Thai chilies (to taste), slightly crushed

1. In a medium-sized soup pot, heat the broth on medium. Add the lime leaves, lemongrass, ginger, fish sauce, and lime juice.
2. Bring the mixture to a boil, add the chicken and coconut milk, and bring to a boil again.
3. Reduce the heat, add the chilies, and cover; let simmer until the chicken is cooked through, about 3 to 5 minutes.
4. Remove the chilies and the lemongrass stalk with a slotted spoon before serving.

Quick Thai Favorites

Next time you scroll through a Thai menu, why not try a few of these: tom yam koong (lemon-flavored sour shrimp soup); hor mok (a seafood dish with a red curry custard base); tom kha kai (a mild spicy chicken soup with coconut milk); tod man (a savory deep-fried fish or prawn quenelles); chor ladda or chor muang (minced pork or prawn dumplings); kang khieu wan kai (thick green chicken curry); kang masaman (southern Thai beef and potatoes curry); mee krob (deep-fried rice vermicelli).

Pumpkin Curry Soup

1 pound kabocha squash
2 kaffir leaves
4 cups chicken or vegetable stock
1 cup unsweetened coconut milk
2 teaspoons freshly squeezed
   lime juice

2 tablespoons palm sugar
2 tablespoons chili paste, or to
   taste
Fresh Thai basil leaves, as
   garnish

Thai basil has a distinctive flavor similar to licorice or anise. Both Thai basil and kabocha squash can be found at Asian markets.

1. Cut the kabocha in half, remove the seed and stringy pith in the middle. Peel off the greenish skin and cut into 1½-inch chunks. Chop the kaffir leaves.
2. In a large saucepan, bring the chicken stock, coconut milk, kabocha, kaffir leaves, lime juice, and palm sugar to a boil. Reduce the heat to low and simmer, partially covered, until the kabocha is tender when pierced with a fork (about 20 minutes). Stir in the chili paste.
3. Purée the broth in a blender or food processor. Pour into soup bowls and garnish with the Thai basil.

What Is Curry?

Curry is an English word most probably derived from the South Indian word kaikaari. Kaikaari, or kaari, referred to vegetables cooked with spices and coconut. In India curry means gravy. In America many believe curry is an Indian spice, but curry powder is actually a blend of spices, mainly garam masala mixed with ground coriander and turmeric. There is a plant, however, that has leaves that are called curry leaves (meetha neem in Hindi) or kadhi leaves. They look like tiny lemon leaves and grow wild in most forest regions of India and are used as a seasoning.

Bangkok-Style Roasted Pork Tenderloin

Serves 4

This is a great dish to make when you're in a hurry. Serve with a salad, some vegetables, and rice, and you can still have the whole meal ready in less than 30 minutes.

1 teaspoon salt
¼ teaspoon ground ginger
¼ teaspoon ground cardamom
¼–½ teaspoon freshly ground
  black pepper

2 (1-pound) pork tenderloins,
  trimmed
Olive oil
½ cup chicken, pork, or
  vegetable stock, or water

1. Place rack on bottom third of the oven, then preheat the oven to 500°.
2. Combine the spices in a small bowl.
3. Rub each of the tenderloins with half of the spice mixture and a bit of olive oil. Place the tenderloins in a roasting pan and cook for 10 minutes.
4. Turn the tenderloins over and roast for 10 more minutes or until done to your liking.
5. Transfer the pork to a serving platter, cover with foil, and let rest.
6. Pour off any fat that has accumulated in the roasting pan. Place the pan on the stovetop over high heat and add the stock (or water). Bring to a boil, scraping the bottom of the pan to loosen any cooked-on bits. Season with salt and pepper to taste.
7. To serve, slice the tenderloins into thin slices. Pour a bit of the sauce over top, passing more separately at the table.

Sweet and Savory Grilled Coconut-Rice Hotcakes

3 (14-ounce) cans coconut milk
¼ cup, plus 2 tablespoons granulated sugar (keep separate)
2½ tablespoons tapioca starch or arrowroot flour
3 tablespoons uncooked short-grain white rice
⅓ cup finely shredded fresh coconut

2 cups rice flour
2 teaspoons sea salt
2–3 tablespoons peanut or corn oil

Optional filling ingredients:
¼ cup sliced green onions
¼ cup fresh corn kernels
2 tablespoons chopped fresh cilantro leaves

Serves 6

Executive Chef Sean O'Connell of Banyan Tree Phuket offers this wonderful recipe inspired by the restaurant's tropical location. If you can't find fresh coconut, substitute 1/4 cup dried, unsweetened shredded coconut.

1. Do not shake the cans of coconut milk before opening. Spoon off the thickest cream from the top of the cans to yield 1¾ cups. Heat the coconut cream in a saucepan, just enough to smooth out the lumps. Add the ¼ cup sugar to the coconut cream and stir to dissolve. Let cool, and mix in 2 tablespoons of the tapioca starch. Stir until smooth. Set aside.
2. Pour the remaining coconut milk from the cans into a large bowl and stir until smooth. (Heat it if necessary to melt the coagulated parts, and let cool.) Grind the uncooked white rice in a clean coffee grinder as finely as possible. Do the same with the shredded coconut. Add the ground rice and coconut, the rice flour, salt, and remaining 2 tablespoons sugar to the bowl with the thin coconut milk. Stir and mix until well blended and smooth. (This is the main rice batter.)
3. Heat a well-seasoned pancake griddle on the stove. When the griddle is hot, lightly brush the surface with the oil. Wait a few seconds before spooning the rice batter onto the griddle. The batter should sizzle when it hits the hot metal.
4. Immediately add a dab of the sweet coconut-cream mixture over the top to fill the indentations, and sprinkle the center of each hotcake with a little of one of the optional toppings, or leave plain. Cover with a round lid and cook for a few minutes, until the hotcakes are firm and crispy brown on the bottom. Remove gently with a spoon and place on a cooling rack. Regrease the griddle before making the next batch. Because rice flour tends to settle, stir the batter well each time before pouring it onto the griddle. Serve warm.

Lemongrass Chicken Skewers

Serves 4

These chicken skewers are based on a recipe from award-winning chef Jean-Georges Vongerichten, whose French-inspired Thai cuisine has won praise the world over. Vongerichten has a line of tasty sauces and marinades that is available in stores.

5 stalks lemongrass, trimmed
12 large cubes chicken breast meat, a little over 1 ounce each
Black pepper
2 tablespoons vegetable oil, divided
Pinch of dried red pepper flakes
Juice of 1 lime
2 teaspoons fish sauce
Pinch of sugar
Sea salt to taste

1. Remove 2 inches from the thick end of each stalk of lemongrass; set aside. Bruise 4 of the lemongrass stalks with the back of a knife. Remove the tough outer layer of the fifth stalk, exposing the tender core; mince.
2. Skewer 3 cubes of chicken on each lemongrass stalk. Sprinkle the skewers with the minced lemongrass and black pepper, and drizzle with 1 tablespoon of oil. Cover with plastic wrap and refrigerate for 12 to 24 hours.
3. Chop all of the reserved lemongrass stalk ends. Place in a small saucepan and cover with water. Bring to a boil, cover, and let reduce until approximately 2 tablespoons of liquid are left; strain. Return the liquid to the saucepan and further reduce to 1 tablespoon.
4. Combine the lemongrass liquid with the red pepper flakes, lime juice, fish sauce, sugar, and remaining tablespoon of oil; set aside.
5. Prepare a grill to high heat. Grill the chicken skewers for approximately 2 to 3 minutes per side, or until done to your liking.
6. To serve, spoon a little of the lemongrass sauce over the top of each skewer and sprinkle with sea salt.

Sambal Bunchies (Green Beans)

Serves 4

½ pound green beans, washed and cut into 3-inch-long pieces
1 jalapeño chili pepper
¼ lemongrass stalk
2 cloves garlic
½ teaspoon palm or brown sugar
1 teaspoon shrimp paste.
1 cup vegetable oil

1. Wash the green beans, drain, and cut into 2-inch-long pieces. Cut the jalapeño in half, remove the seeds, and finely chop. Finely chop the lemongrass stalk. Smash, peel, and finely chop the garlic.
2. In a food processor, purée the chopped chili pepper, garlic, and the lemongrass pieces. Add the palm sugar and shrimp paste and process again. The sauce should have a paste-like consistency.
3. Heat the wok over high heat. Add 1 cup of oil. When the oil is hot, add the green beans. Let the beans cook in the hot oil for 1 minute, then remove with a slotted spoon. Remove all but 2 teaspoons oil from the wok.
4. Turn the heat down to medium-high and add the shrimp paste mixture. Stir for 30 seconds. Add the green beans back into the pan. Mix with the sauce and serve hot.

If necessary, a deep-sided frying pan can be used in place of a wok. Serve this flavorful side dish with Chili Prawns with Tomato Sauce (page 154).

Herbs and Spice and Everything Nice

Twenty-seven main herbs and spices form the foundation of Thai cooking. There are several basils, including horapa, ga-prow, and manglug, and more than ten types of chilies. Other favorites include garlic, mint, sesame (usually as oil), mace (the outer shell of nutmeg), nutmeg, lemongrass, bay leaves, cloves, cardamon, cinnamon, cumin, ginger, galangal (a fragrant root similar to ginger), gra-shai (a type of ginger added to fish curries), turmeric, kaffir lime, mandarin oranges, and jasmine (used as a scent in drinking water, tea, and desserts).

Pad Thai

Tart tamarind water can be purchased at Asian markets. If unavailable, substitute 3 tablespoons lemon juice mixed with 1 tablespoon tomato sauce.

½ pound dried rice stick noodles (rice vermicelli)
½ pound firm tofu
2 large eggs
⅛ teaspoon salt
2 green onions
1 cup mung bean sprouts
¼ cup vegetable or peanut oil
2 cloves garlic, chopped
1 teaspoon minced ginger
½ pound small shrimp
¼ cup tamarind water

2 tablespoons fish sauce or soy sauce
3 tablespoons fresh-squeezed lime juice
2 teaspoons granulated sugar
2 teaspoons brown sugar
¼ cup warm water
⅓ cup ground unsalted roasted peanuts
2 limes or lemons, cut into wedges

1. Soak the rice vermicelli in warm water for 20 minutes, or until the noodles are softened and slippery. Drain thoroughly. Place the tofu on a plate lined with paper towels, and cover with a book or plate to squeeze out the water. Drain the water from the plate and change the paper towels as needed. Cut the drained tofu into 1-inch cubes.
2. In a small bowl, lightly beat the eggs with the salt. Wash the green onions and cut into 1-inch pieces. Rinse and drain the mung bean sprouts.
3. Heat the wok. Add the oil and heat over medium-high heat until very hot. Add the garlic and ginger and stir-fry for 30 seconds until aromatic. Add the shrimp and stir-fry until they turn pink. Stir-fry for 1 minute, then add the tamarind water, fish sauce, lime juice, and sugars, stirring the entire time.
4. Push the ingredients up to the sides of the wok. Add the beaten eggs into the middle of the pan, and quickly scramble. Add the noodles, mung bean sprouts, and green onion, stirring the entire time. Add as much of the warm water as needed.
5. Sprinkle the crushed peanuts over top. Garnish with the lime or lemon wedges.

Fire Noodles

15–20 (or to taste) Thai bird chilies, stemmed and seeded
5–10 (or to taste) cloves garlic
1 pound presliced fresh rice noodles (available at Asian grocery stores and on the Internet)
2 tablespoons vegetable oil
2 whole, boneless, skinless chicken breasts, cut into bite-sized pieces

2 tablespoons fish sauce
2 tablespoons sweet black soy sauce
1 tablespoon oyster sauce
1 teaspoon white pepper
1½ tablespoons sugar
1 (8-ounce) can bamboo shoots, drained
1½ cups loose-packed basil and/ or mint

Serves 4–6

If you bite into a chili that is just too hot to handle, try sucking on a spoonful of sugar or sucking on a hard candy.

1. Place the chilies and garlic cloves in a food processor and process until thoroughly mashed together; set aside.
2. Bring a kettle of water to a boil. Place the noodles in a large colander and pour the hot water over them. Carefully unfold and separate the noodles; set aside.
3. Heat the oil in a wok or large skillet over medium-high heat. When it is quite hot, carefully add the reserved chili-garlic mixture and stir-fry for 15 seconds to release the aromas.
4. Raise the heat to high, add the chicken, and stir-fry until it begins to lose its color, about 30 seconds.
5. Stir in the fish sauce, soy sauce, oyster sauce, white pepper, and sugar.
6. Add the noodles and continue to stir-fry for 30 seconds, tossing them with the other ingredients.
7. Add the bamboo shoots and cook for another minute.
8. Turn off the heat and add the basil.

Spicy Scallops

Serves 4

These scallops are simple to make but are sure to impress even your fussiest guests. They are also tasty over pasta as a main course. Make sure to use the freshest scallops you can find.

1 teaspoon vegetable oil
1 clove garlic, minced
1 jalapeño, seeded and minced
1 (½-inch) piece ginger, peeled and minced
⅛ teaspoon ground coriander
2 tablespoons soy sauce
2 tablespoons water
8 large scallops, cleaned

1. In a pan large enough to hold all of the scallops, heat the oil over medium heat. Add the garlic, jalapeño, and ginger, and stir-fry for about 1 minute.
2. Add the coriander, soy sauce, and water, stirring to combine; simmer for 2 to 3 minutes. Strain the liquid through a fine-mesh sieve. Allow the pan to cool slightly.
3. Add the scallops to the pan and spoon the reserved liquid over the top of them. Return the pan to the stove, increasing the heat to medium-high. Cover the pan and let the scallops steam for about 2 to 3 minutes, or until done to your liking. Serve immediately.

Thai Beef with Rice Noodles

¾ pound sirloin, trimmed of all
   fat, rinsed, and patted dry
½ pound dried rice noodles
¼ cup soy sauce
2 tablespoons fish sauce
2 tablespoons dark brown sugar
Freshly ground black pepper
5 tablespoons vegetable oil,
   divided

2 tablespoons minced garlic
1 pound greens (such as spinach
   or bok choy), cleaned and cut
   into ½-inch strips
2 eggs, beaten
Crushed dried red pepper flakes
   to taste
Rice vinegar to taste

Serves 2–4

You can
use a bag
of organic
baby spinach
leaves for
the greens
in this recipe
to make it
easier—they
are pre-
washed and
small enough
that you
can skip the
process of
cutting them
into strips.

1. Slice the meat into 2-inch-long, ½-inch-wide strips.
2. Cover the noodles with warm water for 5 minutes, then drain.
3. In a small bowl, combine the soy sauce, fish sauce, brown sugar, and black pepper; set aside.
4. Heat a wok or heavy skillet over high heat. Add approximately 2 tablespoons of the vegetable oil. When the oil is hot, but not smoking, add the garlic. After stirring for 5 seconds, add the greens and stir-fry for approximately 2 minutes; set aside.
5. Add 2 more tablespoons of oil to the wok. Add the beef and stir-fry until browned on all sides, about 2 minutes; set aside.
6. Heat 1 tablespoon of oil in the wok and add the noodles. Toss until warmed through, approximately 2 minutes; set aside.
7. Heat the oil remaining in the wok. Add the eggs and cook, without stirring until they are set, about 30 seconds. Break up the eggs slightly and stir in the reserved noodles, beef, and greens, and the red pepper flakes. Stir the reserved soy mixture, then add it to the wok. Toss to coat and heat through. Serve immediately with rice vinegar to sprinkle over the top.

Crispy Crepes with Fresh Fruits

Serves 4

You can substitute a mixture of tropical fruits for the berries, if you like.

1 package frozen puff pastry sheets, thawed according to package instructions

2 tablespoons confectioners' sugar, divided

2 cups raspberries, blueberries, or other fresh fruit, the best 12 berries reserved for garnish

1 cup heavy cream

¼ cup shredded, unsweetened coconut

1 tablespoon unflavored rum or coconut-flavored rum

1. Preheat the oven to 400°.
2. Place the puff pastry sheet on a work surface and cut into 12 equal-sized pieces. Place the pastry pieces on a baking sheet.
3. Bake the pastry approximately 10 minutes. Remove from the oven and use a sifter to shake a bit of the confectioners' sugar over the puff pastry. Return to the oven and continue baking for approximately 5 minutes or until golden. Place the puff pastry on a wire rack and let cool to room temperature.
4. Place the berries in a food processor and briefly process to form a rough purée.
5. Whip the cream with the remaining confectioners' sugar until thick, but not stiff. Stir in the coconut and the rum.
6. To serve, place 1 piece of puff pastry in the middle of each serving plate, spoon some cream over the pastry, and then top with some purée. Place another pastry on top, garnish with some of the remaining berries, any leftover juice from the purée, and a sprinkle of confectioners' sugar.

Watermelon with Beef and Tangerine Herb

Serves 2

Joseph Poon, chef/owner of Asian Fusion Restaurant in Philadelphia, leads diners on a journey of taste and flavor that includes all the regions of China.

Marinade:

½ tablespoon light soy sauce
3 tablespoons port wine or red
¼ cup water
2 teaspoons sesame oil
1 teaspoon cornstarch

Watermelon beef:

½ pound lean sirloin tip beef, sliced
1 tablespoon soybean oil
1 teaspoon minced garlic
1 teaspoon minced ginger
1 cup seeded and sliced watermelon
1 tangerine peel, soaked in sherry
½ cup snow peas

¼ red bell pepper, cubed
¼ yellow bell pepper, cubed
¼ red onion, cubed

Stir-fry sauce:

½ cup water or veal stock
½ teaspoon oyster sauce
½ teaspoon light soy sauce
1 teaspoon granulated sugar
3 tablespoons port wine or red wine
1 tablespoon hoisin sauce
½ teaspoon cornstarch, dissolved in 1 tablespoon water

Garnish:

4 drops sesame oil
Watermelon wedges

1. Mix together all the marinade ingredients and add the beef. Marinate for at least 30 minutes at room temperature. Sauté the beef in a nonstick pan over medium-high heat until brown on all sides. Set aside.
2. Heat the soybean oil on medium-high in a wok or large sauté pan. Add the garlic, ginger, watermelon, and tangerine, and sauté for 30 seconds. Add all the peas, bell peppers, and onions, stirring constantly to sweat the onions and peppers.
3. Mix together all the stir-fry sauce ingredients except the cornstarch and add it to the wok, stirring to mix. Bring to a boil. Pour in the dissolved cornstarch to thicken the sauce, add the beef, and mix thoroughly.
4. Spoon onto serving plates and top each with a couple drops of sesame oil. Garnish with triangular wedge of watermelon, if desired.

Steamed Tilapia with Mushrooms and Black Bean Sauce

8 to 12 ounces fresh tilapia,
cleaned
1 pinch salt
2–3 Chinese mushrooms,
shredded
1 tablespoon minced ginger

1 tablespoon canned black
beans, drained
½ cup diced green onions
1 teaspoon hot chili oil
¼ cup light soy sauce, or as
needed

Serves 2

Another recipe by Chef Joseph Poon. He suggests "steaming the tilapia a bit longer if it is on the larger size."

Place the fish in a metal steamer over a saucepan filled with boiling water. Sprinkle the salt, mushrooms, ginger, black beans, and green onions on the top of the fish. Steam for 10 to 15 minutes (depending on the size), until the flesh flakes easily when tested with a fork. Drizzle the hot chili oil over top. Serve with light soy sauce for dipping.

Steamed Prawns with Crushed Garlic

½ pound prawns
5 garlic cloves, crushed
½ teaspoon salt

½ teaspoon chicken bouillon
½ cup, plus 2 tablespoons
vegetable oil

Serves 6

This flavorful dish is a signature dish that is enjoyed in many of Hong Kong's finest restaurants.

1. Cut open the top ¼ inch of each prawn and remove the intestine. Rinse clean and set aside.
2. Crush the garlic cloves and place in a heat-resistant bowl. Stir in the salt and chicken bouillon. Bring the oil to a boil and pour it into the bowl of crushed garlic. Stir, and let cool. Spread the mixture on the open tops of the prawns.
3. Fill a steamer with water and bring to a boil. Place prawns on a deep plate and place in steamer and cover. Steam the prawns for 5 minutes. Serve.

Tomato Egg-Flower Soup

Serves 4

Beef and tomato are a natural combination. For a heartier soup, add ½ cup of ground beef or lean beef.

4 cups beef broth
2 medium tomatoes
⅛ teaspoon white pepper
¼ teaspoon salt
½ teaspoon sugar
1 teaspoon Chinese rice wine or
   dry sherry

1 tablespoon cornstarch
4 tablespoons water
1 egg white, lightly beaten
2 green onions, minced
A few drops of sesame oil

1. Bring the 4 cups of beef broth to a boil.
2. Bring a large pot of water to a boil. Blanch the tomatoes briefly in the boiling water. (This will make it easier to remove the peel.) Peel the tomatoes and cut each into 6 equal pieces.
3. When the beef broth comes to a boil, add the white pepper, salt, sugar, rice wine, and tomatoes. Bring the broth back to boiling.
4. Mix the cornstarch and water, and pour it into the soup, stirring to thicken. Turn off the heat.
5. Pour the egg white into the soup and quickly stir in a clockwise direction to form thin shreds.
6. Add the green onions and a few drops of sesame oil. Give the soup a final stir.

Cholesterol Concerns

Using egg whites instead of eggs in the Egg Drop Soup–type recipes helps reduce the amount of cholesterol. Another option is to forgo the egg altogether—heartier soups taste fine without it.

Snail in Black Bean and Orange Peel Sauce

Several large lettuce or cabbage
   leaves
1–1½ pounds fresh snails
1 tablespoon vegetable oil
1 teaspoon chopped fresh garlic
1 teaspoon chopped fresh ginger
½ cup mix of diced red, yellow,
   and green bell peppers
¼ cup diced white onion
1 tablespoon fermented black
   beans
1 tablespoon lemon zest

1 tablespoon dried orange peel,
   softened in water
½ cup Chardonnay
1 cup chicken broth
1 tablespoon oyster sauce
1 teaspoon mushroom soy sauce
1 teaspoon light soy sauce
1 tablespoon granulated sugar
2 tablespoons cornstarch
   dissolved in 4 tablespoons
   water
1 teaspoon sesame oil

Serves 2

In this recipe,
Chef Poon
creates a
unique Asian-
style version
of the classic
French dish,
escargots.

1. Line a bamboo steaming basket with lettuce or cabbage leaves. Place the snails on the leaves and place the basket in a wok half-filled with boiling water. Steam the snails until cooked through (8 to 10 minutes) and place on a serving plate.
2. Heat the oil in a frying pan on high heat. When the oil is hot, add the garlic and ginger and stir-fry until fragrant (about 30 seconds). Add the bell peppers, onion, and black beans. Stir-fry for several minutes, until the peppers and onion are tender. Stir in all the remaining ingredients except the sesame oil and cook for several minutes on high heat. Add the sesame oil at the last minute (otherwise it will lose its favor). Pour the sauce over the top of the cooked snails.

Lemon Chicken

Fresh lemon makes the perfect garnish for this delicately flavored dish. Serve with basmati or jasmine steamed scented rice.

1 pound skinless, boneless
   chicken breasts, cut into
   1-inch cubes
4 tablespoons soy sauce, divided
2 tablespoons cornstarch, divided
1 red bell pepper
1 green bell pepper
1 bunch green onions

6 tablespoons water, divided
1 tablespoon granulated sugar
2 tablespoons freshly squeezed
   lemon juice
¾ teaspoon lemon peel, grated
4 tablespoons vegetable oil,
   divided
1 slice ginger, unpeeled

1. Place the chicken cubes in a medium bowl. Add 2 tablespoons of the soy sauce and 1 tablespoon cornstarch, using your fingers to mix in the cornstarch. Cover and marinate in the refrigerator for 30 minutes. Remove the stems and seeds from the bell peppers and cut into cubes. Chop the green onion on the diagonal into 1-inch pieces.
2. Meanwhile, combine the remaining 2 tablespoons soy sauce, ¼ cup water, sugar, lemon juice, and grated lemon peel. Set aside. Mix the remaining 1 tablespoon of cornstarch in 2 tablespoons of water to make a cornstarch "slurry." Set aside.
3. Heat 2 tablespoons oil in a preheated wok over high heat. Add the chicken cubes into the pan. Brown briefly; then stir-fry until the chicken turns white and is nearly cooked through. Remove and drain on paper towels.
4. Heat the remaining oil in the wok over high heat. When the oil is hot, add the ginger. Stir-fry for 30 seconds until fragrant. Add the cubed green pepper. Stir-fry for 1 minute, and add the red pepper cubes.
5. Push the peppers up to the side. Add the sauce into the middle of the wok. Add the cornstarch slurry to the sauce, stirring quickly to thicken. Add the chicken back into the pan. Stir in the green onions. Stir to lightly glaze the chicken and peppers with the lemony sauce. Serve immediately, removing the ginger before serving.

Pork and Crab Lumpia

2 to 3 tablespoons crabmeat, as
 needed
¼ pound ground pork
1 egg, lightly beaten
1 tablespoon minced green
 onions

1 tablespoon minced water
 chestnuts
1 teaspoon fresh minced ginger
Salt and pepper, to taste
Pinch granulated sugar
8 spring roll wrappers
Vegetable oil, as needed

Serves 4

This recipe from Executive Chef Michael Viloria of Vancouver, British Columbia, is considered a wonderful accompaniment to an elaborate Filipino feast. Serve with Achara (page 180).

1. In a medium-sized bowl, mix together the crabmeat, pork, and egg. In a small bowl, mix together the scallions, water chestnut, and ginger, and add to the crabmeat mixture. Add the salt, pepper, and sugar, and mix thoroughly.
2. Place a wrapper on a flat surface diagonally. Place ⅛ of the mixture onto the wrapper. Shape the mixture into a tube shape and roll the sides of the spring roll wrapper in toward the center. Fold the bottom of the wrapper over the top of the filling and roll it away from you into the shape of a cylinder (instructions on how to roll the spring rolls should be on the package of the wrappers). Repeat with the remaining wrappers and filling.
3. Fill a pot ⅓ of the way with vegetable oil and heat on medium. Deep-fry the lumpias until golden brown (you may have to turn them occasionally so they cook evenly). Serve.

Stuffed Red Peppers

Serves 1

The Chinese version of miso, brown bean sauce is made with soybeans and spicy seasonings such as chili and garlic.

1 red bell pepper
1 cup ground pork
1 tablespoon brown bean sauce
2 tablespoons soy sauce, divided
½ teaspoon sugar

1 teaspoon Chinese rice wine or
    dry sherry
1 green onion, minced
1 clove garlic, chopped

1. Preheat the oven to 300°F.
2. Wash the red pepper; cut off the top and set it aside. Remove the seeds.
3. In a medium-sized bowl, use your hands to mix the ground pork with the brown bean sauce, 1 tablespoon soy sauce, sugar, and rice wine. Add the green onion and chopped garlic.
4. Stuff the red pepper with the ground pork mixture. Add 1 tablespoon soy sauce on top and replace the lid. Place in a heatproof dish in the oven, and bake until the pork is cooked through, about 45–55 minutes.

Achara

Serves 3–4
(as a sauce)

Inspired by a classic Filippino dish, this sweet and tangy treat tastes great served over rice or noodles.

1 habanero chili pepper
1 green papaya
½ large carrot
2-inch piece daikon radish

3 tablespoons granulated sugar
⅓ cup cider or Asian rice vinegar
1 teaspoon salt

1. Deseed the red chili pepper. Peel the papaya and the carrot. Thinly slice the papaya, carrot, daikon radish, and the chili pepper lengthwise to resemble matchsticks.
2. Whisk together the sugar, rice vinegar, and salt. Add to the papaya mixture and refrigerate, covered, for 1 hour to give the flavors a chance to blend. Use within a few days.

Sesame Chicken

10 chicken thighs
3 tablespoons light soy sauce
2 tablespoons Chinese rice wine
  or dry sherry
1 teaspoon grated ginger

1 green onion, chopped
2 tablespoons cornstarch
4 tablespoons white sesame
  seeds
6 cups peanut oil for deep-frying

Serves 6

Made from sweet glutinous rice, Chinese rice wine is found in Asian markets. Use dry sherry as a substitute if rice wine is unavailable (not cooking wine or cooking sherry).

1. Cut the chicken thighs in half across the thigh bone, and place in a shallow dish. In a small bowl, mix together the soy sauce, rice wine, grated ginger, green onion, and cornstarch. Cover and marinate the chicken thighs in the refrigerator for 1 hour, turning over once to make sure all the chicken is evenly coated in the marinade.
2. While the chicken is marinating, toast the sesame seeds. Spread the seeds out in a frying pan and cook on medium heat, shaking the pan continuously, until the seeds are browned. Remove the toasted seeds from the pan and cool.
3. In a large pot, bring the peanut oil to 375°. Carefully slide ¼ of the marinated chicken pieces into the hot oil and deep-fry until golden brown. Remove the chicken from the wok with a slotted spoon and drain on paper towels. Continue deep-frying the remainder of the chicken.
4. Sprinkle the toasted sesame seeds over the chicken and serve hot.

Why Chopsticks, Not Knives, at the Table?

You probably expect to receive a pair of chopsticks when you sit down to a meal in a Chinese restaurant. In fact, the Chinese were using chopsticks long before Europeans were lifting forks and spoons to their mouths. The knife was invented earlier—but as a weapon, not a cooking utensil. It turns out chopsticks were advocated by the famed Chinese philosopher Confucius. His reason? That as an advancing society, instruments used for killing should be banned from the dining table. Thus knives were not permitted, and that is why Chinese food is always chopped into bite-size pieces before it reaches the table.

Lobster Cantonese

Serves 2

The secret
to preparing
this popular
Cantonese
dish is not to
overcook
the lobster
tails.

1 teaspoon fermented black
beans
1 clove garlic, minced
¾ cup chicken broth
2 tablespoons Chinese rice wine
or dry sherry, divided

1 tablespoon soy sauce
2 tablespoons oil for stir-frying
¼ pound ground pork
3 slices ginger, minced
1 green onion, thinly sliced

1 tablespoon cornstarch mixed with 4 tablespoons water
2 lobster tails, cut into ½-inch pieces

1 teaspoon sugar
1 egg, lightly beaten

1. Soak the beans in warm water and rinse. Mash, chop finely, and mix with the garlic clove.
2. Combine the chicken broth, 1 tablespoon rice wine, and soy sauce. Set aside.
3. Add oil to a preheated wok or skillet. When oil is hot, add the garlic and black bean mixture. Stir-fry briefly until aromatic. Add the pork and stir-fry for several minutes, until cooked through.
4. Push the ingredients up to the side of the wok. Add the ginger and green onion in the middle. Stir-fry briefly. Add the sauce and bring to a boil. Give the cornstarch-and-water mixture a quick stir and add, stirring quickly to thicken.
5. Add the lobster, the sugar, and 1 tablespoon rice wine. Stir-fry for about 2 minutes, then stream in the egg. Mix together and serve.

Preparing Fermented Black Beans

Soak the beans until they are softened. Mash the beans by flattening them under the blade of a knife or cleaver, and then mince or chop as called for in the recipe.

Asparagus with Pork

¼ pound lean ground pork
1 tablespoon light soy sauce
2 teaspoons sesame oil
1 green onion, washed and diced
1 teaspoon cornstarch
¼ cup low-sodium chicken broth
1 tablespoon oyster sauce
1 tablespoon dark soy sauce

1 teaspoon granulated sugar
3 ounces fresh shiitake
   mushrooms
½ white onion
4 cups water
1 pound fresh asparagus,
   trimmed
2 tablespoons vegetable oil

Serves 4

To enhance the savory flavor of this dish, use vegetarian oyster sauce, made with mushrooms instead of boiled oysters.

1. In a small bowl, combine the ground pork with the soy sauce, sesame oil, diced green onion, and cornstarch, making sure to add the cornstarch last. Marinate the pork for 15 minutes.
2. Combine the chicken broth, oyster sauce, dark soy sauce, and sugar in a small bowl. Set aside. Wipe the mushrooms clean with a damp cloth and cut into thick slices. Peel and finely chop the white onion.
3. Heat the water to boiling. Add the asparagus and blanch for 1 minute, or until the asparagus turns bright green and is tender but still firm. Plunge into a bowl filled with cold water. Remove and drain thoroughly. Lay the asparagus spears on a large serving platter and keep warm.
4. Heat the oil in a preheated wok or large skillet over medium-high heat. Add the marinated ground pork, using chopsticks or a spatula to separate the individual pork bits. Stir-fry for approximately 1 minute, until the pork changes color and is nearly cooked.
5. Push the ground pork up to the side of the wok or skillet. Add the onion, and stir-fry for 1 minute. Add the mushrooms and stir-fry for 2 more minutes. Turn the heat to high and add the chicken broth mixture to the middle of the pan. Mix everything together. To serve, pour the pork and mushroom mixture over the asparagus.

Straits Sea Bass

Serves 6

Christopher Yeo, owner and executive chef of Straits Restaurants, is among the first restaurateurs to bring authentic Singaporean cuisine to the San Francisco Bay Area. Wolfberry is available at Asian markets.

6 (6-ounce) sea bass fillets,
    1-inch thick
1 red bell pepper, julienned
1 yellow bell pepper, julienned
1 green bell pepper, julienned
12 shiitake mushrooms, julienned
2-inch piece ginger, julienned
6 teaspoons dried longan (or
    litchi)

3 teaspoons wolfberry
6 teaspoons sesame oil
1¼ cups Chinese rice wine or dry
    sherry
5 tablespoons fish sauce
1 tablespoon granulated sugar
Salt and white pepper, to taste

Preheat the oven to 400°. Place the sea bass in an ovenproof baking dish. Cover evenly with the bell peppers, mushrooms, ginger, longan, and wolfberry. Mix together the sesame oil, wine, fish sauce, and sugar. Pour the sauce into the baking dish and sprinkle with salt and pepper. Cover pan with foil and bake for 15 to 20 minutes, until the fish is just cooked through. It should flake easily when tested with a fork.

Garlic and Ginger: Two Chinese Staples

What do garlic and ginger have in common? One is their prominence in Chinese cuisine, but they are also known for their curative properties. Vitamins A, C, and D can be found in garlic, and ginger is rich with vitamin C. Both offer extreme flavors, and complement each other beautifully, despite their differences. When storing peeled ginger be sure to put the unused portion in a covered jar, filling it up with vodka to preserve it. You can also store peeled ginger in a paper bag in the refrigerator for about 1 month.

Pork and Ginger Pot Stickers

6 tablespoons vegetable oil, divided
½ cup finely diced white onion
1 pound ground pork or ground beef
½ cup finely diced garlic chives (also called Chinese chives) or regular chives

1 teaspoon finely diced ginger
1 teaspoon oyster sauce
24 pot sticker wrappers
1 egg yolk, lightly beaten with a few drops of water

Yields 24 pot stickers

Pot stickers are an Asian tradition. This recipe is from Chef Kiong Banh of Twenty Manning in Philadelphia, who learned this from his grandmother.

1. Preheat a sauté pan on high, then add 2 tablespoons of the oil. Sauté the onion for 1 minute. Remove from heat and let cool.
2. In medium-sized mixing bowl, combine the ground pork, garlic chives, ginger, and oyster sauce. Mix well.
3. Lay out 1 wrapper and brush the egg around the edges. Place 1 teaspoon of the pork mixture in the center of the wrapper. Fold into a half-moon shape. Repeat with the remaining wrappers and filling.
4. In a 4-quart pot bring 2 quarts of water to a boil. Blanch the pot stickers for about 1 minute, until they rise to the surface of the water. Remove with a slotted spoon and let stand until dry.
5. Preheat a sauté pan over medium heat and add the remaining oil. Pan–sear the pot stickers until golden brown. Serve.

Tommy Toy's Minced Squab Imperial

Serves 4

In addition to being delicious, part of the fun is eating the Minced Squab Imperial: just pick it up like a taco and dive in. Take a page out of Tommy Toy's book, and provide your guests with lemon-scented hot towels, to clean their hands.

3 teaspoons peanut oil
1 teaspoon chopped fresh ginger
1 teaspoon chopped green onions (white part only)
2 fillets of squab, skin removed, deboned, and diced
3 black mushrooms, soaked in water for 30 minutes and thinly sliced
1 ounce bamboo shoots, diced
1 teaspoon rice wine

1½ teaspoons cornstarch
3 teaspoons chicken broth
1 tablespoon oyster sauce
2 teaspoons soy sauce
½ teaspoon granulated sugar
¼ teaspoon salt
Dash sesame seed oil
1 head crispy lettuce
4 dashes seafood (or hoisin) sauce

1. Preheat a wok, then add the peanut oil and heat on high. When the oil is hot, add the ginger and green onions, and sauté for about 1 minute. Add the squab, mushrooms, and bamboo shoots, and cook for about 1 minute.
2. Add all of the remaining ingredients except the lettuce and seafood/hoisin sauce, and stir-fry for about 2 minutes. Remove from heat.
3. Pull off the 4 largest and freshest leaves from the head (do not cut the lettuce). Spoon equal amounts of the squab mixture into each leaf and add a dash of seafood sauce on top of each serving.

Wok-Seared Beef Medallions with Asparagus Tips

18-ounce filet mignon or eye fillet, cut into 4 medallions
¼ cup balsamic vinegar
3 tablespoons light soy sauce, divided
1 tablespoon olive oil
2 cloves garlic, crushed
1 green onion, chopped

1 pound asparagus tips
1 tablespoon Asian rice vinegar
½ teaspoon granulated sugar
A few drops sesame oil
2 tablespoons vegetable oil
1 clove garlic, finely chopped
Cilantro sprigs, for garnish

Plunging the blanched asparagus tips into ice water helps them keep their bright green color and firm texture. They make an interesting contrast in flavor and texture to the beef medallions.

1. Marinate the filet medallions overnight in the balsamic vinegar, 1 tablespoon light soy sauce, olive oil, crushed garlic, and green onion. Discard the marinade after using.
2. Prepare a bowl with ice-cold water. Fill a large saucepan with enough salted water to cover the asparagus tips and bring to a boil. Blanch the asparagus tips in the water until they turn bright green and are tender (about 2 minutes). Plunge the asparagus briefly into the ice-cold water to stop the cooking process. Remove immediately and drain in a colander.
3. In a small bowl, whisk together the remaining 2 tablespoons light soy sauce, rice vinegar, sugar, and sesame oil. Set the vinaigrette aside.
4. Heat a wok and add 2 tablespoons vegetable oil (not olive oil). When the oil is hot, add the chopped garlic. Stir-fry for 30 seconds. Add the marinated beef medallions. Lay flat for a minute, then fry, stirring occasionally, until the beef is cooked according to your preference.
5. To serve, lay the blanched asparagus on a serving dish. Drizzle with the vinaigrette. Surround with the beef medallions. Garnish with the cilantro.

Tommy Toy's Four Seasons Fried Rice

Serves 6

Another of Tommy Toy's recipes, this is a very simple recipe, perfect for a casual but tasty meal.

2 large eggs
2 teaspoons, plus 1 tablespoon vegetable oil
⅛ pound barbecue pork, minced
⅛ pound minced sirloin or flank steak
⅛ pound chicken, minced
⅛ pound bay shrimp, minced
3 cups cooked long-grain white rice
1 tablespoon soy sauce
¼ teaspoon salt
¼ teaspoon ground white pepper

1. Lightly beat the eggs. Preheat a wok or skillet over medium-high heat until hot but not smoking. Add the 2 teaspoons oil and the beaten eggs. Cook for 1 to 2 minutes, tilting the pan so that the egg covers the surface as thinly as possible, to make a pancake. Allow the egg to cool, then julienne the egg pancake.
2. Add the remaining oil to the wok. Sauté the pork, beef, chicken, and bay shrimp for 1 to 2 minutes. Add the rice to the wok and stir-fry for 2 to 3 minutes, breaking up the rice to separate the grains. Add the eggs, soy sauce, salt, and pepper, and stir-fry until well combined. Transfer to plate and serve.

Soy Sauce—More to It Than You Might Think

The making of soy sauce, known in Chinese as jiang you, is a complex process. It begins with cleaning dried soybeans, then soaking them until soft. They are then steamed, mixed with yeast culture and wheat flour, and incubated for 3 to 5 weeks. They are then fermented with a brine solution for 6 to 24 months, and set out to dry in the sun for 100 days. A "soy master" oversees the entire process. Something to think about the next time you reach for a bottle at a restaurant.

Honey Walnut Shrimp

½ cup chopped walnut pieces
¼ cup sugar
½ pound shrimp
3 cups oil for deep-frying
1 egg, lightly beaten
4 tablespoons cornstarch

1½ tablespoons honey
3 tablespoons mayonnaise
3¾ teaspoons freshly squeezed
   lemon juice
3 tablespoons coconut milk

Yields 2 cups

The sweet flavor of coconut milk nicely balances the tart lemon in this popular restaurant dish.

1. Earlier in the day, boil the walnut pieces for 5 minutes. Drain well. Spread the sugar on a piece of wax paper. Roll the walnut pieces in the sugar and allow to dry.
2. Peel and devein the shrimp. Wash and pat dry with paper towels.
3. Heat oil to 375°F. While waiting for oil to heat, mix the egg with the cornstarch to form a batter. Dip the shrimp in the egg batter. Deep-fry the shrimp until they turn golden brown. Remove from the wok with a slotted spoon and drain on paper towels. Cool.
4. Combine the honey, mayonnaise, lemon juice, and coconut milk. Mix in with the shrimp. Serve on a platter with the sugared walnuts arranged around the shrimp.

Mango Chicken

Serves 4

Turmeric is a distant relative of ginger. In this recipe it gives the chicken a nice yellow color.

4 boneless, skinless chicken breasts
1 egg white
1 tablespoon Chinese rice wine or dry sherry
¼ teaspoon salt
2 teaspoons cornstarch
2 tablespoons rice vinegar

2 tablespoons plus 1 teaspoon brown sugar
1 can mango slices with reserved juice
1 cup oil for frying
1 tablespoon minced ginger
1 teaspoon curry paste
½ teaspoon turmeric

1. Cut the chicken into cubes. Mix in the egg white, rice wine, salt, and cornstarch. Marinate the chicken for 30 minutes.
2. In a small saucepan, bring the rice vinegar, brown sugar, and ¾ cup of reserved mango juice to a boil. Keep warm on low heat.
3. Add 1 cup oil to a preheated wok or skillet. When the oil is hot, velvet the chicken by cooking very briefly in the hot oil, until it changes color and is nearly cooked through (about 30 seconds). Use tongs or cooking chopsticks to separate the individual pieces of chicken while it is cooking.
4. Remove all but 2 tablespoons oil from the wok. (Wipe out the wok with a paper towel if necessary.) When oil is hot, add the ginger, curry paste, and turmeric. Stir-fry for about 1 minute until aromatic. Add the chicken and mix with the curry paste.
5. Add the sauce and bring to a boil. Stir in the mango slices. Mix all the ingredients and serve hot.

Ham with Asian Pear

1½ pounds ham, thinly sliced
2 teaspoons sesame oil
2 teaspoons cornstarch
2 tablespoons soy sauce
2 tablespoons dark soy sauce

2 tablespoons honey
1 green onion
2 tablespoons oil for frying
2 Asian pears, sliced

Although China's Yunnan hams are famous throughout Europe, they are hard to find in the West. Smithfield hams are a good substitute.

1. Marinate the ham for 30 minutes in the sesame oil and cornstarch.
2. Combine the soy sauce, dark soy sauce, and honey. Set aside. Cut the green onion into 1-inch slices on the diagonal.
3. Add 2 tablespoons oil to a preheated wok or skillet. When oil is hot, add the sliced ham and brown briefly. Remove and drain on paper towels.
4. Prepare the wok for steaming. Place the sliced ham on a heatproof dish on a bamboo steamer. Brush ½ the sauce over. Cover and steam, adding more boiling water as necessary.
5. After 25 minutes, drain the ham juices, combine with the remaining half of the sauce, and bring to a boil in a small saucepan. Arrange the pear slices with the ham. Steam the ham for another 5 minutes, or until it is cooked. Pour the cooked sauce over the ham before serving. Garnish with the green onion.

Yin and Yang

Chinese culture is influenced by the philosophy of "yin" and "yang." So it should come as no surprise that Chinese food is also dominated by these two principles. Literally, yin and yang mean the dark and sunny side of a hill. And though most people interpret the terms as meaning opposing forces, they really are complementary. The Chinese believe in a perfect balance between these forces in the environment, and also in food. Any Chinese dish emphasizes the balance between several elements: taste, color, and texture. Certain foods are also thought to have yin or "cooling" properties, while others have "warm," or yang, properties. Even cooking methods are divided. Boiling, steaming, and poaching are all "yin," whereas roasting, deep-frying, and stir-frying are considered "yang."

Dry Ginger Beef

Serves 2

For an added touch, top with a few slices of preserved red ginger before serving.

1 tablespoon soy sauce
½ teaspoon Chinese rice wine or dry sherry
¼ teaspoon sugar
¼ teaspoon baking soda
½ pound flank steak, shredded
½ red bell pepper
2 tablespoons dark soy sauce

1 tablespoon plus 1 teaspoon oyster sauce
1½ teaspoons sugar
½ cup water
4–5 tablespoons oil for frying
2 slices ginger, minced
½ cup mushrooms, sliced

1. Add the soy sauce, rice wine, sugar, and baking soda to the beef. Marinate the beef for 30 minutes.
2. Wash the red pepper, remove the seeds, and cut into thin slices.
3. Combine the dark soy sauce, oyster sauce, sugar, and water and set aside.
4. Add 3 tablespoons oil to a preheated wok or skillet. When oil is hot, add the beef. Lay flat and fry for 2 minutes, then turn over and fry for another 2 minutes. Stir-fry the beef until it turns a dark brown (this will take about 8 minutes). Remove from the wok and drain on paper towels.
5. Add 1–2 tablespoons oil to the wok. When oil is hot, add the ginger and stir-fry briefly until aromatic. Add the mushrooms and red pepper and stir-fry until tender. Add the sauce to the middle of the wok and bring to a boil. Add the beef. Mix everything through and serve hot.

Preserving Foods—A Chinese Tradition

For centuries the Chinese have been employing a clever trick to draw out the shelf life of their foods: preserving. There are many methods of preserving food, from smoking, to salting, sugaring, pickling, drying, soaking in soy sauces, etc. Not only did this enable them to whip up foods quickly, but it also ensured that during hard times they would have a constant supply of nourishment. What began as a means of preserving life (both the foods' and the Chinese peoples') is now a means of flavoring.

Savory Shanghai Noodles

½ pound (8 ounces) fresh cooked shrimp, tails and vein removed
½ teaspoon sugar
½ teaspoon cornstarch
1 bunch spinach
¾ cup chicken broth
¼ cup water

2 tablespoons plus 2 teaspoons oyster sauce
1 teaspoon Chinese rice wine or dry sherry
1¼ cups oil for frying
1 garlic clove, finely chopped
2 slices ginger, finely chopped
½ pound fresh Shanghai noodles
½ teaspoon sesame oil

Serves 2–4

Frying the shrimp briefly in 1 cup of hot oil gives it a soft, velvety texture.

1. Rinse the shrimp in warm water and pat dry. Marinate the shrimp in the sugar and cornstarch for 15 minutes.

2. Wash the spinach and drain thoroughly. Mix together the chicken broth, water, oyster sauce, and rice wine, and set aside.

3. Add 1 cup oil to a preheated wok or skillet. When oil is hot, add the shrimp and fry briefly for 1 minute (if using raw shrimp, fry longer until the shrimp turn pink and firm up around the edges). Remove the shrimp from the wok with a slotted spoon and drain on paper towels.

4. Remove all but 2 tablespoons oil from the wok. Add the spinach and fry until it changes color. Add seasonings such as salt or soy sauce, if desired. Remove from the wok and set aside.

5. Add the garlic and ginger and stir-fry briefly until aromatic. Add the noodles. Stir-fry and toss with the sesame oil. Make a well in the middle of the wok and add the sauce. Bring to a boil. Add the spinach and the shrimp back into the wok. Mix everything through and serve hot.

CHAPTER 14
Japan: Sumo Delights

Edamame Soup à la Chef Nobu

Serves 6

At his res-
taurant in
Scottsdale,
Arizona, Chef
Nobu serves
up his unique
"Tapanese" cui-
sine, a hybrid
of Japanese
sensibility,
global cooking
influences, and
wine-friendly
small plates.

*1 medium-sized yellow onion,
peeled and minced*
1 tablespoon unsalted butter
3 cups chicken stock

½ teaspoon sea salt
Peeled edamame (soybeans)
2-inch piece ginger, minced

1. Sauté the onion in the butter until translucent. Add the chicken broth and bring to a boil. Add the salt and simmer for 1 hour. Add the edamame and cook at medium temperature for 10 minutes.
2. Let cool to room temperature, purée in a blender, and refrigerate overnight.
3. Garnish with the minced ginger and serve.

Scallops Broiled in Sake

Serves 4

Sweet sake
imparts a
wonderful,
while not too
distracting,
flavor.
Kikkoman
is a good soy
sauce to use
in this dish.

2 tablespoons vegetable oil
*¾ pound sea scallops, shelled
and cleaned*
*3 tablespoons Japanese soy
sauce*

2 tablespoons sake
¼ teaspoon Asian sesame oil
Fresh cilantro sprigs

Heat the oil in a frying pan or wok. Sauté the scallops just until they turn color. Stir in the soy sauce and sake. Cook for 1 to 2 more minutes, and add the sesame oil. Garnish with the cilantro. Serve immediately.

Eggplant Miso Soup

½ pound firm tofu
2 carrots
2 eggplants, preferably Asian
2 green onions

5 cups water
1 package dashi soup stock
2 tablespoons miso paste
¼ teaspoon Asian sesame oil

Serves 6

For best
results, use
firm tofu in
this recipe,
as it will hold
its shape in
the hot broth.
Instant dashi
soup stock is
available in
most super-
markets, or
you can use
the recipe on
page 204.

1. Thirty minutes ahead of time, drain the tofu: place the tofu on a plate lined with paper towels. Place a book or plate on top of the tofu to squeeze out the water. Drain the plate and change the paper towels as needed. Cut the drained tofu into ½-inch cubes.
2. Wash the vegetables. Peel and julienne the carrots and eggplants. Chop the green onions.
3. In a large saucepan, bring 4½ cups water to a boil. Stir in the dashi soup stock. Add the vegetables and return to a boil. Reduce the heat and simmer, uncovered, until the vegetables are tender but not mushy (7 to 8 minutes).
4. In a small bowl, mix the miso with ½ cup water to form a paste. Remove the saucepan from the heat. Stir in the miso. Season the soup with a few drops of sesame oil and serve immediately.

Savory Hot Pots

One popular Japanese cuisine is savory hot pots known as nabemono. A simmering pot of broth is placed on a burner in the center of the table with plates of various raw meats and vegetables, which diners poach and serve up themselves. Two varieties are shabu shabu, named for the swishing motion made by the chopsticks of the diners as they cook the various ingredients of their individual portions at the table, and nabe, a hearty meat and vegetable stew that is a treasured treat for sumo wrestlers.

Roasted Tomato Vinaigrette

**Serves 8–10
(as a topping)**

The roasted tomatoes are rich in flavor and are a perfect ingredient for a unique vinaigrette.

4 cups Roma tomatoes
2 red bell peppers
1 tablespoon chopped garlic
1 cup olive oil

3 tablespoons red wine vinegar
Salt and freshly ground black
* pepper, to taste*

1. Preheat the oven to 350°.
2. Cut the tomatoes in half and dice the bell peppers. In a bowl, coat the vegetables with the garlic and 2 tablespoons of the oil. Place on a baking sheet and bake for 10 minutes.
3. Transfer the tomatoes and bell peppers to a blender and purée until very smooth. Add the vinegar and oil and blend lightly. Season with salt and pepper.

Daikon Salad with Cucumber

Serves 6

For an added touch, serve with fresh fruit in season, such as apricots or plums.

½ large daikon radish
1 carrot
1 English cucumber
½ teaspoon salt
4 tablespoons rice vinegar

2 tablespoons mirin
2 teaspoons Japanese soy sauce
1½ tablespoons granulated sugar
2 tablespoons white sesame
* seeds*

1. Peel the daikon radish and grate. Peel and grate the carrot. Peel the cucumber and cut into thin slices. Sprinkle the cucumber slices with the salt and drain for 15 minutes. Pat dry with paper towels.
2. In a small bowl, whisk the rice vinegar, mirin, Japanese soy sauce, and granulated sugar.
3. In a small serving dish, arrange the cucumber slices and the grated daikon and carrots. Drizzle the vinegar dressing over top. Sprinkle with the sesame seeds and serve.

Butterfly Shrimp Tempura

4 cups vegetable oil
12 large shrimp
1 egg
¾ cup ice-cold water

1 cup all-purpose flour
2 tablespoons fresh cilantro
   leaves, as garnish
3 lemons, sliced

Serves 2–4

The Japanese version of deep-frying, tempura is easy to make. In addition to sliced lemon, serve the tempura with soy sauce, cayenne pepper, or salt and black pepper for dipping.

1. Heat the oil to 350° in a deep-fat fryer, large heavy saucepan, wok, or electric fondue pot.
2. Rinse the shrimp under warm running water and pat dry with paper towels. Remove the main shell from the shrimp, but leave on the tails. To butterfly the shrimp, cut a deep slit along the back of shrimp. (Be careful not to cut right through the shrimp.) Press out the flesh on either side of the cut to form the butterfly "wings."
3. In a small bowl, stir the egg into the ice water. Stir in the flour to form a thick, lumpy batter, being careful not to overmix (the batter should resemble a pancake batter).
4. Dip the shrimp into the batter and deep-fry in the heated oil. Fry the shrimp until the batter is golden brown and crispy. Use a slotted spoon to remove the shrimp. Drain on paper towels. To serve, place the tempura on a plate and garnish with the fresh cilantro leaves and lemon slices.

To the Table

Does Japanese cuisine seems full of obscure and unknown foods? If so, you can take heart in knowing that its most important ingredient is very familiar. The answer is found in the Japanese expression for "Let's have a meal" (Gohan ni shimasho). Gohan means cooked rice, so the phrase literally is "Let's eat cooked rice."

California Rolls

**Yields 4 rolls
(32 pieces)**

Sushi fans will love California rolls, which are simply sushi rolled inside out, so that the seaweed is on the inside.

1½ cups short or medium-grain rice
Water, as needed
6 tablespoons rice vinegar
2 tablespoons granulated sugar
1 teaspoon salt
2 avocados
2 tablespoons lemon juice

1 cucumber
½ pound imitation crab
4 teaspoons mayonnaise, preferably Japanese
4 nori (seaweed) sheets
¼ cup toasted sesame seeds
Pickled ginger, wasabi, and soy sauce for dipping

1. Rinse the rice 2 or 3 times, until the water runs clear. In a medium saucepan, add the rice and just enough water to cover. Bring the water and rice mixture to a boil. Turn the heat down to low and simmer, covered, until the rice is cooked through and has absorbed most of the liquid (about 20 minutes). Remove the rice from the heat and let it stand, still covered, for 15 to 20 minutes.

2. While the rice is standing, heat the rice vinegar, sugar, and salt in a small saucepan over low heat, stirring to dissolve the sugar. Sprinkle the mixture over the cooked rice, and slowly work it into the rice, taking care not to mash the grains. (Use a rice paddle if you have one.)

3. Peel the avocadoes, cut in half, and remove the pit in the middle. Cut into 1½-inch strips. Toss the strips with the lemon juice. Peel the cucumber, cut in half, and remove the seeds. Cut the cucumber into thin strips ⅛-inch long. In a small bowl, mix the crabmeat with the mayonnaise in a small bowl.

4. To make the rolls, cover a bamboo sushi rolling mat with a piece of plastic wrap. Lay 1 nori sheet on the mat, shiny-side down. Spread ¾ cup of the sushi rice over the nori, pressing it down firmly. Sprinkle with 1 tablespoon of the toasted sesame seeds. Lay another sheet of plastic wrap on top. Carefully turn the nori over. Remove the plastic sheet that was on the bottom.

continues >>

5. Lay ¼ of the avocado and cucumber strips on the nori. Spread 1 teaspoon of the crabmeat and mayonnaise mixture over. Carefully roll up the nori into a cylinder, moving the bamboo sheet forward as you do so. Repeat with the remainder of the nori.
6. Cut each nori roll into bite-sized pieces. Serve with the wasabi, pickled ginger, and soy sauce for dipping.

Marinated Teriyaki Salmon

¼ cup olive oil
¼ cup Japanese soy sauce
2 tablespoons mirin (Japanese rice wine)
1 teaspoon brown sugar

1 teaspoon grated ginger
1 clove garlic, minced
1 green onion, chopped
4 salmon steaks, 6 to 7 ounces, skinned

Serves 4

A liqueur made from rice, mirin is the secret ingredient that gives Japanese teriyaki sauce its rich, mellow flavor. Mirin is available in the international cuisine section of many supermarkets.

1. In a medium bowl, combine the olive oil, soy sauce, mirin, brown sugar, ginger, garlic, and green onion. Place the salmon steaks in a shallow 9 × 13-inch baking dish. Pour the marinade over the steaks. Cover the salmon and marinate in the refrigerator for 2 hours.
2. Remove the salmon from the refrigerator. Reserve the marinade.
3. Heat the broiler. Place the marinated salmon fillets, skin-side down, on a greased rack in the broiler. Broil the salmon steaks until opaque throughout (10 to 12 minutes). Brush the steaks frequently with the reserved marinade during cooking.

Green Tea Crepes

Serves 6

Make sure to keep the pan at a medium temperature when cooking the crepes—if the pan is too hot, the batter won't spread out to cover the pan.

1¼ cups silken tofu
¾ cup all-purpose flour
1 teaspoon matcha green tea powder
½ cup granulated sugar
2 cups whole milk

1 teaspoon salt
½ teaspoon almond extract
4 tablespoons melted unsalted butter, divided
3 cups green tea ice cream

1. Mash the silken tofu and purée in the blender. Add the flour, green tea powder, sugar, milk, salt, almond extract, and 2 tablespoons of the unmelted butter to the puréed tofu. Mix at medium speed for 1 to 2 minutes, until a smooth batter is formed.

2. Heat a crepe pan or 8-inch frying pan over medium heat (when you spatter a bit of water in the pan and it sizzles, it is ready). Lightly brush the pan with about 1 teaspoon of the remaining melted butter to prevent sticking. Pour 4 tablespoons of the crepe batter into the pan. Immediately begin tilting and rotating the pan so that the batter spreads out evenly to cover the entire pan. Check for doneness by carefully lifting one side with your fingers—when the crepe is golden brown underneath, turn it over and cook the side until golden brown. Stack the crepes on top of one another, with a piece of wax or parchment paper between each one. Continue until all the crepes are cooked. Let the crepes cool.

3. To serve, spread ⅓ to ½ cup green tea ice cream over each crepe, as needed. Roll up the crepes, brushing with any leftover melted butter. Serve immediately.

Dainty Desserts

Japanese desserts tend to be quite small and are often made with tiny sweetened red beans called adzuki. Another typical dessert is fruits in gelatin, as well as the famed green tea ice cream. Depending on the season, fresh fruits are also common, and often marinated with grated ginger and mirin.

Oyster Mushroom and Jasmine Tea Rice

1 cup Asian scented rice
1¼ cups water
2 teaspoons jasmine tea leaves
½ pound fresh oyster mushrooms
2 green onions
1 tablespoon vegetable oil

2 tablespoons Japanese soy
  sauce
A few drops Asian sesame oil, or
  as desired
1 tablespoon white sesame seeds

Serves 4

Use scented jasmine or basmatic rice in this dish. For an added touch, enhance the nutty flavor of the sesame seeds by toasting them before adding to the cooked rice and mushrooms.

1. Rinse the rice, using your hands, until the water runs clear, without any milkiness. Drain and set aside.
2. In a medium saucepan, bring the water to a boil. Remove from the heat. Place the leaves in a teapot and pour the water over. Let the tea steep for 5 minutes, then strain to remove the leaves.
3. In a large saucepan, combine the rice with the jasmine tea. Let it sit for 1 hour or longer (overnight if possible). To cook, bring the water and rice mixture to a boil. Turn the heat down to low and simmer, covered, until the rice is cooked through and has absorbed most of the liquid (about 20 minutes). Remove the rice from the heat and let it stand, still covered, for 15 to 20 minutes.
4. While the rice is cooking, prepare the vegetables. Wipe the oyster mushrooms clean with a damp cloth. Cut off the stems and cut the tops into ½-inch pieces. Chop the green onions.
5. In a large frying pan, heat the oil on medium-high heat. Add the green onions, cook briefly, then add the oyster mushrooms. Stir in the soy sauce. Cook, stirring, until the mushrooms have softened. Stir in the sesame oil.
6. Use a fork or chopsticks to fluff up the cooked rice. To serve, combine the jasmine tea rice with the sautéed mushrooms. Garnish with the sesame seeds.

Dashi Soup Stock

Yields 4 cups

The secret ingredient that gives dashi soup stock its savory flavor is konbu kelp, which contains the same chemical that is used to make MSG seasoning.

1 (6-inch) piece high-quality konbu (kelp)
4½ cups water

3 tablespoons dried bonito flakes (hana-katsuo)

1. Clean the konbu by wiping it dry with a damp cloth. (Don't wash the konbu under running water, as this removes the flavor.) In a medium saucepan, place the konbu in the water. Soak for 2 hours.
2. Bring the water to a boil. When the water is boiling, stir in the dried bonito flakes. Remove the saucepan from the heat. Let stand for 5 minutes, then remove the dried konbu and strain out the bonito flakes. Use the broth as called for in the recipe. (Refrigerated, it will last for 2 to 3 days.)

Sweet Simmered Squash

Serves 4

The Dashi Soup Stock lends a savory flavor to this vegetable dish.

1 small acorn squash (kabocha)
1½ cups Dashi Soup Stock
3 tablespoons Japanese soy sauce

2 tablespoons sake
4 tablespoons granulated sugar

1. Use a strong knife to cut the acorn squash in half. Remove the seeds from the middle, and cut the squash into 2-inch slices.
2. In a heavy-sided frying pan, heat the Dashi Soup Stock on medium-high heat. Stir in the soy sauce, sake, and sugar. Reduce the heat to medium. Simmer briefly, then add the sliced squash. Simmer, covered, until the squash is tender and the liquid has been nearly absorbed (15 to 20 minutes). Cool and serve immediately.

Savory Crispy Wheat Cake

Serves 4

Another creation by Executive Chef Erdem Dönmez, this dish uses hulled wheat, as do many Turkish recipes, in both savory and sweet dishes.

1 cup hulled wheat
3 cups chicken broth
1 bunch basil, chopped
2 cloves garlic, sliced
1 medium onion, chopped

3 tablespoons olive oil
¼ cup grated Parmesan cheese
3 tablespoons softened butter,
  plus extra as needed for frying
Salt, to taste

1. Soak the wheat in cold water overnight. Cook, covered, over low heat in a medium-sized pot with the broth for about 20 minutes.
2. In a pan over medium heat, sauté the basil, garlic, and onion in the olive oil. Add to the cooked wheat, along with the Parmesan, butter, and salt. Mix well.
3. Transfer the mixture to a rectangular pan large enough to spread the mixture into a layer 1 inch thick. Let cool. When ready to serve, cut into squares and fry in butter until crisp on each side. Serve hot.

Crusading Kitchens

Ever wonder what the crusaders, when they weren't busy plundering and pillaging, stopped to eat? Record has it that the crusaders fell in love with the Arabic cooking style of continuously hanging a large cauldron over a low-burning fire, and every day adding what was available to the pot. These cauldrons were a constant fixture in the crusader camps, delivering thick soups, stews, and dumplings to hungry warriors.

Lamb and Artichoke with "Terbiye"

Juice of 2 lemons
8 small artichokes, trimmed and
   cleaned
1 pound lamb, cut in kebab-size
   pieces
Butter, as needed
20 shallots
Salt and white pepper, to taste
Fresh dill

Terbiye:

½ tablespoon all-purpose flour
3 tablespoons plain yogurt
2 egg yolks
Juice of 1 lemon

Serves 4

This recipe
comes
from Vedat
Basaran, chef
and manager
of the Feriye
Restaurant
in Istanbul.
Terbiye is
a thickener
made of
lemon and
eggs, usually
with an addi-
tion of yogurt
and a little
bit of flour.

1. Fill a pot with water and add the juice from the 2 lemons. Put the arti-chokes in the water and set aside (this keeps the artichokes from turning black before you are ready to cook them).

2. Bring another pot of water to boil and boil the lamb for 2 to 3 minutes. Drain and set the meat aside. Heat the butter in the pot and sauté the shallots on medium until browned. Add the meat pieces and sauté for about 1 minute. Add enough water to the pan to cover the meat and cook for about 30 to 40 minutes over medium heat, covered.

3. Add the cleaned artichokes to the pot and cook until the artichokes are tender, about 15 minutes. Meanwhile, mix together all the terbiye ingre-dients thoroughly.

4. When the artichokes and the meat are tender, take 3 to 4 spoonfuls of the broth and add it to the terbiye mixture (so the mixture will not curdle when it is added to the pot). Add the diluted terbiye slowly to the pot, mixing constantly with a wooden spoon. Add the salt and pepper. Warm over low heat for another minute. Serve garnished with fresh dill.

Vine Leaf Envelopes with Raisins

Serves 4

Another recipe by Erdem Dönmez.

6 ounces goat cheese

1 tablespoon fresh thyme or mint leaves

1 tablespoon chopped fresh basil

2 tablespoons heavy cream (optional)

4 large vine leaves

Olive oil, as needed

3 tablespoons chopped walnuts

2 tablespoons white sultana raisins

1 teaspoon granulated sugar (optional)

Lettuce leaves, to serve

1. Mix together the goat cheese, fresh thyme, basil, and cream, if using. Shape into 4 balls, and flatten a bit. Roll up the balls in the vine leaves (you can fold the leaves around the filling like envelopes if it is easier).
2. Sauté the envelopes in a little olive oil, taking care not to brown them too much. Remove the envelopes from the pan, and sauté the walnuts for about 1 minute; remove, set aside, and then sauté the raisins just to give them a shine, about 1 minute. If desired, add the granulated sugar and caramelize the raisins (this will give them a slightly different texture).
3. Serve the envelopes or the rolls over the lettuce leaves with the walnuts and raisins sprinkled over them.

In Persian Culture, You Are What You Eat

Iranians have long considered food and drink the foundation of both physical and mental health. For example, it was thought that consuming red meat and fats led to evil thoughts, and made one selfish. Consuming a healthy diet of fruits, vegetables, fish, fowl, mixed petals, and blossoms had the opposite effect—your soul would be generous and good. The records on classical Persian cooking are scarce, and most of the techniques have been passed down from generation to generation through the women—the ones who typically do all the cooking.

Blintzes

1 cup ricotta or farmer's cheese
8 ounces cream cheese
1 egg, lightly beaten
¼ teaspoon ground cinnamon
1 teaspoon vanilla extract
3 tablespoons granulated sugar
1 stick unsalted butter

3 large eggs, not beaten
1 cup all-purpose flour
1⅓ cups milk
1 teaspoon salt
¼ cup confectioners' sugar,
  or as needed

1. In a medium bowl, combine the ricotta cheese, cream cheese, lightly beaten egg, ground cinnamon, vanilla extract, and sugar. Refrigerate until needed.
2. Melt the butter in a small saucepan on low heat. To make the crepe batter: combine the eggs, flour, milk, salt, and 2 tablespoons of the melted butter in a blender and mix at medium speed for 1 to 2 minutes, until a smooth batter is formed. (The batter should be thinner and smoother than pancake batter.) Pour into a large bowl, cover, and refrigerate for 1 hour.
3. Heat a crepe pan or 5- to 6-inch frying pan over medium heat. Lightly brush the pan with about 1 teaspoon of the melted butter to prevent sticking. Pour just enough batter into the pan to make a thin crepe (about 3 tablespoons). Immediately begin tilting and rotating the pan so that the batter spreads out evenly to cover the entire pan. Cook until the crepe is lightly browned on top, and just beginning to pull away from the edges of the pan. Carefully lift the crepe from the pan. Stack the crepes on a warm plate. Continue until all the crepes are cooked.
4. To make the blintz, place 1 level tablespoon of the cream cheese filling mixture on the edge of the crepe and roll it up. Continue with the remainder of the crepes. Dust with the confectioners' sugar. Serve immediately.

Jewish Honey Cake

Serves 6

Traditionally served during the Jewish New Year season, sweet honey cake symbolizes the wishes for a good year ahead.

3 large eggs
1¼ cups granulated sugar
4 teaspoons vegetable oil
3 cups sifted all-purpose flour
¾ teaspoon salt
2 teaspoons baking powder
1 teaspoon baking soda
1 teaspoon ground cinnamon

⅛ teaspoon ground cloves
¼ teaspoon ground ginger
1 cup honey
1¼ cups brewed coffee
½ cup chopped walnuts
2 teaspoons grated orange rind
3 tablespoons confectioners' sugar, or as needed

1. Preheat the oven to 350°. Grease a 10-cup bundt pan.
2. In a small bowl, beat the eggs until fluffy. Beat in the sugar and oil.
3. Sift together the flour, salt, baking powder, baking soda, cinnamon, cloves, and ginger. Make a well in the center of the bowl, and add in the beaten egg, honey, and the coffee. Stir in the walnuts and the grated orange rind.
4. Pour the batter into the bundt pan and bake for 60 minutes or until the cake is done and a toothpick comes out clean when inserted in the center. Cool on a cake rack before removing from the pan. Dust with the confectioners' sugar and serve.

Influences on Israeli Cooking

When traveling and eating in Israel, you will notice plenty of other Middle Eastern influences. From Iran came the tradition of cooking meat with fruits and lentils. Lebanon inspired a method of cooking fish with cayenne pepper, paprika, cinnamon, and other spices. And Jordanian lamb and beef kebabs are also very common. Other dishes you might find include Syrian or Kurdish kubbeh—lamb and cracked wheat paste served in fried patties stuffed with meat, onion, and pine nuts—and Egyptian sfeeha—small pastry shells filled with spiced ground lamb, pine nuts, and yogurt.

Potato Pancakes (Latkes)

1 egg, lightly beaten
⅛ teaspoon salt, or to taste
¼ teaspoon black pepper, or to
  taste
4 russet or purple potatoes
½ red onion

2 tablespoons all-purpose flour
⅓ cup vegetable oil, or as needed
2 tablespoons freshly chopped
  chives
½ cup sour cream
½ cup natural yogurt

Serves 4–6

For a more "gourmet" touch, replace the yogurt and sour cream topping with whipped cream infused with an apple liqueur.

1. In a small bowl, lightly beat the egg, stirring in the salt and pepper. Peel and grate the potatoes, squeezing out any excess liquid. Peel and finely chop the onion.
2. In a medium-sized bowl, mix the potatoes and onion with the lightly beaten egg and the flour.
3. In a heavy-bottomed frying pan, heat the oil over medium heat. Carefully add 2 to 3 tablespoons of the potato mixture. Use a spatula to gently press the mixture down into the shape of a small pattie. Brown briefly, then turn and brown the other side. Remove and drain on paper towels.
4. Stir 1 tablespoon of the chives into the sour cream, and the remaining tablespoon into the yogurt. Serve the yogurt and sour cream with the potato latkes.

The Yiddish Kitchen

The dishes that define Yiddish cuisine came out of Central and Eastern Europe. Having evolved in the shtetls (the small towns and villages once inhabited by Jews, before the Holocaust), these are the foods considered by most Americans and Europeans to be typically "Jewish." Among them are gefilte fish (fish balls made of finely minced carp, pike, or a mixture of both, served in their own jelly and often with horseradish), kishke (a peppery blend of bread crumbs, chicken fat, and onions prepared sausagelike in beef casings), and knaidlach (egg and matzo meal–based dumplings). Other popular offerings include kreplach (dumplings filled with ground meat or cheese and boiled or fried) and latkes (fried potato pancakes), often served with applesauce.

Rhubarb Khoresh

Serves 4

Through Asia, rhubarb has been valued since ancient times for its reputed ability to cleanse the blood and purify the system. Sweet cinnamon helps minimize its tart taste.

2 small yellow onions
4 tablespoons vegetable oil, divided
1 pound boneless lamb shoulder, cubed
1 teaspoon ground cinnamon
¼ teaspoon ground turmeric
1 teaspoon salt

¼ teaspoon freshly ground black pepper
2 tablespoons tomato paste
2 cups water, or as needed
2 teaspoons lemon juice
½ pound fresh or frozen rhubarb
6 mint sprigs, for garnish

1. Peel and thinly slice the onions. In a large saucepan or Dutch oven, heat 2 tablespoons of the vegetable oil. Add the cubed lamb and brown over medium heat. Remove the lamb, but do not clean out the pan. Heat 1 more tablespoon of oil in the pan and add the chopped onion. Cook the onion over medium heat until it is soft and translucent (about 5 minutes).

2. Stir in the ground cinnamon, turmeric, salt and pepper, and the tomato paste. Cook for 1 minute, stirring then add the lamb back into the pan with the water and lemon juice. Make sure there is enough water to cover the lamb.

3. Simmer the stew, covered, for 45 minutes. Add the rhubarb to the pan, Continue cooking, covered, until the meat is tender (50 to 60 minutes). If necessary, add 1 to 2 more tablespoons of water. Serve the khoresh hot and garnished with the mint sprigs.

The History of Couscous

The North African nations of Morocco, Algeria, and Tunisia had a major influence on Israeli cuisine, especially when it came to couscous. A stew based on hard wheat semolina, couscous was born in the desert by wandering Berber tribesmen, about 4,000 years ago. Couscous is served in a variety of styles, but is typically topped with simple meats and a variety of vegetables. Algerian versions almost always include tomatoes; Moroccan couscous uses saffron; and Tunisian couscous is highly spiced.

Chicken in Pomegranate Sauce

Serves 4

3 pomegranates, to make 1¼ cups juice

2 cups coarsely chopped walnuts

4 tablespoons olive oil, divided

1 pound chicken pieces, boneless, skinless

1 large red onion, peeled and finely chopped

2 garlic cloves, crushed

2 tablespoons tomato paste

1 cup water

½ teaspoon turmeric

1 teaspoon ground cinnamon

1 tablespoon granulated sugar

Salt to taste

Freshly ground black pepper, to taste

To increase the sourness, add 1 or 2 tablespoons pomegranate juice to the sauce, reducing the amount of water as needed. To increase the sweetness, add extra sugar.

1. Wash the pomegranates, pat dry, and cut in half. Squeeze out the pomegranate juice, either by hand or with a juicer. Strain the juice through a mesh sieve. Reserve 1¼ cups.
2. Coarsely chop the walnuts, and then grind to a paste in the food processor. Mix in the freshly squeezed pomegranate juice. Process until you have a thick liquid.
3. In a large saucepan, heat the olive oil. Add the chicken pieces and cook over medium heat until browned. Remove the chicken pieces and drain on paper towels.
4. In a separate saucepan, heat 2 tablespoons oil. Add the chopped onion and garlic. Cook over medium heat until the onion is softened. Turn the heat down to low and stir in the tomato paste. Stir for a minute, and then slowly add the pomegranate/walnut mixture and the water. Stir in the turmeric, ground cinnamon, sugar, salt, and black pepper.
5. Add the browned chicken to the pomegranate sauce mixture. Simmer, covered, until the chicken is tender and cooked through (about 35 minutes). Serve hot over steamed rice.

Cold Yogurt and Cucumber Soup

Serves 4

This is a perfect soup to serve on hot summer days. Feel free to add a few ice cubes before serving.

1 English cucumber
1 small red onion
3 cups plain yogurt
1 cup light cream
2 tablespoons lemon juice

2 tablespoons finely chopped fresh mint
1 tablespoon finely chopped fresh dill
¼ cup chopped walnuts
1 teaspoon salt
Freshly ground black pepper

1. Peel the cucumber, cut lengthwise and remove the seeds, and finely chop. Peel and finely chop the red onion.
2. In a large bowl, combine all the ingredients. Refrigerate, covered, for at least 3 hours before serving to chill the soup and give the flavors a chance to blend.

Turkish Delight

Serves 6–8

For an authentic touch, serve this exotic Middle Eastern treat with strong coffee.

1 cup water
1 cup granulated sugar
¾ cup corn syrup
½ teaspoon cream of tartar

1 tablespoon lemon juice
1 teaspoon grated lemon rind
¼ teaspoon rose water
½ cup raw shelled pistachios

1. In a heavy saucepan, bring the water to a boil. Add the sugar and the corn syrup, stirring to dissolve the sugar. Stir in the cream of tartar. Reduce the heat and simmer, uncovered, until the mixture has the texture of a softened ball instead of a liquid. Stir in the lemon juice, grated lemon rind, and the rose water. Cook for 5 more minutes, stirring.
2. Pour the mixture into an 8 × 8-inch greased pan. Stir in the pistachios. Cool, stirring occasionally. Cut into squares and serve.

Chicken with Mushrooms

8 ounces button mushrooms
4 chicken breasts, boneless,
    skinless
⅓ cup all-purpose flour
½ teaspoon turmeric
1 teaspoon salt
Pinch of black pepper

¼ cup olive oil, divided
2 cloves garlic
½ red onion
2 tablespoons tomato paste
2 teaspoons granulated sugar
1 tablespoon lemon juice
1 cup dry white wine

Serves 4

The combination of chicken and mushrooms is found in many ethnic cuisines. Here it is enlivened with a sweet and sour sauce made with tomato paste, lemon juice, and sugar.

1. Wipe the mushrooms clean with a damp cloth and cut into thin slices. Rinse the chicken breasts and pat dry with paper towels.
2. In a small bowl, combine the flour with the turmeric, salt, and pepper. In a frying pan, heat 2 tablespoons olive oil over medium heat. Coat the chicken breasts in the seasoned flour mixture and add to the pan. Cook the chicken over medium heat until the chicken is cooked through and the juices run clear when pricked with a fork. Remove the chicken from the pan.
3. Add the garlic cloves and red onion to the pan. Cook over medium heat until the garlic is browned and the onion is soft and translucent (5 to 7 minutes). Add the tomato paste, sugar, and lemon juice. Cook for a minute, stirring, and add the wine. Bring to a boil, then turn down the heat and add the mushrooms. Cook for 5 more minutes.
4. Add the chicken and heat through. Serve hot.

Afghani Lamb with Spinach

Serves 4

Serve this dish over a classic Middle Eastern rice pilaf, made with wild rice, dried fruit, and toasted pine nuts.

⅓ cup olive oil
2 pounds lamb stew meat, cubed
2 small white onions
2 cloves garlic
1 cup crushed tomatoes with
    juice
2 teaspoons ground turmeric
6 cardamom pods
½ teaspoon ground coriander
1 teaspoon cayenne pepper
¼ teaspoon ground cinnamon
3 cups beef broth
10 spinach leaves, washed and
    torn
1 cup water, or as needed
½ cup pine nuts
Cold Yogurt and Cucumber Soup
    (page 214)

1. Heat 1 tablespoon olive oil in a heavy frying pan or Dutch oven. Add the cubed lamb and sear over medium-high heat. Remove the lamb from the pan.
2. Add 1 tablespoon olive oil to the pan. Add the chopped onion and garlic. Cook over medium heat until the onion is nearly softened (4 to 5 minutes). Add the garlic and cook for 1 more minute. Add the canned tomatoes, and the turmeric, cardamom, coriander, cayenne pepper, and cinnamon. Cook for a minute, stirring, then add the beef broth. Add the lamb back into the pan. Turn down the heat and simmer, covered, until the lamb is tender (about 1 hour). Add the spinach leaves and simmer for 5 more minutes, adding as much of the water as necessary to keep the stew from drying out.
3. Garnish the stew with the pine nuts and serve with the Cold Cucumber and Yogurt Soup.

Toasting Pine Nuts

Toasted pine nuts make a delicious garnish for this dish. To toast, place the nuts in a large skillet and shake continuously over medium heat until the nuts turn a light brown.

Lebanese Rice Pudding

1 cup jasmine or Basmati short-grained rice
1½ cups cold water, divided
½ cup golden raisins
5 cups whole milk

½ cup granulated sugar
2 teaspoons ground cinnamon
½ teaspoon caraway seeds
1 tablespoon shelled pistachios

Serves 8

In Lebanon, this rice is traditionally served to celebrate the birth of a child. Authentic rice pudding is made with "pounded rice"—rice that is ground with a mortar and pestle until it has a powder-like consistency.

1. Rinse the rice until the water runs clear and there is no milkiness. Soak the rice in 1 cup of water for 30 minutes to soften. Drain out most of the water, leaving about 1 tablespoon. In a small bowl, soak the raisins in ½ cup water to soften. Drain.
2. In a medium saucepan, heat the milk to a near boil. Add the sugar and the soaked rice. Bring to a boil, stirring constantly to thicken. Stir in the ground cinnamon, caraway seeds, and the pistachios. Reduce heat and simmer, covered, until the pudding has a thick texture similar to porridge.
3. To serve, pour the pudding into bowls and garnish with the raisins. Sprinkle extra pistachios on top if desired.

Turkish Lamb Casserole Cooked in Paper

Serves 6

This is a fun and elegant way to present a basic lamb casserole dish. Feel free to dress up the packages by wrapping them in aluminum foil instead of wax paper, with a spring of parsley or thyme for the "bow."

1 yellow onion
2 new potatoes
2 carrots
4 tablespoons olive oil
2 pounds lamb, cubed
1 tablespoon tomato sauce
1 teaspoon dried thyme

½ teaspoon dried parsley
½ teaspoon granulated sugar
3 tablespoons red wine vinegar
½ cup grated strong cheddar cheese
¼ cup chopped fresh cilantro

1. Preheat the oven to 375°. Grease two 9 × 13-inch baking sheets. Peel and finely chop the onion. Peel and thinly slice the potatoes and carrots.
2. In a heavy frying pan, heat 1 tablespoon olive oil. Add the cubed lamb and cook over medium-high heat until browned. Remove the lamb and clean out the pan.
3. Heat 3 tablespoons olive oil in the pan. Add the chopped onion and cook over medium heat until softened (5 to 7 minutes). Add the sliced potatoes, carrots, and the tomato sauce. Stir in the dried thyme, parsley, and sugar. Add the red wine vinegar. Sauté the potatoes and carrots over medium heat until browned (about 10 minutes). Add the lamb back into the pan and stir everything together.
4. Cut a large sheet of wax paper into six 12-inch squares. Spoon a heaping portion of the stew in the center section of each square. Sprinkle with the cheddar cheese and chopped cilantro. Wrap up each package. Bake for 20 minutes. Cool before serving. Serve in the wax paper.

Middle Eastern Stuffed Grape Leaves

1 bottle grape leaves
½ white onion, finely chopped
1 clove garlic
½ cup uncooked long-grain rice
¼ cup pine nuts
¼ cup currants

¼ cup finely chopped parsley
3 tablespoons tomato sauce
3 tablespoons olive oil
¼ cup water, or as needed
Lettuce leaves
2 lemons, cut into wedges

1. Fill a medium saucepan with hot water. Place the grape leaves in the water and use a wooden spoon to separate the leaves. Remove the leaves from the pan and drain thoroughly. Peel the onion and finely chop. Smash, peel, and mince the garlic.

2. Toast the pine nuts by heating them in a large frying pan, shaking continuously, until the nuts are browned. Cool and coarsely chop.

3. In a large bowl, combine the chopped pine nuts, rice, currants, chopped onion, garlic, chopped parsley, tomato sauce, and olive oil. Add a bit more olive oil if the mixture is too dry.

4. To stuff the grape leaves, lay out a grape leaf with the shiny side down. Place 1 tablespoon of the mixture in the leaf and roll it up. Continue with the remainder of the leaves.

5. Steam the grape leaves in a frying pan or steamer lined with lettuce leaves on the bottom. Sprinkle the leaves with water and steam, covered, until the leaves are tender (about 45 minutes). Garnish with lemon wedges.

Armenian Nutmeg Cake

Serves 6

The Armenian version of a pound cake, nutmeg cake is both sweet and spicy.

2 cups all-purpose flour
½ cup firmly packed brown sugar
2 teaspoons baking powder
1 teaspoon salt
½ teaspoon baking soda
1 teaspoon ground nutmeg
2 sticks unsalted butter
   (8-ounces) plus 1 tablespoon
   butter

1 cup granulated sugar
2 large eggs, lightly beaten
½ cup milk
1 teaspoon vanilla extract
½ cup chopped walnuts
2 tablespoons confectioners'
   sugar

1. Preheat the oven to 325°. Heavily grease an 8-inch square baking pan.
2. In a large bowl, combine the flour with the brown sugar, baking powder, salt, baking soda, and nutmeg. Add the butter, mixing it in with your hands until the mixture resembles fine breadcrumbs. (Press half the mixture into the prepared pan.)
3. Beat the butter with 1 cup granulated sugar until the mixture is creamy. Beat in the eggs and the milk. Beat in the vanilla extract.
4. Carefully fold the dry ingredients into the egg mixture. Stir in the walnuts. Pour the mixture into the pan. Bake for about 1 hour, or until a toothpick inserted in the middle of the cake comes out clean. Cool on a wire rack for 15 minutes. Sprinkle with confectioners' sugar before serving.

Palace-Style Rose Milk Pudding

6 cups whole milk

1 small piece mastic

2 teaspoons granulated sugar

1 tablespoon rose water

1 teaspoon rice flour

2 pounds fresh strawberries, sliced

1 tablespoon chopped fresh mint

Serves 10

From Chef Aydyn Demir of Tugra, the Turkish fine-dining restaurant in Ciragan Palace Hotel Kempinski, Istanbul.

1. In a large saucepan, combine the milk, mastic, sugar, and rose water, and bring to a boil.
2. In a small bowl, mix the rice flour with little bit of cold water, then add the mixture to the boiling milk. Cook for 3 minutes. Pour into small, elegant serving glasses and cover with the strawberries and garnish with mint.

Mare's Milk in the Nomadic Diet

Milk and dairy products were an essential part of the nomadic diet, and it was mare's milk—not sheep's or cow's—that was most highly prized. (Mare's milk has four times more vitamin C than cow's milk.) It was simmered in shallow pans and the cream, which rose to the surface, was consumed, while the remaining milk was dried in the sun and stored as powder. Milk and thick cream were the basic elements of a nomad's breakfast. Mare's milk was also fermented to make a strong alcoholic beverage known as kimiz, which is still widely consumed among the Turkish people of Central Asia.

Slow-Roasted Balsamic Tomato Soup

Serves 6

Slow roasting unlocks the flavors of the tomatoes for a rich, delicious soup.

12 tomatoes, cut into wedges
6 cloves garlic, crushed
1 large onion, crushed
3 sprigs thyme
⅓ cup balsamic vinegar

Salt and crushed black pepper, to taste
½ cup olive oil
4 cups strong vegetable stock

1. Preheat the oven to 350°.
2. Mix together all the ingredients except the vegetable stock and place in a roasting tray. Slow-roast for approximately 30 minutes in the oven until slightly browned. Remove from the oven and place in a pot with the vegetable stock. Simmer on medium heat for 35 minutes. Adjust seasoning to taste, and purée the mixture in a food processor or blender. Serve with chopped fresh basil, if desired.

Preserved Lemons

Yields 12 lemons

Preserved lemons add a tart flavor to many African dishes, including Tagine-Style Beef Stew (page 229) and Egyptian Fava Beans (page 230).

12 lemons

¾ cup sea salt, or as needed

1. Cut a thin strip off both ends of a lemon. Stand up the lemon and cut through the middle, almost to the bottom, taking care not to cut right through the lemon. Spread the two cut halves of the lemon apart and add up to 1 tablespoon salt on the flesh. Close up the lemon. Continue with the remainder of the lemons.
2. Place 1 tablespoon salt on the bottom of a sterilized glass jar. Pack in the lemons. Cover tightly. Leave the preserved lemons for at least 1 week, shaking the jar occasionally to distribute the lemon juice. Remove from the jar and store in a sealed container in the refrigerator. (The lemons will last for 2 to 3 months.) Use as called for in a recipe.

African Squash and Yams

1 medium onion
2 medium sweet potatoes (yams)
1 butternut squash
2 tablespoons vegetable oil
¾ cup thin coconut milk

¼ cup thick coconut milk
1 teaspoon brown sugar
½ teaspoon grated lemon rind
½ teaspoon salt
¼ teaspoon ground cloves

Serves 6

Starchy foods such as yam make a frequent appearance in African cooking. This recipe blends two starches with the delicate flavor of coconut milk.

1. Peel and chop the onion. Peel the sweet potatoes and cut into 1-inch chunks. Peel and remove the seeds from the butternut squash. Cut into 1-inch chunks.
2. In a large frying pan, heat the vegetable oil. Add the onion and cook over medium heat until soft and translucent (5 to 7 minutes). Add the sweet potatoes and the butternut squash. Cook for 1 minute, then add the thin and thick coconut milk. Stir in the brown sugar, grated lemon rind, salt, and the ground cloves. Reduce heat to low and simmer, covered, for 30 minutes, or until the vegetables are tender. Serve immediately.

A Basic Native African Meal

Africa is a continent, and thus its cuisine cannot be summarized in a few lines or a chapter of a cookbook. But there are some basic tenants of the African table, and some general cooking principles. For starters, starch is a major focal point of the African meal, with a stew of meat and/or vegetables cooked to go with it. Common main root vegetables include yams and cassava, and other typical ingredients are steamed greens, spices, and peanuts (called "groundnuts" in Africa), which can be a simple garnish or the main ingredient, as in peanut soup.

Orange Salad with Orange Flower Water

Serves 6

Particularly prominent in Egyptian cooking, orange flower water is made from distilled orange blossoms. It is relatively easy to find, and usually comes in a beautiful, deep blue bottle.

½ cup unblanched almonds
6 ripe, juicy oranges
½ teaspoon granulated sugar
¼ teaspoon ground cinnamon
10 pitted dates, sliced lengthwise
2 teaspoons orange flower water
4 fresh mint sprigs, for garnish

1. In a small saucepan, add the almonds and cold water. Bring to a boil. Boil for 1 minute, then remove the almonds and place in a bowl filled with cold water. Remove the skin by holding the almond between your thumb and forefinger and pressing until the skin slips off. Continue with the remainder of the almonds. Chop the blanched almonds into thin slivers.

2. Peel the oranges, removing all the pith, and slice. Toss the sliced oranges with the sugar and ground cinnamon. Place the oranges in a serving bowl. Add the sliced dates and the blanched almonds. Sprinkle the orange flower water over top. Cover and chill for 1 hour. Garnish with the fresh mint leaves just before serving.

A Lean Bird with a Mean Kick

Ostrich, a bird with a very powerful kick (just ask anyone who has gotten in the way), is a fabulous meat to eat. Many entrepreneurs tried their hand at running ostrich farms and selling the meat, but it never became the craze many thought it would in America. Fortunately, you can find the meat at many specialty stores.

Moambé Stew

2 yellow onions
1 garlic clove, crushed
2 large tomatoes
½ pound fresh spinach leaves
1 jalapeño chili pepper
2 pounds stewing beef, cut into
    bite-sized pieces

⅓ cup freshly squeezed grapefruit
    juice
2 tablespoons peanut oil
1½ cups water
½ teaspoon salt
¼ teaspoon ground cumin
¼ teaspoon cayenne pepper
1 cup smooth peanut butter

Serves 6

Traditionally, this African stew dish would be served with palm oil instead of peanut oil, and palm butter in place of the peanut butter.

1. Chop the yellow onion and smash the garlic clove. Blanch the tomatoes briefly in boiling water. Drain, peel off the skins, and chop. Wash the spinach leaves, drain, and tear into shreds. Cut the chili pepper in half, remove the seeds, and chop thinly. (Wear plastic gloves while working with the chilies and wash your hands afterward.) Crush the garlic.

2. In a shallow 9 × 13-inch glass baking dish, combine the stewing beef, grapefruit juice, garlic, and chili. Cover and marinate in the refrigerator for 1 hour, turning occasionally.

3. In a large saucepan, heat the peanut oil over medium heat. Add the beef and cook over medium to medium-high heat until browned (about 5 minutes). Cook the meat in 2 batches if necessary. Remove the meat from the pan but don't clean out the pan.

4. Add the onions and 3 tablespoons water. Cook over medium heat until the onion is soft and translucent. Add the tomatoes and 1½ cups water. Stir in the salt, ground cumin, and cayenne pepper. Heat to boiling. Add the stewing beef. Reduce the heat and simmer, covered, for 15 minutes. Stir in the peanut butter and spinach leaves. Simmer for 45 minutes more, or until the beef is cooked. Add more water if necessary to prevent the stew from drying out. Serve hot.

Greens with Peanuts

Serves 4–6

Many Congo dishes feature cassava leaves that come from the cassava plant (also called the yucca plant). Feel free to replace the spinach leaves in this recipe with cassava leaves if they are available.

1 cup unsalted peanuts, without skins
¼ teaspoon salt
2 pounds spinach leaves
1 jalapeño chili pepper
½ white onion

1 red bell pepper
1 tablespoon peanut oil or palm oil
2 cups water
2 cups chickpeas
1 teaspoon granulated sugar

1. Heat oven to 350°. Spread the peanuts out in a 9 × 13-inch baking sheet. Roast for 15 minutes, or until the peanuts are browned. Cool. Use a blender or food processor to crush the cooled peanuts with the salt. Process 2 or 3 times until the peanuts have a crumb-like texture.
2. Wash the spinach leaves and pat dry with paper towels. Tear into shreds. Cut the chili pepper in half, remove the seeds, and chop thinly. (Wear plastic gloves while working with the chilies and wash your hands afterward.) Peel and chop the onion. Cut the red bell pepper in half, remove the seeds, and cut into strips.
3. In a large saucepan or deep-sided frying pan, heat the peanut oil. Add the onion and cook over medium heat until it is softened (5 to 7 minutes). Add the chili pepper and the red bell pepper and cook briefly, until the skin of the chili begins to blister. Add 1¼ cups water and bring to a boil. Stir in the crushed peanuts and the spinach.
4. Reduce the heat and simmer, covered, until the spinach is wilted and tender. Add the chickpeas. Stir in the sugar. Heat through and serve hot.

Making Your Own Peanut Paste

To make your own homemade peanut paste, first shell the peanuts, then roast in a large skillet on the stove, stirring often. Remove the skins and place the peanuts in a saucepan. Add enough water to partially cover them and bring to a slow boil, stirring often. Reduce heat. Mash the peanuts into a paste with a potato-masher.

Tagine-Style Beef Stew with Lemons

2 pounds stewing beef, cut into
    chunks
Salt and pepper, to taste
2 cloves garlic
1 red onion
1 (14-ounce) can plum tomatoes
1 tablespoon palm or peanut oil
2 cups water
2 cups beef broth

1½ teaspoons ground cumin
½ teaspoon cayenne pepper, or
    to taste
2 teaspoons turmeric
1 (3-inch) cinnamon stick
1 cup golden raisins
½ cup chopped cilantro leaves
2 Preserved Lemons, cut into
    slices (page 224)

Serves 4 to 6

A North African specialty, tagine is a spicy stew traditionally served in a clay cooking pot. Serve the tagine over cous-cous or boiled rice.

1. Season the stewing beef with salt and pepper. Crush the garlic cloves. Peel and chop the red onion. Cut the plum tomatoes into quarters, but reserve the juice from the can.
2. In a large saucepan or Dutch oven, heat the oil. Add the beef and cook over medium-high heat until browned. Remove the beef from the pan, but do not clean out the pan.
3. Add the chopped onion and garlic. Add 1 tablespoon water and cook the onion over medium heat until soft and translucent. Add the beef broth and 1 cup water. Bring to a boil, then stir in the ground cumin, cayenne pepper, and turmeric. Add the cinnamon stick.
4. Add the beef back into the pan. Turn down the heat, cover, and simmer. After the stew has been simmering for 1 hour, add the raisins, plum tomatoes, and chopped cilantro. Simmer, covered, for 30 more minutes, adding the remaining 1 cup of water as needed. Taste and add salt and pepper, as desired. Serve hot, garnished with Preserved Lemons.

Egyptian Fava Beans (Fool Medames)

Serves 6–8

A member of
the pea family,
fava beans
are a popular
ingredient
in Egyptian
dishes. Feel
free to use
lima or pinto
beans as a
substitute
if they are
unavailable.

4 cups fresh fava beans,
  unshelled
2 Preserved Lemons (page 224)
1 small white onion, chopped
2 cloves garlic
2 ripe tomatoes
¼ cup olive oil

1 teaspoon ground cumin
1 teaspoon ground coriander
½ teaspoon turmeric
2 tablespoons chopped cilantro
  leaves
Salt and freshly ground black
  pepper, to taste

1. Shell the fava beans by cutting a slit down the side of each bean and removing the tough outer pod. Rinse the Preserved Lemons and pat dry with paper towels. Remove the pulp and chop finely. Peel and finely chop the onion and garlic. Wash and dice the tomatoes.
2. Heat the olive oil in a large saucepan over medium heat. Add the onion and garlic. Cook over medium heat until the onion is soft and translucent. Add the fava beans and tomatoes. Stir in the ground cumin, ground coriander, turmeric, and the chopped cilantro.
3. Cook until the beans have softened but are not mushy (3 to 5 minutes in total). To serve, toss the bean mixture with the chopped lemons. Season with salt and pepper as desired.

Lamb Kebabs

2 pounds boneless leg of lamb
1½ cups plain yogurt
2 cloves garlic, crushed
2 slices ginger, minced
Juice from 2 freshly squeezed
  lemons

½ teaspoon ground cinnamon
¼ teaspoon mild curry powder
½ teaspoon salt
½ teaspoon freshly ground black
  pepper

Serves 6

Marinating the lamb in yogurt helps to tenderize it. When grilling the lamb, be careful not to cook it too long or it will toughen.

1. Cut the lamb into 1½-inch cubes, and place in a 9 × 13-inch shallow glass baking dish. In a large bowl, combine the yogurt, garlic, ginger, lemon juice, ground cinnamon, curry powder, and the salt and pepper. Spoon the yogurt marinade over the lamb cubes. Marinate the lamb, covered, in the refrigerator for 4 hours, stirring occasionally.

2. Preheat the grill. Thread the marinated lamb kebabs onto skewers. (Reserve the yogurt marinade.) Cook over medium heat, turning, until the meat is cooked according to your preference (8 minutes for medium-rare). Baste the lamb frequently with reserved marinade while grilling. Serve hot.

On Alcohol in Africa

Outside of Muslim Africa you can find many types of alcoholic beverages. Most famous are the wine regions of South Africa, which produce exceptional whites and reds. South Africa also produces an unusual beverage—a tangerine-based liqueur called Van der Hum. And the famed Kenyan beer Tusker is exported for those who want to try it without a transatlantic flight. But most famous is the Ethiopian honey wine, Tej, invented centuries ago (bees, it turns out, are the earliest domesticated creature). Wine made from their honey somewhat resembles mead made in Old England.

Cucumber Salad with Fresh Mint

Serves 6

Although they are more commonly associated with Middle Eastern cuisine, chickpeas are also found in North African dishes. If you can't find chickpeas at the supermarket, try looking for them under their other name, garbanzo beans.

2 tablespoons pine nuts
2 cucumbers
1 tablespoon virgin olive oil
3 tablespoons balsamic vinegar
1 teaspoon granulated sugar

½ teaspoon marjoram
1¼ cups chickpeas
1 can mandarin orange segments
2 tablespoons freshly chopped mint

1. Chop the pine nuts into thin slivers. Peel and grate the cucumbers. Drain the liquid from the cucumbers by placing them in a sieve and sprinkling the salt over. Place a small plate on top of the cucumbers to help push out the liquid, and let drain for 1 hour. Toss the drained cucumber slices with the olive oil, balsamic vinegar, sugar, and marjoram.
2. Place the chickpeas in a serving bowl. Add the mandarin orange segments and arrange the seasoned cucumber slices and slivered pine nuts on top. Sprinkle with the freshly chopped mint.

African Cooking Terms

Efo. Gombo. Foofoo. These may sound like the babblings of a small child, but in fact they are African cooking terms. Here are a few of the more unusual-sounding terms used in Africa: efo (a multipurpose name for greens, including mustard, collards, chard, and turnip), elubo (yam flour), foofoo (mashed yam, or yam, corn, and plantain pudding), gombo (the West African word for okra).

Moroccan Stuffed Chicken

½ cup toasted almonds
½ cup golden raisins
½ cup plus 2 tablespoons orange
    juice
4 tablespoons butter
1½ cups water
10 saffron threads

1 cup couscous
1 tablespoon liquid honey
½ teaspoon ground cinnamon
¼ teaspoon ground ginger
¼ teaspoon cayenne pepper
1 teaspoon salt
3½-pound roasting chicken

Serves 4

Always make
sure to tuck
the wing tips
under the
body when
roasting a
chicken.

1. To make the couscous stuffing: chop the toasted almonds into slivers. Plump up the raisins by placing them in a small bowl with the orange juice. Let the raisins sit in the juice for 30 minutes. Drain.
2. In a medium saucepan, melt the butter. Add the water and saffron threads and bring to a boil. Stir in the coucous. Stir briefly and remove from the heat. Let the couscous stand for 15 minutes.
3. Stir the toasted almonds, raisins, honey, ground cinnamon, ground ginger, and cayenne pepper into the couscous. Use your hands to make sure the ingredients are thoroughly mixed together.
4. Preheat the oven to 425°. Clean the chicken cavity, rinse, and pat dry with paper towels. Rub salt over the outside skin. Spoon the couscous stuffing into the cavity of the chicken, and pack loosely. Use poultry skewers to close the cavity opening. Tie the legs together with string. Place the chicken on a rack in a roasting pan. Roast uncovered, basting frequently with the chicken juices, for 1 to 1¼ hours. (The chicken is done when the temperature in the thickest part of the thigh reaches 175°.)

Almond Paste

**Yields about
1 cup**

Almond paste makes an appearance in many Moroccan dessert recipes; it can also be enjoyed spread on freshly baked bread.

*1½ cups blanched whole
  almonds*

½ cup walnut oil
¼ cup liquid honey

1. Toast the almonds by heating them in a frying pan over medium heat, shaking the pan continuously, until they turn golden. Cool and chop finely.
2. Process the almonds in the food processor until they have formed a fine paste. Stir in the walnut oil and process again. Stir in the liquid honey.

Ethiopian Bread

Ethiopian bread is known as injera. Made from teff, the smallest form of millet, it is ground into flour, then made into a thin fermented batter. It is poured onto a griddle in a large spiral, where it blends into a large, 24-inch circular flatbread. Cooked in minutes, the spongy bread acts as the plate for the dish and replaces a spoon.

BLT: Buster Crab, Lettuce, and Tomato Sandwich

Serves 1

This is one of the signature recipes of Restaurant August in New Orleans. Chef John Besh plays on the name of the great American "BLT" sandwich, substituting buster crab for the bacon, resulting in a simple gourmet seafood version of the classic original.

1 buster crab, cleaned
Salt and pepper, to taste
¼ cup cornmeal
¼ cup seasoned flour
¼ cup canola oil
¼ cup grape tomatoes, peeled
1 dash 25-year-old balsamic vinegar

1 teaspoon extra-virgin olive oil
1 pinch minced chives
Salt and pepper, to taste
1 slice brioche, well-toasted
2 teaspoons aioli
1 pinch micro greens or any sproutlike lettuce

1. Season the crab with salt and pepper. Combine the cornmeal and seasoned flour, and toss the crab in the mixture to coat.
2. In a sauté pan, heat the canola oil over medium heat. Place the coated crab in the oil and cook for 1 minute on each side. Remove from pan and allow to drain on paper towels.
3. Toss the tomatoes with the vinegar, olive oil, chives, and salt and pepper. On serving plate, place the tomatoes on top of the brioche. Place the crab on top of the tomatoes, and top with a dollop of aioli and the micro greens.

What's in a Salad?

A staple of the American diet, salads have been around since ancient times. The 1930s saw the invention of Jell-O, as well as the Cobb (invented at the Brown Derby Restaurant in 1937). In the latter half of the twentieth century, salad enjoyed one of its most significant revolutions, when hippies embraced natural and organic ingredients including nuts and berries, alfalfa sprouts, and sunflower seeds. Today there is almost no limit to what you might find in a salad: chefs choose from a plethora of organic mixed greens, edible flowers, and unique dressings, which keep this simple dish a constantly evolving treat.

Young Garlic Soup with Crème Fraîche and Spring Pea Shoots

1 tablespoon extra-virgin olive oil
½ pound fresh young garlic bulbs, roughly chopped
1 small yellow onion, small diced
1 stalk celery, small diced
1 pound Yukon gold potatoes, peeled and diced
2 quarts chicken or vegetable stock

¼ teaspoon cayenne pepper
1 cup heavy whipping cream
1 sprig fresh thyme, leaves picked from stem
Salt and freshly ground white pepper, to taste
¼ cup crème fraîche (or sour cream or plain yogurt)
¼ pound pea shoots

Serves 8

Another recipe from Chef John Besh of Restaurant August in New Orleans. It can be served hot or chilled. If you can't find pea shoots, substitute watercress for the garnish.

1. Heat the olive oil in a 2-gallon pot over medium heat. Add the garlic, onion, and celery, and cook for 5 minutes.
2. Add the potatoes, stock, and whipping cream to pot. Bring to a boil, lower heat, and simmer for 20 minutes. Add the thyme, cayenne, salt, and white pepper.
3. Purée the soup in a blender, then strain through a fine-mesh sieve. Adjust seasonings to taste. Pour into soup bowls or cups and garnish each with a spoonful of the crème fraîche and pea shoots.

Garlic and Crème Fraîche Are Trés Francais

"I love early spring garlic," muses Chef John Besh of Louisiana's Restaurant August. "It has not yet formed each individual toe, and may look more like a small onion bulb than a head of garlic." Garlic and crème fraîche are featured prominently in the traditional French culinary style. Chef Besh, who trained extensively in Provence, likes to emphasize the historic culinary bond between France and New Orleans, using these ingredients in many signature recipes.

Tomato Marmalade

Serves 8
(as a spread)

Chef Besh's Tomato Marmalade is a wonderful gourmet solution to having a surplus of the fruit on hand at summer's end.

½ teaspoon cumin seeds
10 peppercorns
1 cup granulated sugar
1½ cups red wine vinegar

10 tomatoes, peeled, seeded, and diced
2–4 jalapeños, seeded and finely diced

1. Tie the cumin seeds and peppercorns together in a cheesecloth sack.
2. In a saucepan over medium heat, cook the sugar and vinegar to a syrup consistency.
3. Add the tomatoes, jalapeños, and cheesecloth sack to the saucepan. Cook slowly over low heat until the mixture reaches desired thickness. Use immediately, or pour into sterilized jars to save.

Sweet Corn and Cipollini Onion Soup

Serves 8

Another of Chef Scott Johnson's favorite dishes, this combines the sweetness of corn with the sweetness of cipollini onions.

3 cups whole sweet corn kernels
2 cups diced cipollini onion
1 cup diced potatoes
2 teaspoons olive oil

1 teaspoon dried thyme
1 bay leaf
3 cups chicken broth
Salt and pepper, to taste

1. In a soup pot over medium heat, cook the corn, onion, and potatoes in the oil. Sauté for 5 to 10 minutes. Add the thyme, bay leaf, chicken broth, salt, and pepper. Simmer for 30 to 40 minutes.
2. Transfer to a blender or food processor and purée until smooth. Adjust seasoning to taste, and serve.

Red Velvet Cake

3 cups all-purpose flour, divided
1 teaspoon salt
1½ teaspoons baking soda
3 tablespoons cocoa powder
2¼ cups granulated sugar,
   divided

1 cup unsalted butter, divided
2 large eggs
1½ teaspoons vanilla extract,
   divided
2 cups buttermilk, divided
4 tablespoons red food coloring

The white icing on this cake contrasts nicely with the red filling. The red color comes from food dye; the cake is actually chocolate-flavored.

1. Preheat the oven to 350°. Grease 2 round 9-inch cake pans.
2. In a large bowl, combine the 2½ cups flour, salt, baking soda, and cocoa powder. In a separate bowl, use an electric mixer to cream 1¼ cups sugar and ½ cup unsalted butter. Beat in the eggs and 1 teaspoon vanilla extract. Gradually add in 1 cup buttermilk.
3. Make a well in the middle of the flour and add in the liquid ingredients. Combine with the flour, taking care not to overmix the batter. Stir in the red food coloring. Pour the batter into the prepared cake pans. Bake for 30 minutes, or until the cake springs back when a toothpick is inserted in the middle. Cool for 15 minutes and turn the cakes out of their pans.
4. To make the icing, whisk together ½ cup flour and 1 cup buttermilk. Bring to a boil. Reduce the heat to medium, and continue whisking until the mixture thickens. Remove from the heat and cool.
5. Cream together ½ cup unsalted butter and 1 cup sugar. Beat in ½ teaspoon vanilla extract. Gradually beat in the cooled milk mixture until it is light and fluffy. Spread the icing over the cake and serve.

Snapper with Jumbo Lump Crabmeat

Serves 4

This recipe, by Chef Matthew Murphy of Victor's Grill at the Ritz-Carlton, New Orleans, combines the richness of snapper and crab, finished with a warm Bacon Dressing.

¾ pound red snapper fillet
¼ cup olive oil, plus extra for brushing
Salt and freshly ground black pepper, to taste
1 lemon
3 ounces jumbo lump crabmeat
2 tablespoons Chardonnay

2 tablespoons butter
1 small zucchini, cut on a bias
1 red bell pepper, sliced thickly
1 tablespoon cane vinegar
2 tablespoons Bacon Dressing (see sidebar on this page)
½ cup baby spinach

1. Brush the snapper with a little olive oil and season with salt and pepper. Squeeze the lemon over it. Cook the snapper in a medium-sized sauté pan over medium heat, turning once, until fish is cooked through and opaque. Add the crabmeat and chardonnay. When warm, add the butter and stir to melt. Remove from heat.

2. Toss the vegetables with the olive oil, salt and pepper, and the cane vinegar. Grill until cooked through. Place a medium-sized metal bowl on the grill and add the Bacon Dressing and baby spinach and toss. Add the grilled vegetables and toss to mix. Serve alongside the fish.

Bacon Dressing

To make the Bacon Dressing, combine ¼ pound cooked, chopped bacon (together with the fat), ¼ cup balsamic vinegar, ¾ cup shallot stock, and 1 teaspoon of honey.

Bourbon Molasses Glacé

2 cups bourbon
1 cup light corn syrup

½ cup molasses

Reduce the bourbon by ⅓ in a deep pot (because you will be releasing the alcohol, be careful not to expose it to an open flame). Add the corn syrup and molasses, and cook for 5 minutes.

This is a delicious sauce that goes with many meat dishes. It is especially good with the Pecan-Crusted Chicken (page 242).

Serves 4

Buttery Mashed Potatoes

2 pounds medium Yukon gold
  potatoes
1 pound European-style butter
  (such as Plugra brand) or
  regular unsalted butter, at
  room temperature

½ cup plus 1 tablespoon heavy
  cream
Salt and freshly ground white
  pepper, to taste

Chef Matthew Murphy of the Ritz–Carlton in New Orleans uses only Yukon for mashed potatoes because "they have an excellent amount of starch, and have a perfect texture to be mashed."

1. Place the potatoes (skin on) in a pot and cover with cold water. Bring to a simmer and cook for about 20 minutes, until tender and easily pierced with a fork. Drain and peel away the skin.
2. Using a potato ricer, mash the potatoes and butter together. Fold in the cream and salt and pepper. Your mashed potatoes should be fluffy and light. At this point you may add different flavors, such as olive oil, pesto, white truffle, etc.

Pecan-Crusted Chicken

Serves 4

Serve this
with Bourbon
Molasses
Glacé (page
241).

2 tomatoes, halved
3 cloves garlic, chopped
Salt and freshly ground black
   pepper, to taste
2 eggs
2 cups whole milk
2½ cups pecan halves
3 cups all-purpose flour
4 (7-ounce) skinless, boneless
   chicken breasts

½ cup clarified butter
4 teaspoons extra-virgin olive oil
¼ pound onion, diced
1 pound baby spinach
1 tablespoon unsalted butter
1 tablespoon creole spices
1 recipe Buttery Mashed Potatoes
   (page 241)

1. Preheat the oven to 180°. Sprinkle the tomato halves with a little of the chopped garlic, salt, and pepper. Place on a baking tray and bake for about 20 minutes. Remove from oven and let cool. These can be reheated when assembling the dish.

2. While the tomatoes are cooking, make an egg wash by beating together the eggs and milk. Set aside. In a food processor, chop 2 cups of the pecans and 2 cups of the flour together until the pecans are fine and well mixed with the flour. Season the chicken breasts with salt and pepper. Dredge each breast in the remaining 1 cup flour, then dip into the egg wash, and then coat in the pecan flour. Make sure the chicken breasts are completely coated.

3. After the tomatoes have been removed from the oven, increase oven temperature to 375°. In a large cast-iron skillet over medium to high heat, warm the clarified butter. Add the chicken breasts and cook until they are a nice golden color on bottom. Turn the breasts over, and transfer the pan to the oven. Bake for about 8 to 10 minutes, until golden brown on top.

4. While the chicken is cooking, warm the olive oil in a pan and add the onions, then the remaining garlic. (Adding the onions first helps the garlic to cook better.) Cook until onions begin to soften, then add the spinach. When it begins to wilt, remove from heat and season to taste.

continues >>

5. Melt butter in a skillet. Add the pecans and toss with the butter. Sprinkle in the creole seasoning, and toss to coat all the pecans evenly. Cook over medium heat, stirring frequently, for 2 to 3 minutes.
6. To serve, spoon the mashed potato in the center of serving plates and place the spinach to the side. Place the chicken breast on top of the spinach. Arrange the roasted tomatoes beside the chicken and drizzle the sauce around. Spoon the pecans on top of the mashed potatoes.

Balsamic Vinaigrette—A Classic

Whisk together ½ cup balsamic vinegar, 3 tablespoons Dijon mustard, 3 tablespoons honey, 2 finely minced garlic cloves, 2 finely minced small shallots, a bit of salt, and freshly ground pepper to taste. Then very gradually whisk in 1 cup of extra-virgin olive oil (yields 1⅔ cups).

Lollypop Veal Chop

4 (12-ounce) veal chops
Olive oil, as needed
Course salt and freshly ground
   black pepper, to taste
8 cloves garlic

½ bottle Cabernet wine
1 cup Chambord
1 cup fresh raspberries
1 cup granulated sugar

Serves 4

1. Rub the veal chops with olive oil and salt and pepper. Let marinate in the refrigerator while preparing the sauce.
2. Combine all the remaining ingredients in a saucepan. Cook over medium heat until the mixture is a syrup consistency, about 2 hours. Remove from heat and let cool. Strain the syrup through a fine-mesh sieve, holding the candied garlic cloves to the side. Set aside the syrup and garlic.
3. Grill the veal chops over medium heat to desired doneness, basting with the raspberry syrup. Serve the chops with the remaining sauce and garnish with the candied garlic cloves.

This dish comes from Chef Paul O'Connor of Alchemy Restaurant at CopperWynd Resort and Club in Fountain Hills, Arizona.

Roasted Butternut Squash Soup

Serves 4

This hearty and flavorful soup is very low in fat and is a favorite of Washington, DC's 2004 Chef of the Year, Jeff Tunks of the restaurant DC Coast.

1 large butternut squash
¼ cup olive oil
1 small yellow onion, thinly sliced
1 clove garlic, chopped
1 quart chicken stock

1 bay leaf
1 sprig fresh thyme
Salt, to taste
1 smoked chicken breast, diced
1 tablespoon minced fresh chives

1. Preheat the oven to 350°. Split the squash in half lengthwise and remove the seeds. Place cut-side down in ½ inch of water in a baking dish. Roast until tender, about 30 to 45 minutes. Remove from oven and remove the skin.
2. In a large soup pot, heat the olive oil on medium. Add the sliced onion and sauté until tender. Add the garlic and sauté for 1 minute (do not brown). Add the roasted squash, the chicken stock, bay leaf, and thyme, and simmer for 20 minutes.
3. Remove and discard the bay leaf and thyme stem, and purée the soup until smooth. Season with salt.
4. Place a quarter of the diced chicken and the minced chives in the center of each soup plate. Ladle 1 cup of the hot soup around the chicken. Serve immediately.

Cooking in Early American Kitchens

Early colonial housewives didn't have it easy. Their day typically began at 4 a.m., at which time they fetched wood, built a fire, milked the cows, and gathered eggs. Most of their day focused on the main meal—dinner, served in the afternoon. Working until sunset, many American housewives during this period perished from major kitchen accidents caused by their aprons or dresses catching on fire. This was because they cooked in large fireplaces, which held boiling pots. Later "cranes" were introduced, which helped hoist large pots over the fire, but preparing the meals was still dangerous business.

Jumbo Lump Crab Cakes

1 pound jumbo lump crabmeat
1 egg
Juice of ½ lemon
1 tablespoon mayonnaise
1 tablespoon minced fresh chives
Pinch cayenne pepper

Salt, to taste
¼–½ cup fresh brioche crumbs
6 tablespoons olive oil
Corn-Pickled Okra Relish
  (page 246)
Spicy Remoulade (page 246)

Serves 5 (as an appetizer)

This is among the most popular dishes served by Jeff Tunks at his restaurant, DC Coast, in Washington, DC.

1. Preheat the oven to 350°.
2. Gently remove the shells from the crabmeat, being careful not to break up the lumps.
3. In a large mixing bowl, combine the egg, lemon juice, mayonnaise, chives, cayenne, and salt. Gently fold in the crabmeat. Add the brioche crumbs sparingly to lightly bind the meat. Form into 5 cakes.
4. Sauté the crab cakes in olive oil until golden brown. Transfer to a baking sheet and bake for 10 minutes. On individual plates, mound a generous spoonful of okra relish, top with a crab cake, then top with the remoulade.

The Revival of Comfort Food

It's hard to say exactly what defines an "American" meal, at least these days. But not so long ago the following might have been considered typical American family dishes: mashed potatoes, pot roast, fried chicken, chili, roast chicken, pork chops and gravy, sloppy joes, spaghetti, meat loaf, and beef stew. "Comfort foods," as many of these are now known, are actually making a gourmet comeback. Restaurants such as Jones in Philadelphia elevate comfort food to the level of upscale dining. Favorites include creamed corn, turkey dinner (served year-round), and homemade apple pie. But this is not exactly how Mom used to make it—it's even better.

Corn-Pickled Okra Relish

**Serves 5
(as a garnish)**

Serve with
Jumbo Lump
Crab Cakes
(page 245).

2 ears fresh white corn, husks on
½ small red onion, minced
1 clove garlic, minced
12 pickled okra, sliced
1 tomato, diced

¼ cup olive oil
2 tablespoons red wine vinegar
Salt and freshly ground black
  pepper, to taste
1 tablespoon chopped cilantro

1. Preheat the oven to 350° or prepare outdoor grill.
2. Roast or grill the corn in the husk for 20 to 25 minutes. Let cool. Remove the husk and cut the kernels off the cob. Combine the corn with the remaining relish ingredients.

Spicy Remoulade

**Serves 5
(as a garnish)**

Serve with
Jumbo Lump
Crab Cakes.

4 tablespoons mayonnaise
1 teaspoon horseradish
1 teaspoon Creole mustard
½ teaspoon Tabasco
1 tablespoon chili sauce

Juice of ½ lemon
Salt and freshly ground black
  pepper, to taste
½ teaspoon Worcestershire sauce

Mix together all the ingredients until smooth. Serve atop crab cakes.

Roasted Tomato, Zucchini, and Goat Cheese Tarts

4 green zucchini, sliced
2 tablespoons olive oil
2 teaspoons chopped garlic
1 quart heavy cream
4 eggs
Salt and freshly ground black
   pepper, to taste

10 tomatoes, halved, deseeded,
   and juice drained off
2 tablespoons extra-virgin olive
   oil
Herbes de Provence
8 ounces goat cheese
¼ bunch basil
10 puff pastry shells

Serves 10

Award-winning Chef Frédéric Castan serves this savory appetizer at Sofitel Chicago Water Tower Hotel's stylish Café des Architectes. Serve with a salad of mixed baby winter greens tossed in a balsamic vinaigrette.

1. Sauté the zucchini in the olive oil. Add the garlic and then the cream. Let cook for 30 minutes and blend together. Add the eggs and season with salt and pepper.
2. Preheat the oven to 250°. Mix together the tomatoes, extra-virgin olive oil, herbes de Provence, and salt. Roast on a baking sheet in the oven for approximately 3 to 4 hours, until they are dry.
3. When the tomatoes are done, increase oven temperature to 350°. Mix the goat cheese with the basil. In each tart shell, place a layer of tomatoes on the bottom, add a layer of goat cheese, and cover with the zucchini mix. Place on a baking sheet and bake for 15 minutes.

Elegant Cream of Celery Soup

Serves 4

A mascarpone béchamel sauce lends extra richness and flavor to a basic creamed soup recipe. For an extra gourmet touch, garnish the soup with black truffle shavings just before serving.

4 stalks celery
½ sweet Vidalia onion
4 shallots
2 tablespoons olive oil
3 cups water
½ cup chicken broth

3 tablespoons butter
2½ tablespoons all-purpose flour
1 cup light cream
¼ teaspoon celery salt, to taste
⅛ teaspoon paprika, or to taste
2 tablespoons mascarpone

1. String the celery and cut on the diagonal into thin strips. Peel and finely chop the onion and shallots.
2. Heat the olive oil over medium heat. Sauté the celery, onion, and shallots until softened. Cook for 1 more minute, then remove the vegetables from the pan.
3. In a large saucepan, bring the water and chicken broth to a boil. Add the vegetables. Turn the heat down to low while preparing the béchamel sauce. (Do not cover the saucepan.)
4. In a small saucepan, melt the butter in a small saucepan over low heat. Add the flour, whisking continuously until the flour is mixed in with the butter (2 to 3 minutes). Slowly add the light cream. Continue whisking over medium heat until the sauce is thick and bubbly. Add the celery salt and paprika. Remove from the heat and slowly stir in the mascarpone, 1 tablespoon at a time.
5. Carefully pour the béchamel sauce into the celery soup. Turn up the heat and cook for 1 more minute to thicken. Serve immediately.

A Mild-Mannered Onion

Cipollini onions are very mild in flavor, and impart a certain sweetness. The cipollini onion comes from Italy and is harvested in the United States and sold at specialty and farmer's markets. It is a small heirloom onion, shaped like a saucer, and can be found fresh, with the green top still on, or dried like the common yellow onion.

Shiitake Mushroom Soup

¼ cup butter
½ cup diced yellow onion
½ cup chopped celery
1 pound shiitake mushrooms, washed
2 cups chicken stock

2 sprigs fresh thyme
1 sprig rosemary
1 cup cream
Salt and freshly ground black
    pepper, to taste

Serves 4

This is from Chef Scott Johnson of Canoe Bay. Canoe Bay is one of the most romantic hideaways in the Midwest.

1. In a large pot over medium heat, melt the butter. Add the onion, celery, and mushrooms. Cook until the onions are translucent. Reduce heat to low and add the chicken stock, thyme, and rosemary. Let cook until reduced by half.
2. Purée the soup in blender, then return it to the pot. Heat the cream in a saucepan until hot, then fold it into the soup. Season with salt and pepper, and serve.

Cranberry Salad

1 pound cooked wild rice
⅓ cups dried cranberries
½ cup walnuts, toasted
1 apple, diced
¼ cup maple syrup

2 tablespoons cider vinegar
½ cup olive oil
Salt and freshly ground black
    pepper, to taste

Serves 8

This is the perfect afternoon dish to enjoy outside on the deck, or as a refreshing part of a picnic lunch.

In a large bowl, mix together all the ingredients.

CHAPTER 18
Oh Canada: Taste of the Provinces

Merrit Venison Carpaccio

Serves 8

Executive Chef Wayne Martin, at the the Four Seasons in Vancouver, takes advantage of the availability of high-quality venison from a local farm in Merrit, British Columbia, for this recipe. Fleur de sel is a sea salt from Brittany, France.

8 baby carrots
4 baby gold beets
4 baby striped beets
16 fine green beans
4 stalks asparagus
1 small shallot, finely chopped
4 large leaves basil, chopped
1 ounce toasted pine nuts
Juice of 1 lemon

2 tablespoons (or more, as needed) extra-virgin olive oil
Fleur de sel or sea salt, to taste
Freshly ground black pepper, to taste
¾ pound center-cut venison tenderloin
1 cup Mountain Huckleberry Vinaigrette (page 253)
A few chervil leaves

1. Blanch all the vegetables separately until they are easily pierced with a knife. Transfer to a bowl filled with ice water to cool. Remove from the water and peel the carrots. Trim off the tops of the beets. Peel the beets and cut into quarters. Cut the beans in half. Cut the asparagus into 4 pieces each. Set aside.
2. Toss the shallot with the vegetables, along with the basil, pine nuts, lemon juice, 1 tablespoon of the olive oil, salt, and pepper.
3. Slice the venison into 8 equal pieces and place in between 2 pieces of cling film. Gently pound out the meat into as thin a sheet as possible. Brush the venison with the remaining extra-virgin olive oil, and season with salt and pepper.
4. To assemble, place the venison on serving plates and place the mixed vegetables on top. Drizzle the vinaigrette over everything and garnish with the chervil leaves.

Mountain Huckleberry Vinaigrette

¼ cup huckleberries
1 shallot, peeled and roughly
  chopped
2 teaspoons raspberry vinegar
2 tablespoons olive oil

1 teaspoon honey mustard
¼ cup water
Salt and freshly ground black
  pepper, to taste

Serves 8

Serve this delicious dressing over Merrit Venison Carpaccio (page 252).

Mix together all the ingredients and serve.

BC Farms Provide Unique Organic Choices

British Columbia is filled with specialty produce stores and farms such as the Glorious Garnish and Seasonal Salad Company, providing professional and home chefs with colorful, fresh organic produce. You can find nearly everything there: beets, green beans, carrots, and asparagus. The bright mustard-colored gold beets and red-and-white-striped variety add dramatic color to this dish. Red beets, which may be easier to find, are a suitable substitute. The huckleberries add a distinct West Coast touch and can also be found at many specialty produce markets in the Lower Mainland. Frozen or preserved huckleberries can be substituted, as can fresh or frozen local blackberries.

Brine-Marinated Salmon

Serves 6–8

The Sutton Place Hotel's Executive Chef Kim Thai's recipe highlights the "it" food in British Columbia—salmon.

6 cups water
1 tablespoon salt
⅔ cup brown sugar
½ cup honey
½ orange, sliced
½ lime, sliced

½ lemon, sliced
4 sprigs dill
1 (4-pound) fillet fresh Atlantic salmon or wild sockeye, dressed

1. Place all the ingredients except the salmon into a stockpot. Bring to a boil. Remove from heat immediately. Once the mixture is cool, submerge the salmon in it.
2. Marinate in the refrigerator for approximately 24 hours. Then cook the fillet as you prefer. One suggestion: smoke the fillets over a 250° wood fire for approximately 2 hours, until the fillets are firm to the touch. Peel off the skin and serve.

Horseradish Vodka Dip

Serves 6

This dip from Executive Chef Kim Thai goes great with the Brine-Marinated Salmon.

5 tablespoons sour cream
⅓ teaspoon horseradish
2 tablespoons vodka
1 teaspoon honey

6 drops Tabasco
Salt and freshly ground white pepper, to taste

Mix together all the ingredients and refrigerate. Serve cold with salmon.

Salt Spring Island

Coined the "Organic Capital of Canada," Salt Spring Island (just off Vancouver Island) hosts a bevy of regional farmers, artisans, and organic specialists. The Salt Spring Island Farmers' Market is a must-see for those looking to taste the region's best organic produce. Locals sell vegetables, herbs, jellies, and baked goods all with ingredients from their farms, every Saturday from mid-April to mid-October, in the town of Ganges.

Duck Confit in Phyllo with Caramelized Apples

1 pound duck confit meat
⅓ cup minced shallots
5 leaves fresh basil, chopped
12 sheets frozen phyllo dough, thawed in the refrigerator

½ cup unsalted butter, melted
2 Golden Delicious apples
1 tablespoon olive oil

Serves 6 (as an appetizer)

This comes from Executive Chef Patrick Bourachot of the Fairmont Le Chateau Montebello in Quebec. Purchase 13/4 pounds whole duck confit leg at a gourmet shop or high-end butcher, to yield the 1 pound required.

1. Prepare the duck confit by removing the bones, skin, and fat. Shred the meat by pulling it apart with your fingers. Place the meat in a bowl, add the shallots and chopped basil, and mix well to combine. Set aside.
2. Preheat the oven to 350°. Line a baking sheet with parchment paper.
3. Place 1 sheet of the phyllo dough on a clean work surface and brush butter across the surface. Place a second sheet on top of the first and spread with butter. Repeat with a third and fourth phyllo sheet, but do not brush final layer with butter. Prepare 2 separate stacks of phyllo squares the same way.
4. Cut each square in half, for a total of a 6 rectangular phyllo sheet stacks. Spread ⅙ of the confit mixture along the short edge of 1 phyllo rectangle and roll up into a log about 1 inch thick. Place on the prepared baking sheet. Repeat with remaining confit mixture and phyllo rectangles to make six logs in total.
5. Brush the logs lightly with the remaining melted butter and bake until warm and golden, about 7 minutes.
6. Peel the apples and remove the cores, then cut each apple into 8 wedges. In a nonstick fry pan, heat the oil and fry the apples until lightly browned on each side, about 2 minutes per side. To serve, cut each baked confit "log" in half diagonally, and garnish with caramelized apple wedges.

Warm Dungeness Crab and Brie Melt

Serves 2

This is a new take on tuna melts from Executive Chef Michael Viloria of Delta Vancouver Suites.

4 ounces Dungeness crabmeat
2 tablespoons mayonnaise
1 teaspoon lemon juice
Pinch lemon zest
Pinch salt

Pinch pepper
2 Scallion Scones
  (page 257)
2 ounces Brie cheese
Pickled Okanagan Apples

1. Preheat broiler. Mix together the crabmeat, mayonnaise, lemon juice and zest, salt, and pepper.
2. Split the scones in half and place on a baking tray. Place the crab mixture on both halves of the scone. Slice the Brie cheese and place on top of the crab mixture (it is best to slice the cheese when it is cold, directly from the refrigerator, because of its soft texture). Broil until the cheese melts. Serve with the pickled apples.

Pickled Okanagan Apples

Serves 2

These are delicious served with Scallion Scones (page 257) or Warm Dungeness Crab and Brie Melt.

1 Okanagan apple
2 tablespoons apple cider vinegar

1 teaspoon salt
2 teaspoons granulated sugar
Pinch white pepper

1. Peel and slice the apples thinly.
2. Mix together all the remaining ingredients in a bowl, add the apples, and let marinate for 5 minutes before serving.

Belgian Endive Salad with Maple Vinaigrette

7 tablespoons grape seed oil
7 tablespoons maple syrup
4 tablespoons cider vinegar
2 tablespoons whole-grain mustard
1 tablespoon Dijon mustard

Salt and freshly ground black pepper, to taste
12 slices baguette
12 slices Brie
6 Belgian endive leaves
1 tablespoon pecans

Serves 4

1. Preheat broiler on medium heat. Combine the oil, maple syrup, vinegar, both mustards, and the salt and pepper. Mix the vinaigrette well and set aside.
2. Place the baguette slices on a baking sheet and top each with a slice of the Brie. Broil until the cheese has melted. Cut up into croutons.
3. Cut the endives into slivers. In a bowl, toss the endive with the pecans and the vinaigrette. Serve with the Brie croutons.

Jean-Paul Giroux of the restaurant Le Saint-Augustine in Quebec suggests also using this vinaigrette with smoked salmon or cooked ham.

Scallion Scones

2 cups all-purpose flour
½ cup granulated sugar
1 tablespoon baking powder
½ teaspoon salt
1 scallion, minced

½ cup butter
1 egg
⅓ cup whole milk, plus a bit extra for brushing

Yields 12 scones

1. Preheat the oven to 425°.
2. Mix together flour, sugar, baking powder, salt, and scallion. Cut the butter into the flour mixture with a fork. Add the egg and milk, and mix to form the dough.
3. Sprinkle flour on a work surface and roll out the dough to a thickness of 1½ inches.
4. Cut the dough into rounds with a cookie cutter or the mouth of a drinking glass. Brush the surface of the dough with a little bit of milk. Bake for 15 minutes or until golden brown.

For an unusual accompaniment, try serving these scones with Pickled Okanagan Apples (page 256).

Red Laver Sea Lettuce "Kimchi"

Serves 10

From Executive Chef Jonathan Chovancek comes this Canadian version of the classic Korean condiment. If you cannot purchase fresh sea lettuce, it is available dried in most Japanese grocery stores.

1 pound white cabbage, cut into ½-inch squares
2 tablespoons kosher salt
4 ounces fresh Red Laver sea lettuce, washed and julienned
½ cup apple cider vinegar
¼ cup wild flower honey
2 cloves garlic, sliced thinly
3 teaspoons grated fresh ginger
2 teaspoons dried red pepper flakes
2 teaspoons fennel seeds, toasted

1. Spread the cabbage onto a baking sheet and cover evenly with 1 tablespoon of the kosher salt. Leave to dry and cure uncovered for 24 hours.
2. When the cabbage is cured, remove from the tray, discarding extra liquid. In a large, nonreactive bowl, mix the cabbage with the sea lettuce.
3. Place the vinegar, honey, remaining salt, garlic, ginger, red pepper flakes, and fennel seeds in a nonreactive saucepan and bring to a boil. Remove from heat and let cool completely.
4. Pour the cooled liquid over the cabbage mixture and place in a nonreactive, sealable container. Refrigerate for 2 weeks.
5. When ready to use, remove the cabbage mixture from the liquid with clean tongs. Do not rinse. Use as you would pickles. Keep refrigerated.

Some of British Columbia's Best Chefs Float

Imagine checking into a luxury resort floating in the middle of a fjord. Then imagine feasting on king crab claws, poached wild Pacific winter-spring salmon, and flourless dark chocolate hazelnut cake. Some of Canada's best chefs are chopping, blanching, and sautéing in world-class resorts such as King Pacific Lodge, a Clayoquot Wilderness Resort.

Ahi Tuna Tartar

½ pound fresh yellowfin tuna
   (ahi tuna)
1 tablespoon toasted pine nuts
¼ green apple, peeled and diced
½ teaspoon chopped fresh ginger
1 tablespoon chopped fresh
   parsley

¼ teaspoon fresh-squeezed
   lemon juice
1 teaspoon soy sauce
½ teaspoon Dijon mustard
1 teaspoon olive oil
½ teaspoon wasabi powder
Salt and cracked black pepper, to
   taste

Serves 3

Chef Sean Riley of Glowbal Grill and Satay Bar in Vancouver says, "Be sure to use only fresh sashimi-grade ahi tuna, and mix ingredients together just before serving. Also keep all items cool when preparing." Serve with crostinis and sliced avocado, if desired.

1. In a stainless steel bowl, mix together the tuna, pine nuts, green apples, ginger, parsley, and lemon juice. Chill in the refrigerator for at least three hours.
2. In a separate bowl, whisk together the soy sauce, mustard, olive oil, and wasabi. Mix with the tuna mixture.
3. Season to taste with salt and cracked black pepper. Serve cold.

Canada's Varied Cuisine

From tasty Alberta beef to Manitoba's vast agriculture, Canada is an enormous country with a myriad of provinces and styles of cuisine. The Northwest Territories offer total diversity—from dining in chic modern restaurants, to tasting foods that sustained the Inuit in cozy rustic cabins. New Brunswick is the place for seafood, with five-star restaurants as well as wharf-side fish and chip stands. And in Nova Scotia you are never more than a half-hour from the sea. Prince Edward Island diners enjoy a cross between the rugged, seafaring culture of the East Coast and the elegant Victorian era, and in Quebec you will discover something altogether different—French-style restaurants that rival Parisian bistros.

Nasturtium-Wrapped Halibut
with Lobster Ragout

Serves 4

This elegant recipe, created by Chef Randy Akey of Kingsbrae Arms in New Brunswick, Canada, is a tribute to Canada's bounties— from the sea and the shore. Serve with Wild Boar and Orzo Salad (page 261).

2 (1-pound) cooked lobsters
1 small peeled onion
3 stalks celery
1 teaspoon dried thyme
4 bay leaves
1 teaspoon peppercorns
3 sprigs parsley
1 large shallot, diced
½ red bell pepper, diced
2 tablespoons chopped fresh
    cilantro

1 tablespoon finely chopped
    garlic
¼ cup whipping cream
1 tablespoon cornstarch, mixed
    with 1 tablespoon water
Sea salt and cracked pepper, to
    taste
12 nasturtium leaves
4 (5-ounce) fillets fresh Atlantic
    halibut

1. Shuck the cooked lobsters, cut into bite-sized pieces, and set aside. Place the lobster bodies and shells in a stockpot and cover with water. Add the onion, celery, thyme, bay leaves, peppercorns, and parsley. Bring to a boil and simmer the lobster broth for 1 hour.
2. Sauté the shallot and bell pepper. Add 2 cups of the lobster broth, the cilantro, and garlic. Simmer for 5 minutes, then add the cream. Stir the cornstarch slurry into the pot and cook until thickened. Add the lobster meat and season with salt and pepper.
3. Preheat the oven to 400°.
4. Heat the nasturtium leaves in the microwave for 10 seconds to wilt. Place them topside down. Salt and pepper the halibut on both sides, then carefully wrap each portion with 3 wilted nasturtium leaves so the fillet is completely covered. Place in a baking dish and bake for 12 minutes.
5. Divide the lobster ragout among 4 large pasta bowls. Serve the nasturtium-covered halibut on top.

Wild Boar and Orzo Salad

3 ounces wild boar bacon

1 large shallot, peeled and diced

½ red bell pepper, diced

3 baby yellow beets, peeled,
   blanched, and sliced

1 cup orzo pasta

2 cups chicken stock

Fresh-chopped thyme, rosemary,
   sage, and chives, to taste

Salt and pepper, to taste

¼ cup sour cream

Serves 4

Serve this with the Nasturtium-Wrapped Halibut with Lobster Ragout (page 260).

1. Cut the wild boar bacon into small dice and sauté in a deep skillet over medium heat. Add the shallot, red bell pepper, beets, pasta, and chicken stock. Cook over medium heat for 8 to 10 minutes, until the pasta is al dente.

2. Add the chopped herbs, season with salt and pepper, and add the sour cream. Serve warm.

Okanagan Valley

Located in south-central British Columbia, the Thompson Okanagan is a long valley, dominated by Lake Okanagan, running seventy miles down the center of the valley. Over the past ten years the valley's wine industry has blossomed and now boasts over 60 boutique producers. A large number of the wineries are concentrated in the southern part of the valley, between Penticton and Oliver, and include Tinhorn Creek Vineyards, Burrowing Owl, Hawthorne Mountain, Blue Mountain, and Inniskillin Wineries. Meanwhile, a few of the larger producers are in the Kelowna area, including Mission Hill, Summerhill, Quail's Gate, Calona, and Cedar Creek. Visitors can sample local vintages and eat meals highlighting local produce in a series of boutique restaurants overlooking Lake Okanagan.

CHAPTER 19

Mexico: Thinking Outside the Taco

Tuna Ceviche

Serves 4

Chef Erick
Anguiano of
Ikal del Mar
serves up
one of the
best ceviche
menus in
Mexico. Here
is a recipe
that no one
who visits can
resist.

1 tablespoon olive oil
1 garlic clove, chopped
1¾ pounds tuna
2 tablespoons fresh-squeezed lime juice
1 tablespoon fresh-squeezed grapefruit juice
2 tablespoons dry red wine

½ white onion, diced
1 pound tomatoes, diced
1 tablespoon finely chopped fresh cilantro
Salt and freshly ground black pepper, to taste
½ red onion, sliced

1. Heat the olive oil in a sauté pan. Add the garlic and sauté for a few minutes, until aromatic and just slightly golden.
2. Cut the tuna into 4 squares, and mix with the lime and grapefruit juice in a glass bowl. Let marinate for 2 minutes. Add the red wine, white onion, tomato, cilantro, salt, and pepper. Mix well. Place the tuna mixture on serving plates and top with the garlic and its sautéing oil. Place sliced red onion on top, and serve.

Mexi-terranean?

The cuisine at Ikal del Mar has been described as "Mexi-terranean," an eclectic culinary mix combining the flavors of the Mediterranean and the vibrant tastes and colors of Mexico. Azul, the restaurant where these delectable ceviches are made, also offers Mayan-influenced dishes such as Mayan tortilla soup, and sea bass topped with a Mayan black bean sauce.

Broiled Sea Bass Fillet over Tomatillo Rice

¼ cup extra-virgin olive oil, plus extra for garnish
4 (7-ounce) sea bass fillets
2 teaspoons kosher salt
1 teaspoon fresh-cracked black pepper
1 pound green tomatillos

1 sweet Vidalia onion, peeled and quartered
2 cloves garlic, peeled
1 bunch fresh cilantro, leaves chopped, plus extra sprigs for garnish
4 cups cooked basmati rice

Serves 4

This recipe, from Casa del Mar in Los Cabos, suggests sea bass, but you can use any fresh, firm fish such as snapper, grouper, or mahi-mahi.

1. Drizzle the olive oil onto each fish fillet and season with kosher salt and pepper. Pan-fry for 4 minutes each side over medium heat.
2. Preheat broiler on high. Peel off and discard the husks from the tomatillos and rinse under cold, running water. Place the green tomatoes, onions, and garlic on a baking sheet and roast for 7 minutes. Chop the roasted ingredients and combine in a medium-sized bowl. Add the cilantro and season with salt and pepper. Add the cooked rice and mix to combine.
3. Place a scoop of tomatillo rice in the center of each serving plate. (Line the plates with a flat corn husk or a square of banana leaf, if desired.) Place the sea bass fillets over the rice. Garnish with fresh cilantro sprigs and drizzle extra-virgin olive oil around the rice and fish mounds.

From the Sea

Being able to use fresh fish from the Sea of Cortez or the Pacific Ocean is a unique advantage in Los Cabos. Combining them with Mexican ingredients such as tomatillos and fresh cilantro is a signature culinary experience at Casa del Mar, one of Mexico's finest resorts.

Cold Avocado Soup, Atlixco Style

Serves 8

This recipe comes from El Careyes Beach Resort, located in the state of Jalisco. Atlixco is one of the most important avocado-producing regions of Mexico.

For the broth:

5 quarts water
4 chicken legs with thighs
6 chicken wings
1 white onion, sliced
1 head garlic, unpeeled and halved
3 carrots
6 stalks celery
2 bay leaves
6 mint leaves
6 black peppercorns
Salt, to taste

For the soup:

½ cup butter
1 white onion, puréed
2 cloves garlic, puréed
½ leek, puréed
1 carrot, peeled and puréed
6 ripe California avocados, peeled
1 cup crème fraîche or heavy cream
1 cup plain yogurt, beaten
Salt, to taste
2 tablespoons fresh-squeezed lime juice
½ cup olive oil
¼ cup finely chopped white onion
2 tablespoons finely chopped cilantro

1. To prepare the broth, bring the water to a boil in a stockpot. Add all the remaining broth ingredients. Simmer over low heat until the mixture foams. Skim off the foam and simmer for 2 hours. Remove from heat and let cool for 1 hour. Strain through a fine-mesh sieve and discard the solids. Skim off fat, and refrigerate. If the broth separates, reheat slightly before using.

2. To prepare the soup, melt butter in a saucepan. Add the puréed onion, garlic, leek, and carrot along with 3 cups of the broth. Cook until thick, about 25 minutes. Remove from heat and let cool.

3. Meanwhile, blend the avocados with 6 cups of the broth (blend in batches, if necessary) in a blender or food processor. Strain through a fine-mesh sieve. Add the crème fraîche and yogurt. Stir in the vegetable mixture, and add salt to taste. Add the lime juice and olive oil. If the soup is too thick, add a little more broth. Chill in the freezer for 1 hour.

4. To serve, pour the cold avocado soup into soup bowls fitted in liners filled with crushed ice (if available). Garnish with the chopped onion and cilantro.

Five-Minute Recado

½ cup achiote paste
½ cup freshly squeezed lime juice
½ cup orange juice
2 tablespoons white vinegar
2 tablespoons tequila
1 teaspoon freshly ground cumin

¼ teaspoon Tabasco sauce, or to
   taste
½ teaspoon freshly ground black
   pepper
1 clove garlic, minced

In a food processor or blender, process all the ingredients until smooth. Cover and refrigerate overnight to give the flavors a chance to blend.

Fish Tacos

4 fish fillets, such as cod
3 tablespoons lime juice
3 tablespoons olive oil
1 green onion, chopped
1 clove garlic, minced

2 teaspoons granulated sugar
1 tablespoon ancho paste
12 soft corn tortillas
2 cups Mexican salsa, various
   types

1. Rinse the fish fillets and pat dry. In a small bowl, whisk together the lime juice, olive oil, green onion, minced garlic, sugar, and ancho paste. Rub the mixture over the fish. Place the fillets in a large baking dish. Cover and marinate in the refrigerator for 2 hours.
2. Heat the grill. Remove the fish from the refrigerator. Discard the marinade. Grill the fish over medium heat until it is opaque and cooked through. Chop the fish.
3. Serve the fish with the warmed corn tortillas and at least 2 types of salsa.

Cold Coconut Soup

Serves 8

Coconuts are native to the coastal state of Colima. This soup, made at El Tamarindo Golf Resort, uses this abundant ingredient to make a delicious first course.

1 quart whole milk
2 cups finely shredded fresh coconut
2 cups fresh coconut water
2 cups canned coconut milk
½ cup granulated sugar
Salt, to taste
1½ cups heavy cream
Ground cinnamon, for garnish

1. Bring the whole milk to a boil in a medium-sized saucepan. Reduce to a simmer, and stir in the shredded coconut. Simmer for 20 minutes.
2. Remove from heat and blend in a blender or food processor. Return the mixture to the saucepan and add the coconut water and coconut milk. Season with sugar and salt. Add the cream, beating occasionally with a whisk. Cook over medium heat for 25 minutes or until the soup thickens slightly. If the soup is too thick, add a little more cream. Cool the soup on a bed of crushed ice and refrigerate.
3. To serve, pour the chilled soup into hollowed-out coconut shells. Sprinkle cinnamon on top.

Mexican Cheeses: The Whole Enchilada

You may not hear much about Mexican cheeses, but they exist, and are an intricate part of authentic Mexican cuisine. Queso means "cheese" in Spanish, and Hispanic cheeses can be grouped into three basic types: fresh cheeses (best known for being moist, crumbly, and prized for their ability to become soft when heated), melting cheeses (which resist separating when heated), and hard cheeses (usually a finely grated or crumbled dry cheese that finishes off a dish). Here are a few examples: (fresh) queso blanco, queso cresco, and panela; (melting) queso asadero, Oaxaca, quesadilla, and Chihuahua; (hard) queso cotija, and queso enchilado.

Veal Medallions in Almond Stew

6 tablespoons olive oil, divided

2-inch cinnamon stick

⅓ cup whole skinned almonds

2 tablespoons white sesame
seeds

2 small cloves

2 peppercorns

2½ ounces semisweet yeast
bread, torn into pieces

2 pinches dried oregano

2 pinches dried thyme

3½ cups chicken or veal broth

½ pound tomatoes, slightly
charred and skinned

½ white pearl onion, grilled

2 cloves garlic, roasted and
peeled

1 tablespoon whole capers,
rinsed

10 pitted green olives

Pickled jalapeños, to taste

12 (2½-ounce) veal medallions

Salt and freshly ground black
pepper, to taste

All-purpose flour, as needed

Corn tortillas, warmed

Serves 6

This recipe comes from Chef Horacio Reyes of Hotel Hacienda Los Laureles in Oaxaca, Mexico, who learned this recipe from his grand-mother.

1. Heat 4 tablespoons of the olive oil in a skillet and fry the cinnamon, almonds, sesame seeds, cloves, peppercorns, yeast bread, oregano, and thyme until golden. Transfer the mixture to a blender. Add the broth, tomatoes, onion, and garlic, and blend well.

2. Heat the remaining 2 tablespoons olive oil in a pan. Add the blended ingredients and the capers, olives, and pickled jalapeños. Cook for 10 minutes over medium heat, scraping the bottom of the pan often to avoid sticking. (Add more broth if the mole gets too thick.) Continue cooking until the stew turns a bright orange color and is reduced.

3. In the meantime, preheat the oven to 350°. Season the veal with salt and pepper, and flour lightly. Sear in an ovenproof pan over medium-high heat on the stovetop for 1 to 2 minutes on each side. Transfer the pan to the oven and cook according to desired doneness, about 15 minutes for medium-rare.

4. To serve, place pieces of the cooked veal on warmed plates and cover with the stew. Serve with warm corn tortillas.

Roasted Vegetable Salad

Serves 4

Roasted vegetables lend a sweet, smoky flavor to this simple salad dish. For best results, use fresh corn right off the cob.

2 fresh cobs of corn
4 cloves garlic
2 red bell peppers
4 teaspoons olive oil
3 tablespoons lime juice
2 tablespoons orange juice

3 tablespoons virgin olive oil
¼ teaspoon ground cumin
½ teaspoon freshly ground black pepper
1 tablespoon chopped cilantro
1 tablespoon minced red onion

1. Preheat the broiler. Remove the silk from the corn cobs without removing the husks. Use string to tie the husks around the corn cobs. Cover in cold water and soak for 5 minutes. Peel the garlic.
2. Brush each bell pepper with 2 teaspoons olive oil. Lay the peppers on a broiling pan. Broil, turning frequently, until the skins are blackened and charred (about 20 minutes). Place each pepper in a sealed plastic bag for 15 minutes. Peel off the skins, and remove the stems and the seeds. Cut the peppers lengthwise into strips.
3. To roast the garlic, reduce the oven temperature to 400°. Place the garlic cloves on a baking sheet. Roast until softened (about 20 minutes). Remove and cool.
4. To roast the corn, reduce the oven temperature to 375°. Place the corn on a baking sheet and roast, turning frequently, until the husks are browned (about 20 minutes). Cool. Remove the husks. Remove the corn from the cob.
5. In a small bowl, whisk together the lime juice, orange juice, virgin olive oil, ground cumin, freshly ground black pepper, chopped cilantro, and the minced red onion. Drizzle over the roasted vegetables.

Jicama with Lime

2 red chili peppers
2 tablespoons sea salt

3 tablespoons freshly squeezed
  lime juice
2 pounds jicama

Serves 6

Serve this spicy snack with margaritas on a warm afternoon.

1. Cut the red chili peppers in half, remove the seeds, and finely chop. Toss with the sea salt and the lime juice. Purée in a blender or food processor until smooth. Refrigerate the sauce for 1 hour to give the flavors a chance to blend.
2. To serve, peel the jicama and cut into 1-inch slices. Arrange on a serving tray. To eat, dip the sliced jicama into the lime mixture.

Ceviche de Pescado

3 pounds fresh snapper fillets
3 cups fresh-squeezed lime juice
  (approx. 5–6 limes)
3 tablespoons kosher salt
1 cup diced white onion
½ cup diced radish
½ cup diced jalapeño

1 cup seeded and diced Roma
  tomato
2 avocados, sliced
Freshly ground black pepper
Lime slices, for garnish
½ cup chopped fresh cilantro, for
  garnish

Serves 6–8

Chef Alex Padilla of Consuelo Mexican Bistro provides this recipe, which was inspired by fishermen from different beaches in Mexico.

1. Check for bones and cut the fish into ¼-inch cubes. Combine lime juice with the fish cubes. Add of the kosher salt and marinate for at least 2 hours in the refrigerator.
2. Combine marinated fish, white onion, radish, and jalapeño. Spoon into a clear margarita glass. Top each with the tomato, avocado slices, and freshly ground black pepper to taste. Garnish with the lime slices and cilantro. Serve immediately with tostadas.

Mole Poblano with Chicken

Serves 4–6

For best
results,
use milder,
sweeter
chilies that
complement
the rich choc-
olate.

2 dried guajillo chilies
2 dried ancho chilies
¾ cup whole blanched almonds
¼ cup white sesame seeds
4 medium tomatoes
½ small red onion
1 clove garlic
1 cup chicken stock
¼ cup lightly packed seedless
    raisins
1 teaspoon ground cumin

½ teaspoon ground coriander
½ teaspoon ground cinnamon
¼ teaspoon chili powder, or to
    taste
2 tablespoons olive oil
3½-pound chicken, cut into 6
    serving pieces
2 ounces unsweetened chocolate,
    chopped
1 tablespoon chopped fresh
    Mexican oregano, optional

1. Cut the chilies in half, remove the seeds, and finely chop. Cover the
    chilies in hot water and let sit until softened (about 30 minutes). Toast
    the almonds and the sesame seeds by heating them in a frying pan
    over medium heat, shaking the pan continuously, until they turn golden.
    Cool and chop finely. Dice the tomatoes. Peel and mince the red onion
    and garlic.
2. In a blender or food processor, process the toasted nuts, softened chilies,
    chicken stock, raisins, minced garlic, ground cumin, ground coriander,
    ground cinnamon, and the chili powder until smooth.
3. Heat the olive oil in 12-inch heavy-bottomed skillet over medium-high
    heat. Add the chicken pieces and cook until lightly browned, cooking
    the chicken in 2 batches if necessary. Remove the chicken from the
    frying pan. Do not clean out the pan.
4. Pour the mole sauce into the frying pan. Cook for 1 minute, then add
    the unsweetened chocolate. Cook over low heat, uncovered, and stir
    frequently, until the chocolate melts. Be careful not to let the chocolate
    burn.

continues >>

5. Add the chicken back into the pan. Reduce the heat to low and simmer, covered, until the chicken is cooked through and the juices run clear when pierced with a knife (about 30 minutes). Baste the chicken frequently with the sauce during cooking. Sprinkle the mole with the fresh oregano and serve.

Mole

The word *mole* (pronounced MOH-lay) is from the Nahuatl word *molli*, meaning "concoction, or mixture." Red mole is from central Mexico in the Puebla and Oaxaca regions, also known as the Land of Seven Moles. Other mole colors include brown, black, green, and yellow. Generally, mole is a smooth sauce blended of onion, garlic, several varieties of chilies, ground seeds, and a small amount of chocolate. Not all moles contain chocolate.

Plantains with Whipped Cream

2 large, ripe plantains
½ cup heavy whipping cream
2 tablespoons orange juice

1 teaspoon pure Mexican vanilla extract
Mint sprigs, for garnish

Serves 2 to 4

Sweet whipping cream provides a nice counterbalance to starchy plantains.

1. Fill a saucepan with enough salted water to cover the plantains and bring to a boil. Add the plantains and cook, uncovered, in the boiling water until they are tender (about 20 minutes). Remove from the water and cool. Peel the plantains and cut into thin slices.
2. Use an electric mixer to beat the whipping cream with the orange juice and the vanilla extract until it forms stiff peaks. Spoon the whipping cream over the plantain slices and serve. Garnish with the mint sprigs.

Pasta with Chilies

Mild, sweet guajillo chilies add a Mexican touch to Italian pasta in this fusion dish. Feel free to dress it up by sprinkling a bit of grated cheese on top and a sprig of fresh cilantro.

8 ounces linguine
2 guajillo chilies
4 shallots
2 large cloves garlic
2 ripe tomatoes
8 ounces Italian sausage

1 tablespoon butter
3 tablespoons finely chopped
    fresh basil leaves
Salt, to taste
Freshly ground black pepper, to
    taste

1. Fill a large saucepan with just enough salted water to cover the pasta. Bring to a boil. Add the pasta and cook, uncovered, until al dente (10 to 15 minutes). Drain thoroughly. Remove the seeds from the guajillo chilies and chop. Peel and finely chop the shallots and garlic. Peel the tomatoes, deseed, and slice.
2. Remove the Italian sausage from its casing. Cook the sausage in a frying pan over medium-high heat until thoroughly browned. Remove from the pan, but leave 2 tablespoons of drippings in the pan. Drain the sausage on paper towels.
3. Reduce the heat to medium and add the garlic and shallots. Sauté until the garlic is browned, and the shallots are softened. Melt the butter in the pan and add the chilies. Cook until the skin from the chilies begins to blister.
4. Add the tomatoes and cook until softened. Toss the cooked sauce with the linguine. Stir in the fresh basil. Season with salt and freshly ground black pepper as desired.

Working with Hot Chilies

Make sure to wear rubber gloves when handling dried or fresh chilies, and be very careful not to touch your eyes or face after touching them. Keeping chilies under running water while you work keeps the fumes from getting in your eyes. And wash your hands carefully with soap and water after handling either fresh or dried chilies.

Ancho Chili Fudge Pie

Serves 8

2 tablespoons light cream
3 ounces unsweetened chocolate
3 ounces semisweet chocolate
½ cup all-purpose flour
½ teaspoon salt
¼ cup granulated sugar
¾ packed cup brown sugar
 (or piloncillo)

2 large eggs
1 tablespoon Mexican vanilla
 extract
½ cup unsalted butter, melted
¼ cup chopped pecans
¼ cup chopped pistachios
2 tablespoons ancho paste
9-inch unbaked pastry shell

Made from poblano chilies, ancho chili paste makes an excellent addition to everything from soups and stir-fries to desserts. It is available in most specialty stores.

1. Preheat the oven to 350°.
2. Fill the bottom of a double boiler with water and place over medium heat. Combine the light cream and the chocolate in the top of the double boiler and melt. (If you don't have a double boiler, melt the chocolate in a metal bowl placed above a saucepan half-filled with barely simmering water.)
3. In a large bowl, combine the flour, salt, and the sugars. Lightly beat the eggs with the vanilla extract. Add the beaten egg and the melted butter to the flour. Stir in the melted chocolate, nuts, and the ancho paste. Spoon the mixture into the pastry shell. Bake until lightly browned (about 1 hour).

Ancho Chilies

The word *ancho* means "wide" in Spanish. It is the dried form of the poblano chili. When dried, it is very dark in color and has a deep, rich, sweet taste. The ancho is part of the "holy trinity" of chilies used to make traditional mole sauces.

CHAPTER 20
Bermuda and the Caribbean: Island Eats

Guava Mousse

Guava
fruit comes
in many
sizes—this
recipe calls
for the larger
fruit that is
approximately
the same size
as apples.

¼ cup warm water
1 package unflavored gelatin,
    such as Knox
5 large green guavas
¾ cup plus 2 tablespoons whole
    milk, divided

1 vanilla bean
1 cup light cream
½ cup granulated sugar
2 tablespoons confectioners'
    sugar, for garnish
8 mint sprigs, for garnish

1. Pour the warm water into a small bowl. Pour the gelatin over the water and let it stand for 5 minutes to soften.
2. Cut the guavas in half. Scoop out the flesh, removing the section containing the seeds. In a blender or food processor, purée the guava fruit with 2 tablespoons milk until smooth. Measure out 1 cup of puréed guava. Discard the remainder or use in another recipe.
3. Cut the vanilla bean in half lengthwise. Remove the seeds. In a medium-sized saucepan, bring ¾ cup milk, the light cream, vanilla bean, vanilla seeds, and granulated sugar to a near boil. Continue cooking for 2 to 3 minutes, stirring to dissolve the sugar. Remove the vanilla bean.
4. Remove the saucepan from the stove element and stir in the softened gelatin. Continue stirring until the gelatin is completely dissolved (about 5 minutes).
5. Combine the gelatin mixture with the puréed guava and process until smooth. Pour into four 6-ounce custard cups. Cover and chill in the refrigerator for 4 hours. To serve, dust with the confectioners' sugar and garnish with mint sprigs.

Conch Chowder

½ green bell pepper
½ red bell pepper
3 large red potatoes
1 white onion
4 cloves garlic
2 stalks celery
1 jalapeño chili pepper
4 tomatoes
1 pound conch, cleaned
⅓ cup lime juice
¼ cup tomato paste
3 tablespoons olive oil

¼ teaspoon cayenne pepper, or
    to taste
1 tablespoon chopped fresh
    parsley
4 cups water
¼ cup rum
1 bay leaf
Salt and freshly ground black
    pepper, to taste
2 tablespoons chopped fresh
    cilantro leaves

Serves 4–6

Conch chowder is the Bahamian version of Manhattan clam chowder, made with conch snails instead of clams and seasoned with tart lime juice.

1. Cut the bell peppers in half, remove the seeds, and cut into cubes. Peel and dice the potatoes. Peel and finely chop the onion and garlic. String the celery and cut on the diagonal into thin slices. Cut the jalapeño chili pepper in half, remove the seeds, and finely chop. Peel the tomatoes, deseed, and cut into thin slices.

2. Cut the conch into 1-inch pieces. Marinate the conch pieces in the lime juice and tomato paste for 1 hour.

3. In a large saucepan, heat the olive oil over medium heat. Add the onion, garlic, celery, bell peppers, and the chili pepper. Brown the vegetables. Add the tomatoes, pushing down gently with the back of a spoon to release their juices. Stir in the cayenne pepper and chopped parsley.

4. Add the water, conch pieces and the lime juice marinade, potatoes, rum, and the bay leaf. Bring to boil, then reduce the heat and simmer, uncovered, until the potatoes are tender when pierced with a fork (about 30 minutes). Taste and add salt and pepper if desired. Remove the bay leaf. Sprinkle with the fresh cilantro and serve hot.

Chicken and Soba Noodle Salad

Serves 3

This light chicken salad is one of the many delicious dishes served on Richard Branson's private Necker Island resort.

¼ pack soba noodles
3 tablespoons sesame oil
3 skinless, boneless chicken breasts, cut into strips
2 tablespoons Thai fish sauce

½ bunch chives, chopped
½ red onion, sliced
10 cherry tomatoes, cut in half
Juice of 1 lemon
1 dried red chili, finely chopped

1. In a pot of salted, boiling water, cook the soba noodles for 7 minutes. Drain the noodles and run cold water over them until cold. Add 2 tablespoons of the sesame oil to the noodles.
2. Cook the chicken in a pan with the remaining 1 tablespoon sesame oil. Remove from heat and let cool.
3. Mix together all the ingredients, and serve.

Grilled Portobello Mushroom Caps

Serves 4

Serve this dish with the Balsamic Dressing (page 281).

4 portobello mushrooms, stems removed
4 tablespoons olive oil
4 tablespoons balsamic vinegar
Salt and freshly ground black pepper, to taste

4 slices goat cheese
4 handfuls mixed salad leaves
4 tablespoons Balsamic Dressing (page 281)

1. Preheat the oven to 350°.
2. Put the mushrooms in a baking tray, topside down. Drizzle with the olive oil and balsamic vinegar, and season with the salt and pepper. Bake in the oven for about 6 minutes.
3. In the meantime, place the salad leaves in the middle of 4 serving plates, top each plate with a slice of goat cheese, and drizzle with the dressing. Place the cooked mushrooms on top of the salad.

Balsamic Dressing

2 tablespoons balsamic vinegar
6 tablespoons olive oil
1 teaspoon minced onion

1 teaspoon minced fresh thyme
Salt and freshly ground black
    pepper, to taste

Combine all the ingredients and mix well. Serve over greens.

Serves 4

A good balsamic dressing is a must to have on hand. It is ideal to use on almost any combination of greens.

Seared Asian-Style Glazed Tuna

1 tuna fillet, about 9 inches long
    and 1 inch thick
¼ cup light soy sauce
1 teaspoon lime juice
1 clove garlic, minced

½ teaspoon brown sugar
2 tablespoons white sesame
    seeds
1 tablespoon olive oil
2 limes, cut into wedges

Serves 2

Serve this simple dish with Asian Salad (page 282) for a complete meal for two.

1. Place the tuna fillet in a shallow 9 × 13-inch glass baking dish. In a small bowl, whisk the soy sauce, lime juice, garlic, brown sugar, and sesame seeds. Pour the marinade over the tuna. Cover and marinate in the refrigerator for 2 hours.
2. Heat the oil in a frying pan on high heat. Sear the tuna for about 30 seconds on each side. Return the tuna to the refrigerator and chill. To serve, cut the chilled tuna into thin slices and garnish with the lime wedges.

Asian Salad

Serves 2

Serve with
Seared Asian-
Style Glazed
Tuna (page
281) for a
complete
Asian-style
dinner for
two.

1 mango
1 mild green chili pepper
½ red bell pepper
½ yellow bell pepper
½ cucumber

2 tablespoons chopped red onion
½ cup shredded red cabbage
Easy Asian Salad Dressing (see
*   sidebar on this page)*

1. Peel and shred the mango. Cut the chili pepper in half, remove the seeds, and finely chop. Remove the seeds from the bell peppers and dice. Peel and slice the cucumber.
2. Combine all the ingredients and drizzle with the Asian Salad Dressing.

Easy Asian Salad Dressing

Mix together 2 tablespoons fish sauce, 2 tablespoons freshly squeezed lemon juice, 2 tablespoons virgin olive oil, 1 teaspoon palm sugar, a few drops sesame oil, and a pinch of ground cinnamon. Serve over the salad.

Guava Fritters with Banana Syrup

2 bananas, sliced
1 cup maple syrup
¾ cup cornstarch
3 cups plus 3 tablespoons all-
    purpose flour
2 teaspoons baking soda

Pinch salt
Sparkling water, as needed
Vegetable oil, as needed
2–3 guavas, peeled, seeded, and
    cut into wedges

Serves 4

This recipe comes from Glowbal Grill and Satay Bar in Vancouver, British Colombia.

1. Combine the bananas and syrup in a saucepan over low heat and warm gently for a few minutes. Remove from heat and let cool slightly. Process in a blender or food processor until smooth.
2. Mix together the cornstarch, 3 cups of the flour, the baking soda, and salt. Add sparkling water as needed to reach the consistency of a batter.
3. Heat enough oil to cover the guavas in a deep-fryer to a high temperature. Coat the guava wedges in the remaining 3 tablespoons of flour, then dip into the batter mix, and deep-fry until golden brown. Serve with the banana and maple syrup sauce.

No Fryer? No Problem.

As a fryer substitute, you can use a deep saucepan. Fill it with about 2 inches of quality vegetable oil and heat on medium for approximately 10 to 15 minutes. Test the oil with a small amount of the fryer batter placed gently into the pan, so as to not splash.

Bermuda Fish Chowder

Serves 10

This dish, from Chef David Garcelon in Bermuda, is a local specialty that has won several contests on the island.

¼ cup olive oil
2 sprigs fresh thyme
1 tablespoon dried oregano
1 tablespoon dried marjoram
1 tablespoon ground cinnamon
¼ cup finely diced celery
½ cup finely diced carrots
½ cup finely diced onion
4 cloves garlic, minced

½ cup chopped tomatoes
2 pounds diced whitefish (perch, cod, or bass)
2 quarts fish stock
¼ cup black rum
½ cup Worcestershire sauce
1 ounce Gravy Master
1 tablespoon salt

1. Heat the oil on medium in a sauté pan. Add the herbs, cinnamon, and all the vegetables except the tomatoes and sauté until soft. Add all the remaining ingredients and cook over low heat for 45 minutes to 1 hour.
2. Purée the soup lightly with a hand blender, leaving chunks.
3. Adjust seasonings to taste and serve.

Bermuda Fish Chowder

Though a Bermuda national dish, Bermuda Fish Chowder was originally a British recipe that came over with the first colonists. The soup was quickly adopted by Bermudians and today is made with a rich stock (from fresh local fish, including fish heads and tails). Other ingredients are water, bacon fat, parsley, salt and ground pepper, potatoes, onion, carrots, celery, bay leaves, peppercorns, cloves, tomatoes, and thyme.

Bermuda Onion Soup

½ cup butter
2½ pounds Bermuda onions, chopped
½ pound apples, chopped
4 cloves garlic, minced
¼ pound celery, chopped
½ pound potatoes, peeled and chopped

½ tablespoon ground coriander
1 bay leaf
1 tablespoon salt
½ teaspoon pepper
1 quart water
1 cup heavy cream

Serves 10

Another signature soup by Chef David Garcelon of the Fairmont Southampton in Bermuda. This soup is based on the Bermuda onion, which was one of Bermuda's best-known exports in the nineteenth century.

1. Melt the butter in sauté pan over medium-low heat. Sauté the onions, apples, garlic, and celery until soft. Add all the remaining ingredients except the cream, and cook over low heat for 45 minutes to 1 hour.
2. Remove and discard the bay leaf. Purée soup in a blender or food processor until smooth. Strain the soup through a fine-mesh sieve. Add the cream and adjust seasonings to taste.

Bermuda: From Agriculture to Tourism

Though today Bermuda relies on business and tourism as its main sources of revenue, in the not-too-distant past it was agriculture that fed its wealth. Once steamers began traveling to and from New York, Bermudians were able to export their goods: tomatoes, celery, potatoes, arrowroot, Easter lillies, and, most importantly, Bermuda onions. The Bermuda onion became so popular that the colony became known as "the Onion Patch," and true Bermudians still refer to themselves as "Onions."

Jerk Marinade

Yields 1 cup

Chef Walter Staib, culinary consultant for Sandals Resorts International, created this wonderful jerk marinade.

¾ pound Scotch bonnets, stems removed, deseeded, and roughly chopped
1 large onion
4 bunches green onions (white and green parts), chopped
½ pound thyme, leaves removed and stems discarded

½ cup minced fresh ginger
6 cloves garlic, minced
4 tablespoons freshly ground allspice
Salt and freshly ground black pepper, to taste
1 cup soy sauce
½ cup vegetable oil

1. Combine all the ingredients except the soy sauce and oil in food processor or blender, and purée. Transfer the mixture to a mixing bowl and add the soy sauce and oil. Store in a glass jar or clay pot.
2. To use with chicken, beef, or pork, place the meat in the marinade and let sit overnight. Remove the meat from the marinade and grill at a high temperature until cooked through. For fish, lobster, or shrimp, place the fish or seafood in the marinade for 1 hour only. (Do not overmarinate or it will break down the fibers in the fish and seafood, resulting in a mushy consistency when cooked.) Remove from the marinade and grill at a high temperature until cooked through.

What a Jerk

It all began with the Indians. The Arawak tribe had a traditional method of using Jamaican pimento (today's allspice) to season and smoke meat, mostly wild pigs. That spice, combined with hot chilies (from South America and the Caribbean), pirates who brought a medley of new spices, and escaped slaves who were experts at slow-roasting in pits, resulted in what we now call jerk. The escaped slaves, known as Maroons, are believed to have perfected this way of preserving and cooking meat during their years living in the Blue Mountains, fighting the British troops.

Avocado, Crab, and Sour Cream Timbale

½ onion, chopped

1 clove garlic, minced

2 scallions, chopped

1 tablespoon butter

8 ounces lump crabmeat

Salt and freshly ground black
 pepper, to taste

1 avocado, peeled and chopped

2 teaspoons fresh-squeezed lime
 juice

4 tablespoons sour cream

1 tablespoon chopped fresh
 parsley

1 tablespoon chopped fresh
 cilantro

1 tablespoon chopped fresh basil

Dressing:

2 teaspoons fresh-squeezed lime
 juice

2 teaspoons balsamic vinegar

½ cup olive oil

Pinch salt, pepper, and
 granulated sugar

Serves 4

This is a favorite dish of Sandals Grande St. Lucian Beach Resort and Spa. In this recipe, Chef Walter Staib uses avocados—a major staple throughout the Caribbean.

1. Sauté the onions, garlic, and scallion in the butter until soft. Add the crabmeat and cook for 2 minutes. Season to taste with salt and pepper. Chill in the refrigerator.
2. Season the avocado with the lime juice and salt and pepper.
3. Mix together the sour cream and all the herbs.
4. Assemble the timbales: Lightly oil 4 timbale molds (2½ inches in diameter and 3 inches high). Divide the avocado among the molds and press down. Next add the crabmeat and press down. Add the tomato and press down. Finally, top off with the sour cream, filling the molds and smoothing off the top. Chill in the refrigerator for 1 hour.
5. Blend together all the dressing ingredients. Slide the timbales onto serving plates and drizzle the dressing around them.

Risotto with Lobster and Parmesan

Serves 6

This recipe, by Executive Chef Ciaran Hickey of the Four Seasons Resort Great Exuma, uses spiny lobster found in the reefs of the turquoise Bahamian waters. Plain lobster also works fine.

2 shallots, diced
Vegetable oil, as needed
1 pound risotto rice
2 tablespoons dry white wine
2 pints shellfish stock
½ pound spiny lobster meat, diced

1 zucchini, diced
½ cup (1 stick) butter
½ cup Parmesan cheese, grated, plus extra for garnish
Salt and freshly ground black pepper, to taste
A few springs parsley, for garnish

1. In a large pan, cook the shallots in a little oil to release the flavor, then add the risotto.
2. Cook the risotto for about 4 minutes, and add the wine. Cook for a few minutes, then add a bit of the shellfish stock. Stir and cook until the stock is absorbed. Continue adding the stock a bit at a time and stirring until the liquid is absorbed.
3. In a small pan, sauté the diced lobster with the zucchini in a little oil, then add to the risotto.
4. Add the butter and Parmesan to the pan, and season with salt and pepper. Serve in a pasta bowl. Garnish with fresh parsley and extra Parmesan cheese.

The Making of Rum

Rum is made from fermented and distilled sugar-cane juice or, more commonly, molasses. First water is added, then yeast is introduced until the desired alcohol level is reached. Next it is distilled either in copper pot stills or columnar stills. Modern rum production only became a commercial enterprise in the 1600s, after the English and French had established their colonies. Alas, the thriving rum production relied largely on the labor of African slaves, who toiled in the sugar-cane plantations.

Gourmet Cooking Glossary

al dente: "To the tooth," in Italian. Pasta is cooked just to a firm texture.

allemande: In French cooking it means "in the German style." Sauce Allemande is made from veal stock, cream, egg yolks, and lemon juice.

aromatics: Seasonings to enhance the flavor and aroma—usually herbs and spices.

au jus: The natural pan drippings or juice that comes from a roasting pan after deglazing.

bain-marie: A "water bath." Food is placed in a container that is placed in a shallow dish filled with hot water, then heated in an oven or on the stovetop.

baste: To brush or spoon liquid fat or juices over meat, fish, poultry, or vegetables during cooking to help keep moisture on the surface area.

beat: Briskly whipping or stirring with a spoon, fork, wire whisk, beater, or mixer.

bias: To slice a food crosswise at a 45-degree angle.

bind: To thicken a sauce or hot liquid by stirring in ingredients such as roux, flour, butter, cornstarch, egg yolks, vegetable purée, or cream.

blanch: To partially cook vegetables by parboiling them, then cooling quickly in ice water.

blend: Mixing together two or more ingredients to obtain a distributed mixture.

bouquet garni: A bundle of seasonings, such as bay leaf, thyme, and parsley. It's used to season braised foods and stocks.

braise: To cook slowly in liquid in a covered pot.

brown: A quick sautéing/searing done either at the beginning or end of meal preparation.

brush: To coat food with melted butter, glaze, or other liquid using a pastry brush.

butterfly: To cut food down the center without cutting all the way through to open and then spread it apart.

caramelize: The process of cooking sugar until it begins to color. Also, while slowly cooking some vegetables (e.g., onions, root vegetables), the natural sugars are released and the vegetables will caramelize in their own sugars.

chiffonade: Cutting lettuces and other leafy vegetables or herbs into julienne strips.

chinoise: A very fine, conical wire-mesh strainer. Using a chinoise removes small impurities from the liquid that is strained.

chop: To cut into irregular pieces with no set size.

coat: Cover evenly.

confit: Pieces of meat slowly cooked in their own gently rendered fat until very soft and tender.

cure: Marinating to preserve an ingredient with salt and/or sugar and spices.

cut in: Working butter into dry ingredients for equal distribution. This is done with the help of a pastry blender and is important in making flaky pie crusts.

dash: A measure approximately equal to $\frac{1}{16}$ teaspoon, a pinch or less.

deglaze: Adding liquid to a pan in which foods have been sautéed, fried, or roasted to dissolve the baked-on bits stuck to the bottom of the pan.

dice: To cut food into cubes.

dredge: Completely coating in flour and shaking off the excess.

drippings: The liquids and bits of food left in the bottom of a roasting or frying pan after meat is cooked.

drizzle: Pouring a liquid, such as melted butter, olive oil, or other liquid, in a slow trickle over food.

dust: Sprinkling flour to lightly and evenly coat.

egg wash: A mixture of beaten eggs, yolks, whites, or both with milk or water used to coat baked goods to give them a shine when baked. Also may be used as a sealant for pieces of dough.

fillet: A boneless and skinless piece of meat cut away from the bone, usually fish.

fillet: To remove the bones from fish or meat for cooking.

flambé: To ignite liquid that contains an alcoholic substance so that it flames.

fleure de sel: A very high-quality French sea salt.

foie gras: A fattened duck or goose liver.

fold: To gently combine two or more ingredients using a bottom-to-top motion with a spoon or spatula.

fritter: A deep-fried sweet or savory food coated or mixed in a batter.

ganache: A chocolate filling or coating made with chocolate, egg yolks, and heavy cream. Most often used as a filling for truffles and as a coating for cakes.

garnish: A decorative piece of an edible ingredient placed as a finishing touch to dishes or drinks.

glaze: A liquid that gives an item a shiny surface.

grate: To shred food into fine pieces by rubbing it against a coarse surface, usually a grater.

herbes de Provence: A blend of herbs consisting of chervil, tarragon, chives, rosemary, and lavender.

infusion: Extracting flavors by soaking them in liquid heated in a covered pan.

jointed: Something, such as chicken, cut at the joint.

julienne: To cut into thin strips about 2 inches long.

jus: The natural juices released by roasting meats that have collected on the bottom of the roasting pan.

knead: To work dough with the heels of your hands in a pressing and folding motion until it becomes smooth and elastic.

marinate: Submerging a food in a seasoned liquid in order to tenderize and flavor the food.

medallion: Small round or oval pieces of meat (sometimes lightly pounded), such as chicken, tenderloin, pork, and veal.

mince: To chop or dice food into tiny irregular pieces.

mirepoix: A mixture of vegetables: 2 parts onions, 1 part celery, 1 part carrots. It may also contain leeks and mushrooms (in which case the amount of onions would be less).

pan-broil: Cooking food in a heavy-bottomed pan without added fat, then removing any fat as it accumulates so it doesn't burn.

parchment: A nonstick, silicone-coated, heat-resistant paper used in cooking.

pare: To peel or trim food of its outer layer of skin, usually vegetables.

pinch: A small inexact measurement, about $\frac{1}{16}$ of a teaspoon.

poach: To simmer in liquid that is just below the boiling point.

ramekin: A small ovenproof dish used for individual servings.

reduce: To slowly or rapidly cook liquids down so that some or most of the water evaporates.

reduction: Simmering a sauce so that moisture is released, causing the remaining ingredients to concentrate, thickening and strengthening the flavors.

render: Cooking something greasy, such as bacon, to release the fat

roast: A method of cooking in an oven where the item isn't covered, allowing the dry heat to surround the item.

roux: A cooked mixture of equal parts flour and oil, fat, or butter used to thicken liquids.

sauté: To cook food quickly in a small amount of fat in a pan over regulated direct heat.

score: To tenderize meat, fish, or shellfish by making a number of shallow, often diagonal cuts across its surface.

sear: Frying meat quickly over high heat to seal in the juices.

season: To enhance the flavor of foods by adding ingredients such as salt, pepper, and a variety of other herbs and spices.

simmer: Cooking food in a liquid at just below the boiling point so that small bubbles rise to the surface.

steep: To soak dry ingredients in liquid until the flavor is infused into it.

stir-fry: Quickly frying small pieces of meats and vegetables over very high heat with continuous stirring in a small amount of oil.

stock: The liquid that results from simmering bones, vegetables, and seasonings in water or another liquid.

sweat: Cooking vegetables over low heat to release their natural juices.

zest: The thin outer part of the rind of citrus.

What Is Gourmet? Chefs Quoted

Chefs are artists, and artists have their own unique vision of what sets their creations apart. I caught up with a few chefs and asked them how they defined the word gourmet. Here is what they said.

"Gourmet conjures up the thought of a true eating experience cooked by chefs who have a real passion for food. Whatever the style or setting, the food will always shine through in its depth of flavor and the way the ingredients have been assembled and presented."

—CHEF GLEN WATSON, Sofitel St. James, London

"Gourmet means food and ingredients you would not see in an everyday store. The presentation is given great care and is prepared in an appropriate, refined manner. The flavors should last on the palate, developing layer upon layer of flavor. The meal/courses build upon each other as it continues."

—CHEF EDWARD FARROW, Julien Restaurant at the Langham Hotel, Boston

"What food is really all about is the flavor, the taste, the aroma. Although we think of it as more upscale cuisine, gourmet doesn't have to mean difficult. In fact, the simplicity of the dish is often an element of gourmet cooking, and the simple flavors are what people really like. Gourmet cooking is to be enjoyed everyday—it's a feast, a fête, and a dream."

—CHEF ROLAND PASSOT, co-owner and chief culinary officer of the Left Bank Brasserie

"Gourmet is simplicity."

—CHEF CHRIS YEO, chef and owner of Straights

"Well, when my mother-in-law introduces me, she always says, 'This is my son-in-law—he's a gourmet chef!' I guess, to me, it sounds a bit pretentious. But I know she's trying to tell people that what I do is an art—that I'm not just flipping burgers."

—CHEF TERENCE FUERY, Ritz-Carlton, Philadelphia

"Gourmet means opulence. When something is gourmet it's the best of the best—but then again, fresh olives, and feta are gourmet too. . . . I would say it's a fancy word for really good."

—CHEF AUDREY CLAIRE, Twenty Manning and Audrey Claire, Philadelphia

"Gourmet? It's a luxury—like when you drive a Mercedes, you feel good. When you eat gourmet food, you feel great."

—BILLY MIGNUCCI, owner of Di Bruno's, a gourmet specialty cheese shop in Philadelphia

"Excellence in service. We have an advantage at the Four Seasons of knowing that we have the right people, so that the guest's experience begins the moment he or she enters the door. As for the meal, it should showcase a unique change in ingredients."

—CHEF MARTIN HAMANN, Four Seasons, Philadelphia

"To me gourmet is something that is made by hand and with love. Whether it's exotic or not, if a person doesn't put love into it, it will not make an impression."

—HELEN YIN, owner of Fork, Philadelphia

"A gourmet to me is someone who can appreciate the subtleties and nuances of how chefs combine ingredients, spices, and seasonings, cooking techniques, and presentation to create dishes that are a treat to the taste buds and the eye. This is why I was inspired to combine my two favorite cuisines, Chinese and French, to create the dishes we serve here at Tommy Toy's Cuisine Chinoise."

—CHEF TOMMY TOY, Tommy Toy's Cuisine Chinoise, San Francisco

"Gourmet is a style of cooking that is seemingly paired with expensive food ingredients or expensive fine wine. One would have to fully understand haute cuisine to become a gourmet. A chef worth his salt should have the culinary skill to take an ingredient which does not have to be fancy or complicated and turn it into gold. Alchemy at its best! But, gourmet at its best is when the cooking comes from the heart."

—CHEF ANDREW TURNER, Bentley Hotel, London

"The quality of the products is what makes gourmet truly 'gourmet.' This is the most important thing, because people should enjoy the natural flavors of food. Food should not be masked with heavy sauces and spices. With quality products, one only has to lightly season and cook it properly."

—CHEF TROY THOMPSON, Jer-ne Restaurant and Bar, Ritz-Carlton, Marina del Rey

Wine Accompaniments

Red Meat Dishes

Food	Wine
Chili con carne	Beaujolais (an easy-drinking red); Zinfandel (a red to stand up to your chili)
Grilled steak	Cabernet Sauvignon (an ultimate match); Shiraz/Syrah (a good choice at a better price)
Hamburger	Any red wine you like that is inexpensive
Roast beef	Pinot Noir and Merlot (softer reds than for your grilled steak). If you are wild about Cabernet Sauvignon, then have a Cabernet from Bordeaux
Steak au poivre (steak with black peppercorn sauce)	BIG REDS: Zinfandel from California and Rhône reds are perfect
Tenderloin	Same as for roast beef: Pinot Noir and Merlot are the good choices

Poultry Dishes

Food	Wine
Chicken (roasted)	Almost any wine you like—this is a very versatile dish
Chicken (highly seasoned)	Chenin Blanc, Riesling, or other unoaked white
Turkey	Rosé, sweet or dry; rich and heavy whites
Duck and goose	Pinot Blanc or Viognier among whites and Merlot or Rhônes among reds
Game birds	Pinot Noir

Other Meat Dishes

Food	Wine
Ham	Rosé; fruity Pinot Noir; Pinot Gris; Gewürztraminer
Lamb (simple)	Cabernet (especially from Bordeaux); Rioja red from Spain
Lamb (with herbs and garlic)	Cabernet Sauvignon, Spanish reds, Rhônes
Pork	A light Italian or Spanish red; Viognier, Pinot Gris, Gewürztraminer or some other rich white
Sausage	Gewürztraminer or a rustic red
Veal	Richer whites, such as Chardonnay; light reds
Venison (deer)	A big red wine: Cabernet, Nebbiolo, Syrah, or Zinfandel will do well

Seafood Dishes

Food	Wine
Anything with a cream sauce	White Burgundy (clean, crisp Chardonnay)
Lobster	Champagne; dry Riesling; white Burgundy
Oysters	Muscadet, a French white, is ideal with oysters; Chablis (dry French Chardonnay) or Champagne
Salmon	Sauvignon Blanc
Shrimp	Light and dry white wine
Swordfish	Light to medium white wines of all sorts
Tuna	This fish is versatile like chicken; anything but a big red is okay. A light red is probably the ideal match.
White fish (sole, for instance)	Sauvignon Blanc, light Chardonnay

Pasta Dishes

Food	Wine
Red sauce	Barbera; Chianti or another Sangiovese-based red
Vegetables	Grüner Veltliner, Sauvignon Blanc, or other crisp whites
White sauce	Pinot Grigio

Some General Food-Wine Categories

Category	Characteristics	Examples
Fish Whites	Crisp, light, and acidic	Muscadet, Macon, Pinot Grigio, Sauvignon Blanc
Turkey Whites	Rich and heavy whites to accompany holiday meals	Viognier, Pinot Gris, Gewürztraminer
Fish Reds	Light and acidic reds with little tannin	Sangiovese, Lighter Barbera, Lighter Spanish reds, Lighter Merlot, Red Burgundy, and other Pinot Noir
Peppersteak Reds	Big, bold reds that stand up to strongly flavored dishes	Château neuf-du-Pape, Cabernet Sauvignon, Malbec, Syrah/Shiraz